Technology, Innovations and Growth

Technology, Innovations and Growth

Jati K. Sengupta

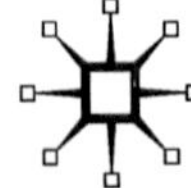

First published 2011 by
PALGRAVE MACMILLAN

Palgrave Macmillan in the UK is an imprint of Macmillan Publishers Limited, registered in England, company number 785998, of Houndmills, Basingstoke, Hampshire RG21 6XS.

Palgrave Macmillan in the US is a division of St Martin's Press LLC, 175 Fifth Avenue, New York, NY 10010.

Palgrave Macmillan is the global academic imprint of the above companies and has companies and representatives throughout the world.

Palgrave® and Macmillan® are registered trademarks in the United States, the United Kingdom, Europe and other countries.

ISBN: 978–0–230–28550–7 hardback

This book is printed on paper suitable for recycling and made from fully managed and sustained forest sources. Logging, pulping and manufacturing processes are expected to conform to the environmental regulations of the country of origin.

A catalogue record for this book is available from the British Library.

A catalog record for this book is available from the Library of Congress.

10 9 8 7 6 5 4 3 2 1
20 19 18 17 16 15 14 13 12 11

Printed and bound in Great Britain by
CPI Antony Rowe, Chippenham and Eastbourne

To Ramakrishna Sarada

With Devotion and Love

Contents

Figures and Tables

Figures

Tables

Preface

A new paradigm of growth theory is the focus of this volume. Innovations, technology diffusion and tests of endogenous growth theory are the key components of this new approach. For the last two decades the industrial economies have undergone some dramatic changes. Technology, innovations and information networks have expanded worldwide. Markets have expanded, knowledge diffusion has spread far and wide due to the growth of computer industry. There has been a dynamic shift from large-scale manufacturing to the design and use of new information technology. New forms of innovations outside the Schumpeterian framework have spread in the form of knowledge capital and learning by doing and expanded the various forms of efficiency not visualized before

On the empirical front the newly industrializing countries (NICs) of South east Asia like China, South Korea and Taiwan have performed growth miracles. They have shown that competitive and innovation efficiency can be achieved so as to sustain a high rate of economic growth by the developing economies. This volume discusses this new perspective of growth both theoretically and empirically.

Three important features of this volume are: (1) to explore a comprehensive theory of innovations extending the Schumpeterian perspective; (2) to discuss the various forms of knowledge diffusion and their empirical basis in terms of the NIC experiences, and (3) to explain the various facets of the growth miracles in NICs like China, Taiwan, South Korea and recently India.

Two important tests of endogenous growth theory are performed here. One is the empirical study of several countries and the other is an econometric time series test based on dynamic regression models. The econometric tests are discussed in Chapter 6, which is contributed by my student Ishita Nandi. This forms a part of her doctoral dissertation completed under my supervision. I am most thankful to her for this valued contribution. She also took care of typing the whole manuscript.

Many of my Ph. D students have helped me to understand the new growth theory and the various facets of the growth miracles in Asia and the world. They came from all over the world from countries such as US, UK, Japan, China, Taiwan, South Korea, Peru, Chile, Mexico, India and even Lebanon and Iran. I take this opportunity to offer my most sincere thanks and gratitude.

Finally, I express my deep appreciation to my wife for her constant support and encouragement. My four grandchildren Jayen, Aria, Shiven and Myra provided me with pleasant diversions and childlike questions which I enjoyed most.

1
Technology and Economic Growth

Technology has a general and a specific meaning. Solow (1957) used the specific concept of technology as a shift of the production frontier or the production possibility frontier. It tends to reduce costs and improve the long-run productivity of firms and industries. In its general and broader meaning, technology characterizes the organizational structure of an industry that includes all its managerial skills and investments in R&D. Schumpeter (1942) used the concept of innovations to include both general and specific meanings of technology.

The shift of the production function over time may be specified as

$$Y = F(X_1, X_2, X_3, X_4, X_5, X_6) = F(K, L, H_1, H_2 H_3, t) \qquad (1.1)$$

where Y is output and X_i are the various inputs or sources of productivity, e.g., physical capital (K), labor (L), human capital (H_1), R&D expenditure (H_2), externalities in the form of knowledge diffusion (H_3) and the time trend (t). Denoting time derivatives by a dot over a variable, one could express output growth over time as

$$\dot{Y} = \frac{dY}{dt} = \sum_{i=1}^{6} F_{X_i} \dot{X}_i = F_K \dot{K} + F_L \dot{L} + F_{H_1} \dot{H}_1 + F_{H_2} \dot{H}_2 + F_{H_3} \dot{H}_3 + F_t \qquad (1.2)$$

where $F_{X_i} = \delta F / \delta X_i$ denotes marginal productivity of each input. Solow's technical progress considers a rise in $\dot{Y}$ due to time alone, i.e., it is a residual after growth accounting due to K, L, H_1, H_2 and H_3:

$$F_t = \dot{Y} - \left(F_K \dot{K} + F_L \dot{L} + F_{H_1} \dot{H}_1 + F_{H_2} \dot{H}_2 + F_{H_3} \dot{H}_3 \right) \qquad (1.3)$$

The other case of output growth may be due to innovation in the form of R&D investment when F_{H_2} rises, other things being equal.

By Duality any production frontier implies the existence of a cost frontier. Hence a steady state decline of unit costs of output may be caused by a rise in technological progress – either embodied in the various inputs, or, as a residual.

Consider an industry with two groups of firms represented by $y_1(t)$ and $y_2(t)$, where the first group alone exhibits technological progress. Then the unit cost $c_1(t)$ for firm 1 may be represented as

$$\dot{c}_1(t) = c_1(t)\left[a - b_1 k_1(t) - b_2 k_2(t)\right] \tag{1.4}$$

where $k_i(t)$ may for instance denote R&D efforts by firms $i = 1, 2$. The fixed costs of R&D efforts may be written as a strict convex function $C(k_1(t)) = (b_3 / 2)k_1^2(t)$ with all the parameters a, b_1, b_2, b_3 assumed to be positive. Here the parameter b_2 measures the positive technological spillover that firm 1 receives from the R&D effort exerted by firm 2, denoted by $k_2(t)$. The spillover externality is also denoted by H_3 in the production function (1.1).

The current profit function $\pi_1(t)$ and its long-run discounted value $J_1(t)$ may be written as

$$\pi_1(t) = p(t)y_1(t) - (b_3 / 2)k_1^2(t)$$
$$J_1(t) = \int_0^\infty e^{-rt}\pi_1(t)dt \tag{1.5}$$

subject to (1.3), where $p(t)$ is the industry demand function which may be linearly written as

$$p(t) = \alpha_1 - \alpha_2(y_1(t) + y_2(t)) \tag{1.6}$$

In the short run, unit costs $c_i(t)$ are constant, so that firms seek to maximize short-run profits π_1 by choosing the output levels. In the long run however the decline of unit or marginal costs over time is due to increases in R&D efforts $k_i(t)$. Here the firms maximize the long-run discounted profits $J_1(t)$ in (1.14) subject to the dynamic differential equation 1.3.

Clearly, various types of equilibria are possible here, e.g., competitive equilibria, Cournot-Nash equilibria and collusion or cartel or a market-share division. In this framework technological progress has direct impact on the market structure.

Our objective in this chapter is to analyze the various dimensions of the process of technological change in relation to economic growth of modern industries. Four aspects will be discussed in some detail. First, we analyze the impact of technology on growth of industries. This impact is discussed in terms of productivity gains at the inter-sectoral levels and the role of efficiency gains. This process is very similar to genetic evolution theory, where the Darwinian principle of survival of the fittest tends to support the dominance of the fittest species. Secondly, we discuss the impact of technology on the market structure. Since the scale economies are significant under technological progress, technology tends to increase the potential monopoly power of large industries. This changes the extent and direction of new technological activity.

Thirdly, recent technology in the form of knowledge diffusion, e.g., through software development and networking alliances, has transformed modern industries in so many ways that one has to analyze their global implications in terms of externalities and spillovers.

Finally, recent growth theorists have emphasized the *endogenous* nature of long-run growth, where households, firms and government policies affect the *long run growth rate* of national output. The neoclassical models of economic growth emphasized the point that permanent changes in government policies and the savings rate have only 'level effects' and no 'growth effects'. Solow (1957) used this result in his growth model where technical progress was defined as a residual in the production function (1.3). Here technology alone drives long-run growth and this is assumed exogenous. The Solow model assumed a Cobb-Douglas production function with constant returns to scale as

$$Y(t) = (K(t))^{\alpha} \left(A(t)L(t)\right)^{1-\alpha} ; 0 < \alpha < 1 \tag{1.7}$$

where the level of technology 'A' and labor 'L' are assumed to grow exogenously at rates 'g' and 'n', i.e., $A(t) = A(0)e^{gt}$, $L(t) = L(0)e^{nt}$. Here $Y(t)$ is total output and $K(t)$ is capital. On defining 'k' as K/AL and 'y' as Y/AL, the evolution of k is determined by the savings–investment equilibrium as

$$\dot{k}(t) = sy(t) - (n + g + \delta)k(t) \tag{1.8}$$

where s and δ are the savings and depreciation rates respectively. This equation implies that k converges to a steady state value k^*, where $k^* = \left[s/(n+g+\delta)\right]^{1/1-\alpha}$. On substituting this value into the production function (1.7) one obtains

$$\ln y(t) = \ln A(0) + gt + \left[\frac{\alpha}{1-\alpha}\right]\left[\ln s - \ln(n+g+\delta)\right] \tag{1.9}$$

On differentiating this steady state equation (where $\dot{k}=0$) with respect to the long-run time trend t, one obtains

$$\left.\frac{\dot{y}(t)}{y(t)}\right|_{\dot{k}=0} = g \tag{1.10}$$

This is the 'growth effect', which is a positive constant. Thus technology determines the steady state growth rate of output per capita. The steady state growth rate depends neither on the savings rate nor on the specific form of the production function. It depends solely on the growth of technological progress. Because the Solow model assumes a competitive market where factors are paid their marginal products, it predicts the signs and magnitudes of the regression coefficients on savings and population in (1.8). This equation states that the more productive a country's workers, the faster its technological progress, the higher its savings rate and the lower its depreciation rates and population growth and the higher its per capita income at any point of time in the steady state. But this is the 'level effect'. The growth effect is determined by equation (1.10), which shows that technology alone determines the steady state growth rates. Since Solow assumed technology was completely exogenous, no policy decisions could affect it.

The theory of endogenous growth models rejects this argument of Solow. One important class of endogenous growth models is the AK model where output $Y=AK$ and $\dot{k}=(sY-\delta K)$. The output growth rate is $\dot{Y}/Y = \dot{K}/K = sA - \delta$. In this model, any public policy or household decisions that affect the savings rate s can in turn affect the long-run growth rate. This type of AK model ensures endogenous growth by avoiding diminishing returns to capital in the long run. In order to empirically test the AK model, Jones (1995) conducted simple time series tests for 15 OECD countries over the period 1950–88 using Penn World Tables. His tests show that the AK model is not consistent with the empirical data, i.e., increases in investment rates have not been matched by persistent growth of income. His case appeared to be stronger for the tests involving producer durables equipment. Also, the investment rates are found to influence the growth rates for at most 8–10 years and not for a longer duration of time. We need to examine Jones' (1995) hypothesis in more details for testing the endogeneity of the growth models, when other forms of endogeneity may be present.

1.1.   Technology and efficiency

The technology process comprises several stages. The first is technology creation and diffusion across firms and industries. The second is its impact on cost and productivity in the long run. The third is its impact on new types of dynamic efficiency such as innovations efficiency and access efficiency. Innovation efficiency occurs through racing up the competitive ladder in the timing and knowledge arena. Access efficiency occurs through globalization of markets where separate firms and industries merge across countries and the market structure changes when domination by one or two firms occurs.

The process of technology creation and diffusion comes along with the destruction of old technology. Schumpeter (1942) called this 'creative destruction' by emphasizing the point that the leading firms intending to stay dynamically efficient along the efficient frontier must deliberately adopt this creative process. Since a large part of technology creation is due to significant R&D investments, large firms gain competitive advantage through their resource base. D'Aveni (1994) developed the model of hypercompetition, where the leading edge companies make deliberate attempts to increase their resource base and R&D investments in order to gain their next temporary advantage before other competitors enter the field. By following this process and seizing the next temporary advantage, companies like Apple and Microsoft became leading giants. Schumpeter (1942) in his classic book *Capitalism, Socialism and Democracy* emphasized the same point through his concept of innovation as follows:

> ...But in capitalist reality as distinguished from its textbook picture, it is not that kind of competition (i.e., perfect) which counts but the competition from the new commodity, the new technology

and the new source of supply, the new type of organization (the largest scale unit of control for instance) – competition which commands a decisive cost or quality advantage and which strikes not at margins of profits and the outputs of existing firms but at their foundations and their very lives....

We have noted that technology has both a specific and a general meaning. In its specific meaning as we discussed before, it implies the characteristics of the production and distribution process for firms and industries. A change in this form of technology indicates a shift of the production or cost frontier. In its general meaning it includes all the knowledge and innovations applied to the production and distribution process.

Technology generates several important changes, which affect the long-run growth of an economy. By an *upward shift* of the production frontier it improves the productivity of inputs like labor and capital, thus reducing unit costs. This cost reduction helps to increase profits and decrease prices. Profits spur more investment and price declines to help extend the market. For an open economy, the market expansion leads to an increase in global trade and comparative gains from trade creation and diversion.

Secondly, technological progress helps to expand the scale of production, which implies e.g., that doubling all the inputs generates more than double the output. This scale expansion provides a strong incentive for market expansion and globalization of trade. The recent experiences of Southeast Asian countries such as Hong Kong, South Korea, Taiwan and Singapore bear adequate testimony in this regard. High economic growth rates in these countries have been caused, to a large extent, through an increase in input productivity, investment in modern technology and scale expansion.

Thirdly, technology is *innovation* that takes many forms. The core aspect of these forms is innovation efficiency, which was strongly emphasized in Schumpeter's (1942) approach to economic growth. The Schumpeterian model changes technology at various points in the value chain, thus challenging firms to compete in new, innovative ways. Thus the successful firms in an industry transform their technologies so as to create new strategic assets, which bring them new streams of cash flows and projects. Increased investments follow. This results in higher growth.

Two forms of innovation have been emphasized: R&D and Knowledge Diffusion. Investment in R&D has increased significantly in high-tech industries in the last decade and many firms have formed joint ventures or cooperation in R&D as a way to reduce costs or research and to internalize some of the external benefits of R&D.

The knowledge diffusion works at three levels: basic research, applied research in the private sector and applied research in the academic and state supported research institutes. Most of the non-private R&D investment helps the process of knowledge diffusion in other sectors of the economy and the advances in computer technology accentuate this process significantly. These advances help in the process of creation and dissemination of the results of research on a wider scale. Some R&D investments are directly intended to increase efficiency in the distribution and networking of the marketing framework and recent trends in globalization have helped the dissemination process.

Finally, technology changes the market structure dramatically, especially in the high-tech fields. Advances in computer technology, progress in communications techniques and liberalization of global trade practices have played a most dynamic role in this regard. Reducing unit costs through R&D, creating new strategic assets and generating strong positive feedback in today's information economy have intensified the competitive process and provided incentives for more entry in high-tech fields. Thus small firms have taken advantage of the leader–follower models in order to gain from the scale economies of leading firms. Competition has been most intense in recent times in some of the high-tech industries such as computers, telecommunications and electronic industries. Declining prices and increasing tempo of innovation efficiency have intensified the competitive pressures in these industries. Following Schumpeter's dynamic theory of innovations, D'Aveni (1994) has characterized this state as hypercompetition. He argues that this hypercompetition resembles in many ways the Darwinian world of natural selection and the survival of the fittest, where the rival competitors get crushed if they are not on the leading edge of the innovation efficiency frontier.

Our object in the following sections is to analyze two aspects of technological progress that affects the economic growth of developing economies. First we discuss the Schumpeterian model of innovations affecting economic growth. This is extended so as to characterize the optimal growth path of an industry under non-competitive equilibrium. Secondly, we analyze a model of hyper-competition in the framework of a theory of economic evolution and discuss the relevance of a genetic theory of selection and evolution in the hypercompetitive world. The implications of a changing market structure due to increased entry are analyzed in the framework of increased R&D investment.

In Schumpeter's model of innovation, efficiency is the prime mover of growth of firms in an industry. Competition has two facets: static and dynamic. The former takes technology as given, so firms compete only in terms of prices and costs. Thus greater competition tends to reduce prices and costs. In the limit, some firms may have to exit due to large depletion of cash flows from dwindling strategic assets. Schumpeterian competition however is more dynamic in that it changes technology at various points in the value chain. Thus the successful firms in an industry transform their technologies so as to create new strategic assets yielding increased profits.

Two major forms of innovation are R&D investments for creating new technology and new strategies for developing new products that modify the old. The term 'creative destruction' was used by Schumpeter (1942) to convey these two independent forms of investment. R&D investments tend to reduce average costs. Cost-reducing expenditures are largely fixed costs. In a market system the major impact of cost-reducing R&D investment is profitability. The large-scale economies associated with R&D may entail concentrated and imperfectly competitive market structures, which tend to affect price margins and allocative efficiency. What is important is that R&D expenditures also involve the so-called appropriability problems or externalities. Spence (1984) had developed a dynamic model of industry performance assuming Nash Equilibrium for the market environment. In this model, unit cost $c(t)$ for firm i depends on accumulated knowledge through R&D $z_i(t)$ as

$$c_i(t) = F(z_i(t)) \tag{1.11}$$

where $F(z_i(t))$ is a declining function of $z_i(t)$. Growth of R&D knowledge is assumed to take linear form

$$\dot{z}_i(t) = \frac{dz_i}{dt} = m_i(t) + \theta \sum_{j \neq i} m_j(t) \tag{1.12}$$

where $m_j(t)$ is the current expenditure by firm j on R&D. With output x_i and the inverse demand function $D_i(x)$, the profits gross of R&D expenditures for firm i can be written as

$$E_i(z) = x_i(z)D_i(x(z)) - c_i(z_i)x_i(z) \tag{1.13}$$

where $z = \sum_i z_i$. Spence assumed that there is equilibrium at each point of time in the market that depends on the cost $c = (F(z_1), \dots, F(z_n))$. It could be Nash Equilibrium in quantities or some other form of non-competitive equilibrium. It is assumed that the equilibrium is unique given c and z.

Two important results are derived in the Spence model. One expresses the equilibrium for the industry's total investment in R&D as

$$R\&D = z_n(1 + \theta(n-1))^{-1} \tag{1.14}$$

This shows that the R&D costs of the achieved amount of cost reduction decline as θ increases from 0 to 1. Thus, while spillovers reduce the incentives for cost reduction, they also reduce the costs, at the industry level, of achieving a given level cost reduction. Clearly, the incentives can be restored through government subsidies. Thus spillovers can improve the performance of the market with the incentives appropriately restored.

Secondly, one can analyze the impact of cooperative R&D, which is practiced in many European countries. Fully cooperative R&D with firms produces results identical to that of a monopolist with price (p) cost margins $p/c = 1/w$, where $w = 1/nb$, $b > 1$ being the price elasticity of demand. The reasons are twofold: (1) margins are set by competitive rules and (2) each firm's profits gross of R&D costs are $1/n$ of industry profits and its R&D costs are $1/n$ of industry R&D costs. Therefore the firm wants to maximize $1/n$ of industry profits net of R&D costs. They all agree and maximize net industry profits.

The Spence model can easily be extended to develop optimal R&D investment strategies under the threat of superior entry. The entry threat stimulates the incumbent to innovate in case entry prevention is possible but discourages R&D if inevitable. In case of entry deterrence, the incumbent successfully prevents entry by innovating.

Thus greater technical uncertainty of R&D investments stimulates the start of R&D and can result in the implementation of more expensive research projects.

The dynamics of R&D competition may be analyzed very simply by a model of interaction between two players either as a competition between the incumbent and the new entrant or between two agents in a Cournot duopoly market where the firms may undertake independent ventures of R&D process innovation – or form a cartel for cost-reducing R&D investments.

The competitive interaction may be easily modeled in terms of output x and y of the two players as

$$\dot{x} = x(a - bx - cy)$$
$$\dot{y} = y(d - ex - fy)$$

$$(1.15)$$

with positive constants a to f. If one player is absent, the other obeys the familiar logistic growth law representing the growth of technical innovation. The x and y isoclines are given by $a-bx-cy=0$ and $d-ex-fy=0$, which are straight lines with negative slopes. If the two isoclines do not intersect, then one of the players tends to extinction. This is a case of the dominant firm model, where entry is successfully deterred or blocked by the dominant incumbent firm. When the two isoclines intersect at a unique point $A = (\overline{x}, \overline{y})$ given by

$$\overline{x} = \frac{af - cd}{bf - ce}$$
$$\overline{y} = \frac{bd - ae}{bf - ce}$$

$$(1.16)$$

The Jacobian of (1.15) at A is

$$J = \begin{bmatrix} -b\overline{x} & -c\overline{x} \\ -e\overline{y} & -f\overline{y} \end{bmatrix}$$

$$(1.17)$$

Two situations are distinguished here:

(a)   If $bf > ce$, the denominator in (1.16) is positive, which implies that $af - cd > 0$ and $bd - ae > 0$. This shows that all the eigenvalues of (1.17) are negative. This means all trajectories converge to A. This is the case of stable coexistence.

(b) Otherwise, $c/f > a/d > b/e$. Since $|J| = \overline{xy}(bf - ce) < 0$, we get A as a saddle point. Its stable manifold consists of two orbits converging to point A. All orbits from one basin converge to $A_2 = (0, d/f)$, all those from the other basin point to $A_1 = (a/e, 0)$. This means that depending on the initial conditions, one or the other player gets eliminated, i.e., if one player (e.g., the new entrant) cannot compete to remain on the dynamic efficiency frontier, while the other (the incumbent) does, the entrant gets crushed. This is the so-called *bi-stable* case of competition. The player who survives dynamically becomes the dominant player. Hofbauer and Sigmund (1998) and other ecologists such as Otto and Day (2007) have discussed various types of dynamic interaction models and their stability properties.

1.2.   Technology and market structure

Two most significant influences of technology on the market structure come through R&D investments and knowledge diffusion. The first generates the expectation of high monopoly profits for the efficient firms leading the R&D race – through increased innovations. If we assume that successful innovations arise as a result of a Poisson process with an intensity u, the probability that a firm innovates successfully during the period dt is udt. The expected monopoly profit for the successful firm may then be written as

$$\pi(u, n) = r(n)u - c(u, f) \tag{1.18}$$

where $r = r(n)$ the instantaneous monopoly surplus obtained by the winner and $c(u, f)$ is the firm's cost function depending on intensity u and fixed cost f. Here the monopoly surplus $r(n)$ depends on the number of firms n in the industry. By assuming a convex function $c(u, f)$ as a lower function in intensity u, Folster and Trofimov (1997) maximized the profit function (1.18) with respect to intensity u and the result is an optimal profit function which is S-shaped. This type of profit function implies that the positive external effect of R&D innovations sometimes dominates the negative effect of increasing competition.

   Knowledge diffusion through technology has intensified in recent times through global spread of software technology and direct international investment by multinational corporations. Companies such as Microsoft, Apple, Oracle and Intel have expanded their foreign investment, in China, India and other southeast Asian countries and the trend of outsourcing of jobs of high-tech industries in the US and Europe has continued over time though it has slowed down a bit due to recessionary slump in business in the US. Knowledge diffusion affects market structure in several ways, e.g., it reduces unit cost for other firms and increases their potential for Bertrand-type price competition. The limit-pricing model of a dominant firm develops this theory of potential entry. These and other aspects will be discussed in the following section.

1.3.   Knowledge diffusion

Knowledge diffusion may occur in several ways. Since innovations may take several forms, technology diffuses through international trade and international R&D ventures by multinational corporations. Recent developments in software technology and sharing of R&D investments have intensified this process. The trend in the future is to increase this tempo of diffusion of knowledge technology. The race in R&D competition for new processes and products has been intensified in recent times due to globalization of trade and markets. As a result the expectation of higher profits for the successful innovator who wins the race has accentuated the trend of new investment. Escalating the quality ladder and following a strategy to preempt the future entry have been other means adopted by the large innovators.

A useful way to model the spread of technology and research knowledge is through a stochastic diffusion process. A lognormal diffusion process is more appropriate for knowledge innovations as many empirical studies have found its appropriateness. Let $X(t)$ be the investment in knowledge or its output at time t. We assume the transition probability $f(\tau, x; t, y) = \Pr[X(t) = y; X(\tau) = x]; 0 < y, x < \infty$ for every time point τ and t where $0 \leq \tau < t$ and also that it satisfies the backward and forward Kolmogorov equations. Now consider the coefficients $b(t, x)$ and $a(t, x)$, the infinitesimal mean and variance of the change in $X(t)$ during a small interval Δt of time that characterize a particular process of the diffusion type as $b(t, x) = b_t x$ and

$a(t, x) = a_t x^2 > 0$ where b_t and a_t are functions of time. If we assume $b_t = b_0$ and $a_t = a_0$ where a_0, b_0 are positive constants, then the backward and forward Kolmogorov equations can be written as

$$-\frac{\delta f}{\delta \tau} = \frac{1}{2} a_0 x^2 \frac{\delta^2 f}{\delta x^2} - b_0 x \frac{\delta f}{\delta x}$$

and

$$\frac{\delta f}{\delta t} = \frac{1}{2} a_0 y^2 \frac{\delta^2 f}{\delta y^2} + (2a_0 - b_0)y \frac{\delta f}{\delta y} + (a_0 - b_0)f$$

These diffusion equations imply a lognormal probability density function

$$f = \left\{ \frac{1}{y(2\pi\gamma(t-\tau))^{1/2}} \exp[(-\frac{1}{2\gamma(t-\tau)})[\log y - \log x - \beta(t-\tau)^2]\right\}$$

where $\gamma = a_0$, $\beta = (b_0 - a_0/2)$.

The mean $E[X(t)]$ and variance $V[X(t)]$ may then be derived as

$$\text{Mean} = \left[X(\tau)^k \exp(k\beta_0 + k^2 \frac{\gamma}{2})(t-\tau) \right], \quad k = 1, 2, 3, \ldots$$

$$\text{Variance} = \left[X(\tau)^2 \{\exp(2\beta_0(t-\tau)\}\{\exp a_0(t-\tau) - 1\} \right]$$

On taking $\tau = 0$ as the initial point and $\Pr(X(t) = x_0) = 1$ we obtain

$$\text{Mean} = E[X(t)] = x_0 \exp(b_0 t)$$

$$\text{Variance} = V[X(t)] = x_0^2 \exp(2b_0 t)(\exp a_0 t - 1)$$

i.e., the trend in mean and variance are both exponential functions of time.

Now we extend the model to consider the impact of two exogenous variables ΔR_1 and ΔR_2 denoting the increase in new innovations or R&D expenditure by two groups of firms. Then we obtain $b(t, x) = b_t x$ and $a(t, x) = a_t x^2 > 0$ with $a_t = a_0 > 0, b_t = b_0 + b_1 \Delta R_1(t) + h_2 \Delta R_2(t)$ where a_0, b_0, b_1, b_2 are non-zero constants. The second group of firms' R&D expenditure reflects the impact of the other firms in the industry, i.e., externality effect. In this case we obtain the mean and variance as

$$\text{Mean} = E[X(t)] = x_0 \exp(b_0 t + b_1 \sum_{j=1}^{t} \Delta R_{1j} + b_2 \sum_{j=1}^{t} \Delta R_{2j})$$

$$\text{Variance} = V[X(t)] = x_0^2 \exp 2(b_0 t + b_1 \sum_{j=1}^{t} \Delta R_{1j} + b_2 \sum_{j=1}^{t} \Delta R_{2j})$$

If $b_2 > b_1 > 0$ then the externality effect is higher, implying that the rest of industry allows more diffusion to the given firm group or industry.

In macrodynamic models of growth, learning by doing has provided an important source of knowledge diffusion. One simple way to illustrate Arrow's learning by doing is make the productivity parameter A in Solow's Cobb-Douglas production function

$$Y = F(K, AL) = K^\alpha (AL)^{1-\alpha}, \ 0 < \alpha < 1$$

endogenous as

$$A = ZK^\theta$$

where θ is a positive coefficient.

$$\gamma = \frac{\dot{K}}{K}$$

may be viewed as the exogenous rate of labor augmenting technical change. On defining k as $k = K/AL$ and $n = \dot{L}/L$ as in Solow model we can easily reformulate the extended Solow model as

$$\dot{k} = s(1-\theta)k^\alpha - [\gamma + n + \delta(1-\theta)]k \tag{1.19}$$

where $\dot{K} = sY - \delta K$, δ being the positive rate of depreciation. The steady state equilibrium capital–labor ratio k is then given by

$$\bar{k} = \left[\frac{s(1-\theta)}{n + \gamma + \delta(1-\theta)} \right]^{1/1-\alpha} \tag{1.20}$$

The steady state growth rate of output ALk^α is then equal to

$$\bar{g}_Y = \theta . \bar{g}_K + \gamma + n = \frac{\gamma + n}{1 - \theta}$$

so that income per worker Y/L grows in the steady state as

$$\bar{g}_{Y/L} = \bar{g}_Y - n = \frac{\gamma + n}{1 - \theta} \tag{1.21}$$

It is clear that an increase in learning coefficient θ reduces the steady state value of the capital-effective labor by raising the level of effective labor. The steady state equation (1.21) shows clearly that the higher the learning coefficient θ, the greater is the growth rate of steady state level of per worker income. Thus Arrow's learning by doing is capable of explaining differences in growth rates in per capita income by differences in the ability to learn from experience. Sengupta (2005) and Sengupta and Neogi (2009) have discussed in some detail how the rapid increase in growth rates in southeast Asian countries such as China, Singapore and South Korea have been accomplished by R&D investments and learning by doing.

The externality effect of technology diffusion has been strongly emphasized in the endogenous growth models of Romer (1990) and Lucas (1993). The Romer model writes the production function as

$$Y = K^{\alpha}(AL_1)^{1-\alpha}, L_1 + L_2 = L$$

where total labor L comprises one part L_1, allocated to output and the other part L_2 allocated to research ideas represented by A. Here $A=A(t)$ is the stock of knowledge or the number of research ideas that have been invented over the course of history up to time t. The growth of R&D ideas is assumed to be of the form $\dot{A} = \bar{\delta} L_2, L_2 = L_A$ where L_2 is the number of researchers and $\bar{\delta}$ is their productivity. The productivity parameter $\bar{\delta}$ may be a constant or it may increase over time, i.e., $\bar{\delta} = \delta A^{\phi}$.
Romer assumed $\phi = 1$, so that

$$\dot{A} = \delta L_2 A = \delta L_A A$$

But this specification rules out increasing returns to research inputs or positive knowledge spillovers (diffusion). Empirically the assumption $\phi = 1$ fails to hold for the US and Southeast Asian countries. If g_A is the growth rate of A, i.e., $g_A = \dot{A}/A$ and r is the rate of return on R&D capital, the proportion $\pi_R - L_2/L - L_A/L$ of workforce engaged in R&D can be expressed as

$$\pi_R = \left[1 + \frac{r-n}{\alpha.g_A}\right]^{-1}, \frac{\dot{L}}{L} = n.$$

This shows that the faster the economy grows, the higher the fraction of population engaged in research. Unlike Romer, Lucas introduced the R&D spillover effect, where R&D accumulation in one industry generates induced investment in other industries. The non-rival nature of the R&D input generates increasing returns to scale as this may help industries grow faster.

Bernstein and Mohnen (1994) used a loglinear production function

$$Y_t = F(v_t, K_{t-1}, \Delta K_t, S_{t-1})$$

and the associated dual cost function for the US and Japan over the period 1963–83 to estimate the contribution of two forms of international spillover effects: direct and indirect. Here Y is total real output, v a vector of variable factor demands, K is physical capital and S a vector of R&D spillovers, which is the R&D capital from the other country. The contribution of spillover effect is estimated through the respective input output ratios as

$$\frac{\delta(v_t/y_t)}{\delta S_{t-1}} = \alpha + b\left(\frac{K_{t-1}}{Y_{t-1}}\right)' \beta + c\left(\frac{\Delta K_t}{Y_t}\right)' S\mu\left(\frac{\delta(K_t/Y_t)}{\delta S_{t-1}}\right)$$

where prime denotes transpose. The direct spillover effect on variable factor demand is measured by α, the indirect effects by all capital inputs β and net investment through μ. Their estimates of total factor productivity (TFP) growth are as given in Table 1.1.

This table shows that the direct effect from Japanese R&D capital contributed about 20% to US productivity growth over the two decades 1963–85. Over the same period the US effect accounted for about 60% of Japanese TFP growth in its R&D intensive manufacturing factor. Likewise, over the same period, the international R&D spillovers estimated by the equation above reduced the labor-output

Table 1.1   Decomposition of average annual TFP growth-rates (%)

				Spillover effect	
	TFPG	TFP Scale	Physical capital	Direct	Indirect
USA					
1980–85	−2.413	0.116	0.809	0.632	−4.09
1963–85	0.104	0.219	2.334	0.448	−2.32
Japan					
1980–85	1.394	–	1.118	3.967	−1.44
1963–85	1.935	0.217	2.174	1.868	−1.13

and capital-output ratios for both US and Japanese manufacturing sectors. But for the US, the labor output and capital output ratios declined by 0.04% and 0.02% and in Japan by 3.5 and 0.13 respectively. Thus, the effects from US R&D capital were significantly greater for Japan than the effects arising from Japan generated spillover. One may conjecture that Japan's learning by doing results are repeated by the high growth rates of Southeast Asian countries such as Singapore, South Korea, Taiwan and Hong Kong during the last two decades.

The spillover effect adds an important dimension to the technology by making it endogenous and transferable. Recent spreads of software innovations provide the most important example. Lucas has termed this learning spillover technology which manifests in a most direct form Arrow's learning by doing. In many ways the spillover technology allows dynamic externalities to generate dynamic gains from trade. Thus declining prices of software and computer have helped the newly industrial countries (NICs) in Asia and China to reap the benefits of spillover technology.

1.4.   Endogenous growth: empirical tests

Endogenous growth theory maintains that the key determinants of long-run or permanent growth are determined endogenously within the model, where the agents optimally choose their consumption and savings and also the amount of resources allocated to R&D and hence to the improvements of technology. The central thesis of the endogenous growth literature is that permanent changes in variables that are potentially affected by government policy lead to permanent changes in long-run growth rates. This result is central to the early AK style growth-models due to Romer (1986), Lucas (1993) and Rebelo (1991) as well as the endogenous technological change models due to Romer (1990) and Grossman and Helpman (1991). This type of result contrasts significantly with the neoclassical growth model used by Solow (1957) where the presence of long-run growth depends very critically on the *exogenous* technological progress.

One of the key properties of the endogenous growth models is the absence of diminishing return to capital. The simplest version of a production function without diminishing returns is the *AK* function: $Y=AK$, where A is a positive constant that reflects the level of technology. K may include both physical and human capital (or stock of knowledge). Output per capita is then $y=Ak$ and the savings–investment equilibrium yields.

$$g_k = \frac{\dot{k}}{k} = sA - (n+\delta) \tag{1.22}$$

where s is the savings ratio, n is the growth-rate of labor and δ is the constant rate of depreciation of capital. Since A is constant, there is no technological progress of the Solow-type model. If $sA>(n+\delta)$ then $g_k>0$. In this case k always grows at the steady state rate $\bar{g}_k = sA - (n+\delta)$. Since $y=Ak$, g_y also equals $\bar{g}_k$. Thus the economy described by the AK technology can display positive long-run (or steady state) per capita growth without any Solow-type technological progress. We have to note in particular that the growth rates of capital and output per capita depend on the behavioral parameters of model such as the savings rate and the rate of population growth thus a higher savings rate s or a higher level A due to the government policy may lead to a higher long-run growth rate.

Jones (1995) tested the empirical plausibility of the AK model for 15 OECD countries using data from 1950 to 1988. He found that the notes of investment, particularly equipment investment have risen persistently over time in the long run, while GDP growth rates have not. The time series test performed by Jones suggest that a permanent increase in the investment rate affects growth only over a relatively short horizon of 8 to 10 years. This result is significantly different from the infinite horizon growth note predicted by AK model. Thus the AK models and the Harrod-Domar type models do not provide a good description of long-run growth in advanced industrial countries. This conclusion will be examined in some detail in later chapters.

1.5.   Empirical growth: the NIC experiences

It is useful to examine the fast pace of growth in the last two decades of the NICs of Southeast Asia. The example of China and Taiwan are particularly striking. We already noted the Jones hypothesis about the AK model of endogenous growth that predicts that capital accumulation is the only determinant of long-term growth rate of national output. Nandi (2009) tested the AK model's empirical consistency using macroeconomic data for 112 widely diverse countries for the period 1950–2004. Her conclusion is that rates of investment particularly for equipment have increased persistently over time while GDP rates have not. Hence the AK model is broadly rejected. However, the major exception to this conclusion is China, which supports the AK-type phenomena most consistently. Nandi shows that the Chinese growth and investment rates are both trend stationary with the same direction of trend. The econometric causality tests show that the direction of causality run strongly from high past investment shares of GDP per capita to current growth. This lends strong support to the paradigm that China's growth is predominately driven by the growth of capital accumulation. Sengupta (2005) and Sengupta and Neogi (2009) have critically analyzed the dynamics of China's growth rate and compared it with that of India, where the AK model is not empirically supported.

The case of Taiwan provides another striking contrast. It shows the intensity of knowledge diffusion and the technology of software development to a significant degree. Two important features of R&D development in Taiwan are to be noted. One is that most of the increase in R&D investment was based on firms with 100 employees or less. Hence the technology diffusion helped improve the middle class to a significant degree. Secondly, the state actively pursued the policy of protecting the intellectual property rights associated with software development since 1990s. This provided a favorable climate for R&D investment in the private sector comprising both domestic and foreign enterprises. How has the accumulation of human capital and related R&D efforts helped the growth of productivity in the industrial/manufacturing sector in Taiwan? Wang and Tsai (2002) have estimated the effects of R&D investment in Taiwan's manufacturing firms on productivity growth by estimating the following Cobb-Douglas production function

$$Q_{it} = A_0 e^{\lambda t} L_{it}^{\alpha} K_{it}^{1-\alpha} R_{it}^{\gamma}$$

where Q, L, K and R respectively represent value added, labor, physical capital and R&D capital with i denoting a specific firm. A sample of 136 firms over the period 1994–2000 is used to estimate the parameters as given in Table 1.2.

Two results are most striking. One is that the R&D capital elasticity lying between 0.18 and 0.20 is significant at 1% level of the t-test

Table 1.2 Parameter estimates of production function

	α	γ	λ	R^2
All firms (n=136)	0.485**	0.187	0.037*	0.325
High-tech firms (n_1=43)	0.305	0.297**	0.125**	0.468
Other firms (n_2=93)	0.674**	0.055	0.021	0.326

Note: One and two asterisks denote *t*-values significant at 5% and 1% respectively.

implying a significant impact of R&D on productivity growth. Secondly, if the total sample of n-136 is divided into two groups: high-tech (n_1=43) and the rest (n_2=93) the results are distinctly different – the elasticity for high-tech firms is about six times that of non-high-tech firms.

The production of Information Technology (IT) output like software development and hardware engineering fueled Taiwan's impressive economic growth in the last two decades. IT output grew from less than $100 million dollars in 1980 to more than $5 billion in 1989 and grew over 20% annually in the 1990s, when its GDP growth rate averaged 6.5%. In 1999 it reached $21 billion and if Taiwanese manufacturing in China is included the total IT output exceeded $35 billion in 1999. How did this happen? One basic indicator of Taiwan's technological achievements is its ranking among US patent recipients. In 1980 Taiwan ranked twenty-first, by 1990 it ranked eleventh and in 1995 its rank was seventh. Today Taiwan receives more patents per capita than the other Asians NICs and ranks ahead of all the G7 countries except US and Japan. Not only have the state policies promoting R&D investments in the private sector helped, the agglomeration and scale effects that flowed from the large infusion of entrepreneurial resources from the US provided useful and productive linkages to new technology and markets. The Hsinchu region in Taiwan like Silicon Valley in California provides an industrial environment for Taiwan in which small companies can grow larger, while still remaining a part of the overall decentralized infrastructure of the region.

Table 1.3 Rates of TFP growth

	Growth of output per worker	Contribution (%) of: Physical capital per worker	Education per worker	TFP growth
South Korea				
1973–84	5.3	3.4	0.8	1.1
1984–94	5.2	3.3	0.6	2.1
Japan				
1973–84	4.9	3.0	0.9	0.9
1984–94	5.6	2.3	0.5	2.8
OECD				
(excluding the US)				
1973–84	1.8	1.1	0.6	0.2
1984–94	1.7	0.8	0.2	0.7

The experience of other Southeast Asian countries such as South Korea is very similar in its emphasis on R&D investment and knowledge diffusion. For OECD data (1973–92) the share of R&D as percent of value added in Korea turned out to be 21 for drugs, 18 and 16 for electronics and computers and 11 for electrical machinery. Rates of TFP growth were as given in Table 1.3.

The OECD report for 2001 noted that the Korean overall productivity growth was largely due to the IT manufacturing sector. This sector also helped spread IT knowledge to other industries and sectors. One has to note also that the private sector has taken the lead in R&D expenditure in Korea. The R&D expenditure in average percentage terms has the following breakdown for 1978–97 between the government and the private sector.

	Government	Private
Korea		
1985–90	21.79	78.21
1991–97	19.10	80.90
Japan		
1985–90	54.28	47.72
1991–97	47–16	52.84

Thus it is clear that the accumulation of human capital, learning by doing and R&D innovations have played a dynamic role in the rapid economic development of the Southeast Asian countries. These sources of growth display the multiple facets of technological and innovation efficiency.

The current volume discusses various dynamic models that incorporate the impact of technology and innovations on the industry evolution and overall economic growth. This is supplemented by a detailed empirical analysis of countries such as China and Taiwan and South Korea that have exhibited episodes of rapid economic growth in the last two decades. The dynamics of innovation in Asia is also discussed for countries such as India and China that are likely to play leading roles as technology leaders in the coming decades.

2
Innovations and Industry Growth

Economic efficiency is the key to the growth of an industry. It may take different forms. Productivity gains, unit cost reduction, quality improvement of inputs and outputs and the diversity of output are some of these forms. In the short run a firm operates with a fixed stock of capital. Hence it can reduce unit costs and therefore prices by adopting optimal input and output strategies. In the long run however capital stocks are variable. Investment in capital stocks and innovations then provide the key to efficiency gains through cost reductions, quality improvement and external economies.

Our objective in this chapter is to discuss some specific forms of innovations as they affect industry growth. R&D expenditure is one form where innovations are viewed as knowledge capital. The stock of knowledge capital differs from physical capital, e.g., capital equipment in several aspects. It is complementary to all other inputs and not competitive and it is not subject to diminishing returns to scale. It also exhibits a spillover effect in the form of diffusion of new knowledge, which creates significant external economies. A second form of knowledge capital closely related to R&D investment proportions is 'human capital' which exhibits the feature of learning by doing. Learning by doing exhibits scale economies, improves labor productivity and helps develop improved input and output. Another form of innovation, which has occupied a central place in the high-tech industries of today, is often called information and communications technology (ICT). The major forms of this new technology include new software development and new techniques of communication that help expand the market globally. US multinational firms have used this technology to develop new subsidiaries in other countries such as China, Singapore, Taiwan and India. The future trend is to increase global trade in varieties of goods and services. The dynamics of comparative gains from international trade has been altered in recent times most dramatically. Thus a small country like Taiwan has been greatly successful in generating software patents in New York, which are comparable to US and Japan.

We discuss some analytical models of industry growth – where innovations play key roles. The models characterize efficiency growth and its economic implications.

2.1.   Innovations as knowledge capital

The R&D process as an important form of knowledge capital has been emphasized very strongly in modern endogenous growth theory. Solow's reliance on the neoclassical growth model with decreasing marginal returns to physical capital, perfect competition and exogenous technology cannot fully explain the cross-country variations in per capita income and national growth rates. Romer (1990) and Lucas (1993) have consistently emphasized this point in their endogenous growth theory. Grossman and Helpman (1993) have reviewed the status of endogenous innovations in the modern theory of growth and concluded as follows:

> And what of the endogeneity of technological program? Some might argue that technology is driven by science, which may proceed at a pace and in a direction that is largely independent of economic incentives. But few scholars of industrial innovation accept this view. This is the conclusion of countless studies of particular industries and innovations, including those on machine tools (Rosenberg 1972), synthetic chemicals (Freeman 1982), metallurgy (Mawery and Rosenberg 1989) and semiconductors (Dosi 1984) to name a few. According to these studies firms have invested in new technologies when they have seen an opportunity to earn profits. In fact a large proportion of the scientific research conducted in the OECD countries is financed by private industry. (Grossman and Helpman 1993)

The R&D expenditure process has several distinct features. First of all, there is inherent uncertainty associated with industrial research.

Firms allocating resources to the R&D process buy themselves a chance at developing a new product or process or software. Newcomers may always enter into the research activity unless the entry cost is very high. Hence there is always the potential threat of new entry. Firm's expected gain is derived from the probability of success times the market value of a new product or process. The race for R&D activity between a new comer and the incumbent firm yields an expected monopoly profit for the winner and models of successful R&D innovations may be constructed by using a Poisson process. If successful R&D innovations arise as a result of a Poisson process with intensity u, then the probability that a firm innovates successfully during a period d*t* is *u*d*t*. If there are n firms and each firm has equal chance of winning the R&D race, then the probability that any particular firm becomes a winner in the race is (*u*/*n*) d*t*. The firm's instantaneous expected profit is

$$\pi(n,u) = r \cdot u \cdot n^{-1} - c(u) \tag{2.1}$$

where *r* is the return and $c(u)$ is the cost of R&D research. Maximization of expected profits in (2.1) subject to the potential threat of entry provides the incentive and the rationale for endogenous innovations through R&D capital.

Secondly, the R&D capital sometimes has large spillover efforts. As firms develop new technologies they sometimes enhance scientific discoveries that have more general applicability in other fields. Such discoveries may be difficult to patent and to internalize all external benefits. A most common example is software research and many inventions in communication technology. These external spillover effects tend to make the cost of entry much lower thus opening up intensive competition. The Solow model emphasizing exogenous technology also assumed the existence of perfect competition in the input and output markets. But this does not seem to hold empirically when firms compete in the R&D race and the winner tends to earn large monopoly profits until another competitor innovates and succeeds in bringing out a new product or a new process. Schumpeter learned this as the process of creative destruction. Incumbent firms exit and the newcomers invade the market.

Thirdly, the R&D capital may take different forms, such as basic research (as is performed in many universities and public agencies), applied research and finally commercial research. Cohen and Levinthal (1989) analyzed empirical data of 297 firms in 151 lines of business in the US manufacturing over the period 1975–77. Compared to basic research, the applied scientific research in computer science and related fields had a stronger impact on unit R&D expenditure by the sampled firms. In some industries like pharmaceuticals the process of commercialization of the applied research process, e.g., a new drug, may take quite a long period of time. The impact of R&D investment on the efficiency of the pharmaceutical industry has been very significant however. For example, Sengupta and Sahoo (2006) have considered the following cost efficiency model for pharmaceutical industry.

Min θ subject to

$$\sum_{j=1}^{n} c_j \lambda_j \leq \theta C_h; \quad \sum_{j=1}^{n} R_j \lambda_j \leq R_h; \quad \sum_{j=1}^{n} y_j \lambda_j \geq y_h; \quad \sum \lambda_j = 1; \quad \lambda_j \geq 0 \quad (2.2)$$

where firm h is the reference firm with output y_h and costs C_h and R&D costs R_h. Here C_h is total cost excluding R&D costs. Total cost comprise costs of goods sold, net plant and machinery expenditure and all marketing costs. If the optimal values of the above Linear Programming (LP) model denoted by asterisks are such that $\theta^* = 1$ with

$$\sum_{j=1}^{n} c_j \lambda_j^* = C_h; \quad \sum_{j=1}^{n} R_j \lambda_j^* = R_h, \quad \lambda_j^* \geq 0, j = 1,\ 2,\ 3,\ ...,\ n$$

then the firm h is efficient, i.e., it lies on the cost efficiency frontier. If however, $\theta^* < 1$, then the optimal costs $C_h^* = \sum_{j=1}^{n} c_j \lambda_j^*$ are lower than the observed costs C_h; hence the firm is not on the cost efficiency frontier. Sengupta and Sahoo (2006) have applied this model to the empirical data of 17 companies available from standard and poor for the period 1981–2000. The selected companies comprise such well-known firms as Merck, Eli Lily, Pfizer, Johnson and Johnson, GlaxoSmithKline and so on. On the basis of the model (2.2) a linear regression is run for the following firms over the period 1981–2000 as

$$TC_j = a_0 + a_1 y_j + a_2 R_j + a_3 \theta_j; \quad (j = \text{efficient})$$

Table 2.1 Cost frontier estimates of selected pharmaceutical firms (1981–2000)

Firm	a_0	a_1	a_2	a_3	R^2	F Statistics
ABT	1355**	1.301**	−295.3*	−0.046	0.998	3933.2
BOL	−250.3	1.608**	N	−1375.4	0.996	780.22
GSK	1915.1**	1.335**	−10929.1	−1505.7*	0.993	374.4
PF	1672.7**	1.350**	−46652.7**	0.064	0.998	4196.6
PHA	−16807.7*	2.224**	N	−1.517*	0.985	187.2

Note:
1. One and two asterisks denote significance at 5% and 1% 2-sided *t*-statistics respectively.
2. *N* denotes a high value not significant even at 20% of *t*-statistics.

The results are reported in Table 2.1. Note that the R&D expenditure term R_j here indicates the productivity enhancing aspect; hence its marginal impact on the total cost TC_j is negative.

If instead of total costs (TC) we use average cost (AC) defined by the ratio of TC to output (y) in the LP model (2.2) the number of efficient firms increases (Table 2.2).

Thus R&D investment plays a very significant role in the growth of the pharmaceutical industry. Note that as efficiency measured by θ^* increases for the firms, the total cost gets reduced.

A final point about the role of R&D in knowledge capital: As an input it is complementary to all other inputs like labor and physical capital and it exhibits no increasing returns. R&D ideas are *non-rivalrous*. Goods that are rivalrous must be produced each time they are sold but the non-rivalrous goods need be produced only once. This is because non-rivalrous inputs such as research ideas involve a fixed cost of production and zero or negligible marginal costs. For example, it costs a great deal of fixed cost to produce the first unit of the latest word processor but subsequent units are produced at a negligible cost by copying the software from the first unit. One implication of this fixed cost due to R&D is that the perfect competition rule of price equaling marginal costs assumed in the Solow model results in negative profits and losses. To follow a pricing rule with price equal to average costs would entail positive profits. Thus the pressure for imperfect and monopolistic competition is always present, when

Table 2.2   Number of efficient pharmaceutical firms with efficient TC, AC and R&D

Year	TC	AC	R&D
1981	3	6	6
1990	5	6	6
2000	3	5	5

research ideas generated by R&D enters the production function of competing firms. Jones (2002) discussed several implications of worldwide data on research ideas. First of all, patent counts may provide a simple measure of the number of research ideas produced. But many ideas are neither patented nor produced using resources that are labeled as R&D. In 1880 about 13,000 patents were issued rising to more than 150,000 in 1999. This number exceeded half a million in 2008. Secondly, one has to note that nearly half of all patents granted in 1999 in the US were of foreign origin. We have discussed the remarkable achievement of Taiwan that has been leading in US patents over the last decade. Thirdly, the share of R&D resources allocated to R&D has increased very significantly in the last decade – i.e., it rose from 0.25% of labor force in US to around 0.75% in 1993. For Japan it rose from 0.2% in 1965 to nearly 0.8% in 1990. The newly industrializing countries (NICs) in Asia excluding Philippines and Malaysia achieved a very high level of R&D spending in business as a percentage of total R&D spending. For example, the figures for 2001 estimated by United Nations Development Program (UNDP) are 84% for South Korea, 62.5% for Singapore and 76.4% for Indonesia. The UNDP used the following equation for estimating the impact of R&D on firm performance:

$$\ln \pi = \alpha_0 + \alpha_1 \ln K + \alpha_2 L + \delta \ln R \left(\sum_{i=1}^{n} \beta_i z_i \right)$$

where π is measured as either value added or profits, K and L are physical capital and labor, R is the average number of R&D personnel over the period 1998–2000 and z_i are the different dummy variables for different metropolitan areas of China and Korea. Table 2.3 shows the cross-section estimates.

Table 2.3   Effect of R&D spending on firm performance

Variable	Productivity	Profit
Constant	3.094 (7.67)	1.897 (3.51)
ln K	0.373 (8.01)	0.484 (7.91)
ln L	0.270 (3.71)	0.139 (1.48)
ln R	0.325 (6.05)	0.276 (3.85)
Dummy Variables		
Seoul (Korea)	5.75 (9.48)	4.74 (5.09)
Shanghai (China)	0.83 (4.81)	0.804 (3.45)
Adjusted R^2	0.688	0.580
Sample Size	408	359

Note: *t*-values are in parentheses

The elasticities of productivity and profitability with respect to R&D personnel shown above are all statistically significant at 5% level. The dummy variables show significant effects on productivity and profits associated with the technological clusters in respective metropolitan areas, just as the Silicon Valley in the US.

A production frontier with R&D inputs R may be written as $Y = F(K, L, R)$ where K and L are physical capital and labor. The impact of R on output (Y) may be embodied in the other inputs K and L or, it may be represented as a separate proxy input, although all research ideas are not representable as physical input through such proxy variables as patent or copyrights. When the effects of R is captured in the form of productivity of K and L, the production frontier may be written as $Y = AF(BK,CL)$ where A is Solow's productivity residual and B, C are the productivities of capital and labor respectively. With a Cobb-Douglas form this becomes

$$Y(t) = A_0 e^{g_1 t}(B_0 e^{g_2 t} K(t))^\alpha (C_0 e^{g_3 t} L(t))^\beta \tag{2.3}$$

where A_0, B_0 and C_0 are positive constants and g_1, g_2, g_3 are positive parameters representing productivities. Solow assumed constant returns to scale $\alpha + \beta = 1$ and ignored the parameters B and C. Mankiw, Romer and Weil (1992) considered a slightly different version of the Solow model as

$$Y(t) = K^\alpha(t)(A_0 e^{g t} L(t))^{1-\alpha}, \ 0 < \alpha < 1$$

where C is written as $A_0 e^{gt}$ indicating labor productivity where labor grows at the exogenous rate n, i.e., $L(t) = L_0 e^{nt}$. With $\dot{K} = I - \delta.K$ and $I = sY$ where δ is the fixed rate of depreciation, the growth of per capita capital may be expressed as $\dot{k} = sy = (n + \delta)k$ where y is per capita income, the dot denotes time derivative and it is assumed $\beta = 1 - \alpha$ implying constant returns. On using the steady state values $k*$, $y*$ in the production frontier one obtains

$$\ln y* = \ln D_0 + rt + (1-\alpha)^{-1}(\ln s - \ln D) - (1-\alpha)^{-1}\ln(n+\delta) \tag{2.4}$$

where $D = AB^\alpha C^{1-\alpha} = D_0 \exp(g_1 + g_2 + g_3)t = D_0 e^{rt}$, $r = g_1 + g_2 + g_3$ and ln denotes natural logarithms. On differentiating, the steady state equation (2.4) we obtain

$$\left.\frac{\dot{y}*}{y*}\right|_{k=0} = r = g_1 + g_2 + g_3 \tag{2.5}$$

One has to note two significant differences of this steady state growth rate (2.5) from that of the traditional Solow model. First, the long run impact of $B(t) = B_0 \exp(g_2 t)$ and $C(t) = C_0 \exp(g_3 t)$ indicating the productivity of physical capital and learning effect of labor respectively are as important as Solow's technology parameter $A(t)$. The Asian growth miracle did occur mostly in the form of $B(t)$ and $C(t)$, though technological program in the form of $A(t)$ was negligible. Secondly, the assumption of constant returns to scale may be too restrictive when B and C involve improvement in the quality of inputs such as capital and labor.

In case the R&D input R is a separate variable like human capital (H) in Mankiw, Romer and Weil (1992), assuming the capital accumulation

$$\dot{K} = s_k Y - \delta_k K, \dot{R} = s_r Y - \delta_r R$$

one can derive the steady state equation as follows, provided we assume $\alpha + \beta < 1$ for the existence of the steady state:

$$\ln y* = \ln D_0 + (1 - \alpha - \beta)^{-1}(\alpha \ln s_k) + (1 - \alpha - \beta)^{-1}(\beta \ln s_k)$$
$$+ (1 - \alpha - \beta)^{-1}(\ln n + \delta) + rt$$

This equation is very similar to equation (2.4) and the growth rate of per capita steady state income is $\dot{y}*/y* = r = g_1 + g_2 + g_3$

This shows how R&D affects the growth of per capita income. One could interpret g_2 as the effect of learning by doing through accumulation of capital and g_3 as the impact of R&D as human capital. However, we should make that the steady state does not exist when there is constant or increasing returns to scale.

2.2. Increasing returns and spillover effects

In case of significant increasing returns associated with knowledge as human capital (H), the steady state model of Solow is inapplicable because growth is unbounded. As a consequence the assumption of perfect competition implicit in the model also fails. Another important consequence of the human capital and globalization of international markets is the spillover effect, whereby knowledge in human capital is transmitted across industries and countries. For example, software developed by Microsoft may be developed and improved further by another international company in Taiwan and such knowledge may be used across other industries. One alternative to perfect competition is oligopolistic equilibrium where competitors do not follow the rule of price equaling marginal cost. As an example we consider a model by Cellini and Lambertini (2008) as follows. Two firms with outputs y_i $(i = 1, 2)$ and average costs (c_i) compete with each other and employ research knowledge or human capital k_i at a convex cost function

$$C(R_i) = b_i + \tilde{b}_i R_i^2(t)$$

with b_i and $\tilde{b}_i$ being positive. With price as

$$p(t) = a - \tilde{a}(y_i(t) + y_j(t))$$

and marginal cost $c_i(t)$ as

$$\frac{\dot{c}_i}{c_i(t)} = -\alpha \cdot R_i(t) - \beta_i R_j(t) + \gamma_i, \ i \neq j \qquad (2.6)$$

the profit function π_i of firm i may be expressed as

$$\pi_i(t) = py_i(t) - b_i - \tilde{b}_i(R_i^2(t)) - c_i(t)y_i(t) \qquad (2.7)$$

where production cost $C(y_i) = c_i y_i$ and $p = a - \tilde{a}(y_i + y_j)$. Equation (2.6) assumes that unit cost c_i declines over time as human or knowledge capital $k_i(t)$ increases. This decline may also reflect the spillover effect, since the other firm's knowledge capital $R_j(t)$ $(i \neq j)$ may be as helpful as their own capital $R_i(t)$.

In the comparative static case $c_i(R_i, R_j)$ may be represented as

$$c_i = d_i - a_i R_i - b_i R_j; \quad a_i, b_i d_i > 0.$$

Profit then equals

$$\bar{\pi}_i = [a - \tilde{a}(y_i + y_j)]y_i - (d_i - a_i R_i - b_i R_j)y_i - b_i - \tilde{b}_i R_i^2.$$

On maximizing this profit with respect to y_i and R_i one obtains the optimal or best reply functions of the Cournot duopolists as:

$$\begin{aligned}
y_i^* &= (2\tilde{a})^{-1}[a - c_i - \tilde{a}y_j]; \quad i = 1,\ 2;\ i \neq j \\
R_i^* &= (2\tilde{b}_i)^{-1}(a_i y_i); \quad i = 1,\ 2
\end{aligned} \tag{2.8}$$

Note that the higher the positive value of b_i, greater is the spillover effect, since c_i now declines more due to R_j.

In the dynamic case one maximizes the discounted profit functional

$$J = \int_0^\infty \exp(-rt)\pi_i(t)dt \tag{2.9}$$

subject to (2.6), where $\pi_i(t)$ is given by (2.7). Note that β_i now represents the spillover effect, i.e., any increase of research capital R_j by other firms tends to reduce the proportional rate of costs $\dot{c}_i / c_i$ of firm i.

One using the Hamiltonian H_i of firm i as

$$\begin{aligned}
H_i &= \exp(-rt)[(a - \tilde{a}(y_i + y_j))y_i - c_i y_i - b_i - \tilde{b}_i R_i^2(t) \\
&\quad - \lambda_{ii} c_i(t)(\alpha_i R_i + \beta_i R_j - \gamma_i) - \lambda_{ij} c_j(t)(\alpha_j R_j + \beta_j R_i - \gamma_j)
\end{aligned}$$

we may derive the first-order necessary conditions as

$$\frac{\delta H_i}{\delta R_i(t)} = -2\tilde{b}_i R_i - \lambda_{ii} c_i \alpha_i - \lambda_{ij} c_j \beta_j = 0$$

$$\frac{\delta H_i}{\delta y_i(t)} = a - 2\tilde{a}y_i(t) - \tilde{a}y_j(t) - c_i = 0$$

the adjoint co-state equations as

$$-\frac{\delta H_i}{\delta c_i(t)} = \frac{\delta \lambda_{ii}(t)}{\delta.t} - r\lambda_{ii}(t)$$

$$-\frac{\delta H_i}{\delta c_j(t)} = \frac{\delta \lambda_{ij}(t)}{\delta.t} - r\lambda_{ij}(t)$$

and the transversality equations as

$$\lim_{t \to \infty} \exp(-rt)\lambda_{ij}(t) - c_j(t) = 0; \quad i, j = 1, 2$$

These equations yield the optimal Cournot reaction curves as:

$$y_i^*(t) = (2\tilde{a})^{-1}[a - \tilde{a}y_j(t) - c_i(t)]$$
$$R_i^*(t) = -(2\tilde{b}_i)^{-1}[\lambda_{ii}(t)c_i\alpha_i + \lambda_{ij}(t)c_j\beta_i] \tag{2.10}$$

$$\lambda_{ii}^* = \frac{\delta\lambda_{ii}(t)}{\delta.t} = y_i + \lambda_{ii}(t)[\alpha_iR_i + \beta_jR_j + r - \gamma_i]$$

and
$$\lambda_{ij}^* = \frac{\delta\lambda_{ij}(t)}{\delta.t} = \lambda_{ij}(t)[\alpha_jR_j + \beta_jR_i + r - \gamma_j]$$

Note that the optimal level of knowledge capital $R_i^*(t)$ depends on the adjoint variables or shadow prices $\lambda_{ii}(t)$ and $\lambda_{ij}(t)$. The rate of growth of optimal R_i^* can be computed as

$$\dot{R}_i^*(t) = -(2\tilde{b})^{-1}\left[\dot{\lambda}_{ii}c_i\alpha_i + \lambda_{ii}\dot{c}_i\alpha_i + \beta_i(\dot{\lambda}_{ij}c_j + \lambda_{ij}\dot{c}_j)\right]$$

The Cournot-Nash saddle point equilibrium (y_i^*, c_i^*, R_i^*) defined by the first-order conditions (2.10) is shown to be stable under certain reasonable conditions. This solution has been compared with a cartel solution when the two firms form cooperation in R&D strategies. Cellini and Lambertini (2008) have shown that setting up a monopoly cartel in the R&D stage leads both firms to invest more than in the fully non-cooperation case, since there is no infighting and no spillover effect.

Spence (1984) considered a more general model with n homogenous firms, where unit costs $c_i(t)$ of firm i depends on the accumulated knowledge capital $R = (R_i)$. Let $m_i(t)$ be the current expenditure by firm i on the knowledge capital. Then it is assumed that

$$\dot{R}_i(t) = m_i(t) + \theta\sum_{j \neq i} m_j(t)$$

where the parameter θ captures spillover or externality effects. If $\theta = 0$ there are no spillover or externalities, but for $\theta = 1$ the benefits of each firm's R&D are shared completely. He assumes that there is equilibrium at each point of time in the market that depends on the costs

$$c = (F(R_1), \; ..., F(R_n))$$

or on

$$R = (R_1, R_2, R_3, \; ... \; R_n)$$

where $c_i(t) = F(R_i(t))$ is the R&D cost function. In the symmetric case when firms are alike he derives the important relationship expressing the industry's total investment in knowledge capital as a function of optimal R&D effort at the industry level. This relationship is of the form

$$R \& D^* = nR[1 + \theta(n - 1)]^{-1}$$

If θ is zero then the costs are proportional to the number of firms. With positive θ the unit costs have an upper limit of $1/\theta$ as n increases. Thus while the spillover effects reduce the incentives for cost reduction, they also reduce the costs at the industry level of reaching a given level of cost reduction. Spence has shown that the incentives can be easily restored through state subsidies. Hence, with restored incentives, the spillovers improve the performance of the overall market in terms of higher level of R&D and overall higher level of consumer's surplus with lower prices.

We have to note that the spillover or externality effect has played an instrumental role in expanding the world market in global trade. As different economies have adopted new and modern technologies, the underlying production processes are increasingly characterized by increasing returns (IR). These processes of positive feedback occur due to four basic reasons:

1. diffusion of the learning process;
2. high fixed costs and very low marginal costs;
3. increased network value with the number of uses and
4. high switching costs.

Arthur (1994) and Nachum (2002) have stressed three reasons why the IR processes occur more frequently today than the diminishing returns (DR) processes. The multinational enterprises (MNEs) like Microsoft, Intel and IBM have extensively used the IR processes in opening branches and subsidiaries in China, Singapore, Taiwan and other fast growing countries of Southeast Asia. Very low marginal costs coupled with high fixed costs have helped the MNEs to exploit both scale and scope economies. The scale economies lower unit costs by increasing the scale, where scope economies capture the benefits of integration of operation and cooperation in R&D activities with other subsidiaries. This is different from the cost structure of DR activities, where total costs can spread across units of production more evenly and costs increase as production increases in volume.

There exist several important economic reasons why the IR processes dominate over the DR processes in modern technology-intensive industries today, such as computer hardware and software, telecom industry, pharmaceuticals, bioengineering, drugs and electronics. First of all, knowledge creation is far more important in creating values for IR industries than the DR industries. Secondly, the rate of obsolescence of knowledge is more rapid, for the IR industries and Schumpeter's concept of 'creative destruction' stresses this point. Thus if the stock of knowledge capital of vintage j is denoted by K_j, $j = 1, 2, 3, ..., q$ then the production function with labor augmenting technological progress can be written as

$$Y_j = K_j^{\alpha}(A^j L_j)^{\beta}$$

where labor productivity is denoted by A^j. When R&D is successful, the first prototype of a production unit that yields a labor productivity of A^{q+1} becomes available. This higher labor productivity provides the incentives to finance R&D in a decentralized economy, even though all sectors operate under pure competition. When a new vintage of knowledge capital is found successful, i.e., as q increases by one, the price of older vintage falls and its profit falls. Finally, the older vintage has to exit and thereby the new vintage replaces the old.

Thirdly, many IR industries develop such network connections that prevent rival entry or access to proprietary knowledge. This first mover advantage provides a quasi-monopoly framework and the MNEs take full advantage of this framework. Finally, the scale economies in production and distribution are most important as sources of advantage for the large firms and MNEs compared to the DR industries.

Nachum (2002) used a model with outward foreign direct investment FDI_{it} as the dependent variable for industry i in year t

$$FDI_{it} = f(x_{it}) + e_{it} \tag{2.11}$$

where x_{it} denotes a vector of firm-specific advantages for industry i such as scale, innovative capabilities and so on. The model is estimated with panel data of 650 industries for 10 years 1989–98 (Table 2.4). Industries were divided into IR and DR processes, where the constant returns to scale cases were excluded. The regression equation (2.11) in linear form provides estimates (below) that strongly support the hypothesis about the vital role of innovation in the IR industries.

Here FDI was measured as total capital flows comprised of intercompany loans and reinvested earnings. The IR industries include the knowledge-based industries such as industrial chemicals, communications, software industries and electronics, whereas the DR industries include the traditional manufacturing industries such as primary metals, transportation, meat products and the like.

Table 2.4   FDI model for IR and DR industries in US (1989–98)

Regressors	IR industries	DR industries
Innovation capabilities	15550.9*** (3.214)	59753.5* (2.302)
Scale	0.199*** (3.674)	0.313 (2.854)
Risk	9432.5* (2.055)	−4643.4 (−0.246)
Sales growth	28346.0** (2.448)	13457.9* (2.285)
Other regressors	–	–
N	390	260
Adj. R^2	0.755	0.497
F Value	0.000	0.002

Note:
1. One, two and three asterisks denote significance at 10%, 5% and 1% of t values respectively. Standard errors are in the parenthesis.
2. Other regressors such as firm size, advertising and so on are not reported here.

Note that the scale effect is highly statistically significant at 1% and the risk element is important for the IR industries that allocate more heavily on R&D investments and have the associated uncertainty. Two important features of R&D investments for knowledge capital are to be noted. First, an R&D project takes time to complete and this gestation period may be quite long in some cases, like a new medicine. Even when a new invention is successful, time delays are involved in the FDA approval process. Secondly, the outcome of the R&D process is quite uncertain. Not only is there a chance of failure, there exists also the chance of another rival's entry. Lukach, Kort and Plasmans (2005) have considered an interesting Cournot-Nash type case of quantity competition when there is a positive threat of entry, with the entrant introducing a new technology that may replace, either partially or totally, the old technology of the existing incumbent.

This model has two firms: one Incumbent and the other a potential Entrant. The Incumbent produces with a given technology at a unit cost K. The potential Entrant uses the new technology with a unit cost, which for simplicity is assumed to be zero. The cost of entry is denoted by z. They consider a two-step R&D process with an uncertain outcome at the first step. After completion of the second step the Incumbent is able to produce more efficiently from this moment onwards. At time zero the Incumbent has an opportunity to make an initial irreversible investment $\beta \cdot I$ with $0 < \beta < 1$ whose outcome is stochastic. After having carried out the initial R&D investment at the time point one the Incumbent needs to invest $(1 - \beta)I \pm h$ with probability 0.5 in order to succeed or fail the breakthrough. The total planned cost of R&D is I, the first stage share of the cost is $\beta \cdot I$ and the volatility of the second stage investment is h. It is assumed that the Incumbent has a time lead over the Entrant. The Incumbent anticipates the entry and has one time period advantage. On the basis of the outcome of the first-stage R&D investment at time one the Incumbent being a monopolist decides about completing the R&D project while it still produces with unit cost K. If the Incumbent develops a new technology implying that the unit production cost drops from K to zero, it will start producing with it from period two. If the Entrant decides to enter, it incurs the entry cost z and it will also start its production with zero unit cost as time $t = 2$. We can consider Cournot competition here with the inverse market demand function $p = 1-Q$, where $Q = q_1+q_2$, where the subscripts denotes the Incumbent and the Entrant. Two different equilibrium solutions may emerge. One is symmetric competition with R&D completed by the Incumbent, which has the same zero production cost as the Entrant. The other is the case of asymmetric competition where the Incumbent has cost $K > 0$, while the Entrant has zero cost. On maximizing his profit the optimal output of the Incumbent if it has not completed the R&D project becomes $q_1^* = (1-2K)/3$ while the Entrant will produce $q_2^* = (1+K)/3$. Their corresponding profits are

$$\pi_1^* = \left[\frac{(1-2K)}{3}\right]^2 \text{ and } \pi_2^* = \left[\frac{(1+K)}{3}\right]^2.$$ In the symmetric case both the

Incumbent and the Entrant will produce with the same advanced technology at zero unit cost. Their optimal output will be $q_1^* = q_2^* = 1/3$ with profit levels $\pi_1^* = \pi_2^* = 1/9$.

The authors show that the effect of technical uncertainty in this model is different from the influence of market uncertainty. Many empirical studies have found that increased market uncertainty raises the value of the option to delay the investment and thus leads to lower investment levels. The technical uncertainty considered here cannot be resolved without engaging in research and thus the delay option has no value. Due to the asymmetric nature of the R&D option in this model, increased technical uncertainty gives a greater value to the case of successful implementation of the first-stage R&D, while downward risk is limited. Thus, the greater technical uncertainty positively affects the decision to start an R&D project.

2.3.   Schumpeterian dynamics

Schumpeterian Dynamics of industry evolution have several distinctive features that are relevant for modern growth theory. The first is the dynamic process of creative destruction. Aghion and Howitt (1992) have discussed this aspect in a model of endogenous growth, where the prospect of more research in the future discourages current research by creating a potential threat of more entry. The second important feature of Schumpeterian Dynamics is its emphasis on the impulse and diffusion of new technology. In his *Theory of Economic Development*, Schumpeter (1934) discusses six types of innovations of which the introduction of a new method of production and the opening of a new market or a new product are the most important. According to him, traditional Walrasian theory is helpful in explaining the steady state growth process, where convergence is the dominant characteristic. Diffusion of new innovations requires an analysis of divergence in non steady state system. While traditional theory is useful in studying responses to innovations by the existing firms that are not innovative themselves, a new theory is needed to characterize the behavior of innovating firms. A third feature of Schumpeterian Dynamics is its emphasis on the monopolistically competitive nature of firms innovating in new technology and/or new marks and engaging in R&D investment where the outcome is stochastic. The risk associated with the uncertain outcome is an important part in the decision process of innovating firms.

Palokangas (2007) developed a stochastic model of creative destruction where new technology and/or innovation replaces the old and the optimal decisions by innovative firms generate a stream of productivity improvement for the industry. The model assumes a fixed number n of firms. All firms produce the same consumption good and each firm produces a capital good that is firm-specific. The productivity of labor is assumed to be unity in R&D and 'a' in production activity. The spillover of knowledge from any firm's R&D activity increases the productivity of labor a in production activity. Each innovating firm j uses firm-specific capital K_j to produce good Y_j by using labor L_j, capital K_j and does R&D by labor z_j. I_j is investment in K_j and it is assumed for simplicity that there is no depreciation. Consumption good C_j is produced by converting the residual output $(Y_j - I_j)$ in proportion A^{g_j} where $A > 1$ is a constant and g_j is the serial number of technology. The production function assumes constant returns to scale.

$$Y_j = F(aL_j, K_j) = f(l_j)K_j$$
$$l_j = aL_j / K_j, \quad f' > 0, \quad f'' < 0 \tag{2.12}$$

(prime denotes partial derivatives) where the budget constraint for j is

$$C_j + W_j L_j + vZ_j = A^{g_j}(Y_j - I_j) \tag{2.13}$$

with $W_j L_j$ and $v Z_j$ being wage costs in production and R&D activities that are assumed to be exogenous. Each firm can invest in R&D and improve technology from A^{g_j} to A^{g_j+1}. In a small period of time t the probability that R&D leads to development of new technology is given by $(\lambda \log z_j) dt$, while the probability of no success is $1 - (\lambda \log z_j) dt$, where λ is the productivity of research workers, that is,

$$dq_j = \begin{cases} 0; \text{ probability} = [1 - (\lambda \log z_j) dt] \\ 1; \text{ probability} = (\lambda \log z_j) dt \end{cases} \tag{2.14}$$

where q_j is assumed to be a Poisson process. With no depreciation assumed, investment can be written as $I_j dt = dK_j^d$. After successful development of new technology, a constant share ϕ of the previous vintage capital can be upgraded resulting in higher productivity, that is,

$$\tilde{K}_j = \phi K_j, \quad 0 < \phi < 1 \tag{2.15}$$

Thus the capital accumulation process becomes

$$dK_j = dK_j^d + (\tilde{K}_j - K_j) dq_j = I_j dt + (\tilde{K}_j - K_j) dq_j = \left[\left\{ f(l_j) - w_j L_j \right\} K_j - A^{-g_j}(c_j + v z_j) \right] dt + (\tilde{K}_j - K_j) dq_j$$

This is a stochastic differential equation where

$$dK_j^d = I_j dt = \left[\left\{ f(l_j) - w_j L_j \right\} K_j - A^{-g_j}(c_j + v z_j) \right] dt; \quad W_j = w_j a A^{g_j} \tag{2.16}$$

With a successful R&D project, $dq_j = 1$, capital stock jumps by $(\tilde{K}_j - K_j)$ and the level of productivity in the consumption good sector rises. With no success, dq_j is zero and there is no change in productivity.

With a utility function $U_j = (1 - \sigma)^{-1}[c(\tau)^{1-\sigma} - 1]$ the innovating firm maximizes expected utility by choosing c_j, l_j and z_j subject to the production function (2.12), the capital accumulation process (2.16) and the Poisson stochastic process (2.14), given the productivity adjusted wage rate w_j and the wage rate v in the R&D sector.

$$\underset{c_j,z_j,l_j}{\text{Max}} \; J = E\int_0^\infty e^{-\rho(\tau-t)}U_j\mathrm{d}\tau \tag{2.17}$$

subject to (2.12), (2.16) and (2.14)

Here $\rho > 0$ is the constant rate of time preference and $(1 - \sigma)^{-1}$ is the constant rate of risk aversion.

Several important implications follow from this model. First, the innovation shocks and technology are endogenous here as they depend on the decisions made by the innovative firms. The optimal growth rate may be computed from (2.17) by following dynamic programming algorithms. Second, the risk aversion factor may limit the rate of unbounded growth for the innovating firms that succeed more continually. Third, a more general process than the Poisson may be considered for the R&D process undertaken by the innovating firms. This aspect of generalizing the Poisson process will be discussed in later chapters.

The diffusion aspect of innovations is accelerated by the spillover effects and the externality of knowledge capital. Foreign direct investments, spread of MNEs and growth of computer usage and software research have helped the diffusion process over time to a significant degree in recent times. The experience of rapid economic growth by the Southeast Asian countries often called a 'growth miracle' bear solid testimony in this regard. The diffusion process works in several ways. Foreign direct investment in developing countries, the investment expenditure by the MNEs and increasing spillover effects help other entrepreneurs in the developing countries. Creative destruction brings in new technology. Learning by doing is another important channel. The backward and forward linkages foster intersectional interdependence in the developing countries, where the faster growth in the export sector pulls up the other sectors.

Young (1991) discussed in some detail how learning by doing spreads the dynamic effect of international trade. He noted two important features of the diffusion process. One is that there exist substantial spillover effects in the development of knowledge capital across industries, with technical innovations originating in particular industries and finding important applications elsewhere, as well as instigating further technical change in other economic sectors. An econometric analysis by Jaffe (1986) found that the number of patents an innovating firm received was increasing not only in its own R&D efforts, but also in the R&D efforts of its technical neighbors. Secondly, the development of new productive technologies by R&D efforts initially leads to rapid learning by doing. However, after some time, learning by doing slows and the productive capability of new technologies is exhausted. In Schumpeterian framework this is the time for another round of new innovations. A simple model capturing this dynamic process may be easily formulated in terms of a dynamic path of optimal capital expansion by an innovating firm which seeks to maximize profits $\pi = pY(K,L) - wL - vI$ over time by its decision on the two inputs, physical capital K and labor L and the investment decisions I on the existing physical capital and new creative investment uK as a proportion of capital stock:

$$\text{Max } J = \int_0^\infty e^{-\rho t}[pY(K,L) - wL - vI]\,dt$$

subject to $\dot{K} = I - \delta K - uK, K(0) = K_0$ given

Here δ includes both the constant rate of depreciation of K and the rate of obsolescence (or destruction). The term uK denotes new investment in R&D (creative investment). Unit price of output is given by p. In case of competition p is given but in Cournot-type markets $p = p\,(Y_1,\,Y_2)$ depends on the outputs Y_i of two duopolists, as we discussed before. Denoting the Lagrangian function as

$$\phi = e^{-\rho t}[\pi(t) + \lambda(I - (u + \delta)K - \dot{K})]$$

where dot denotes the time derivative, we may apply the Euler-Lagrange necessary conditions of optimality as

$$\dot{v} = (u + \rho + \delta)v - pF_K$$
$$\dot{K} = I - (u + \delta)K \tag{2.18}$$

At the steady state $\dot{v} = 0; \dot{K} = 0$ and this implies

$$(u + \rho + \delta)v = pF_K$$
$$I = (u + \delta)K \tag{2.19}$$

where F_K denotes the marginal productivity of capital. The steady state equation (2.19) shows that any increase in R&D investment in knowledge capital helps improve the productivity of capital and thereby reduces unit costs in the long run. In the short run however it increases the investment cost. On linearizing the dynamic equations (2.18) one could compute the two characteristic roots of the system as

$$\mu_1, \mu_2 = (1/2)[e \pm (e^2 + 4(u+\delta)(u+\rho+\delta)]$$

with μ_1 being a positive root and μ_2 the negative root. This defines the saddle point equilibrium. It is clear that as u rises, it will raise the positive root that contributes to the non-stationary growth rate. If we assume the production function to be log linear as $Y = AK^\alpha L^\beta$ then

$$pY = (1/\alpha)[(e+u+\delta)v - \dot{v}]K$$

where in the steady state $\dot{v} = 0$ and hence a rise in u increases output and reduces unit production cost.

Schumpeterian Dynamics also emphasized the role of new markets as an important form of innovations. Exploring new markets through globalization of trade and expanding exports has played an important role in the rapid expansion of countries in Southeast Asia. Some of these empirical experiences provide evidence supporting Schumpeterian growth hypothesis.

2.4.   Empirical experiences of innovation dynamics

Innovation efficiency due to R&D investments and advances in knowledge capital has been strongly emphasized by the work of economic historians. For example Rosenberg (1972) provides a comprehensive survey of the relationship between technological advances and US economic growth since the early 1800s. Grossman and Helpman (1993) have reviewed the empirical relations between innovation and growth of industrial countries and stressed two important points. First, the existence of local or national technologies introduces externalities and spillovers that induce dynamic comparative advantage. Such spillovers can generate a self-perpetuating process regardless of the country's relative factor endowments. Secondly, the countries that are integrated into the world market as the NICs in Asia are likely to enjoy access to a larger base of technical and innovation-based knowledge than the others in relative isolation. Trade thus helps in the process of technological and innovation-sensitive dissemination.

The role of R&D investment in raising industrial productivity is most significant in other industries like pharmaceuticals, computer products and services. Sengupta and Sahoo (2006) have discussed both level efficiency and growth efficiency of the US pharmaceutical industry over the period 1980–2000. Their results show that the companies that are leaders in growth efficiency show a very high elasticity of output with respect to R&D spending. Sources of growth efficiency in terms of Solow-type technical progress and R&D efficiency are found as follows.

	Technical progress (%)		R&D efficiency (%)	
	1985–89	1995–2000	1985–89	1995–2000
A. Leading firms	25	30	28	30
B. Other firms	14	16	15	17

This suggests the growing need in India today of increasing R&D investments in computer-related industries, pharmaceuticals and other technology-intensive industries in manufacturing, transport and service sectors. This would improve the long run comparative and competitive advantage for India in world trade. The common belief that increased labor productivity due to cost reducing R&D investments will hamper the growth of employment in manufacturing and IT sector dependent industries may not hold in the long run. Corley, Michie and Oughton (2002) have examined empirical data at finer levels of aggregation (e.g., industry and firm levels) and have found that many high growth manufacturing industries in the US and EU (European Union) showed increases in productivity accompanied by *increases* and not decreases in employment.

These high-growth and high-productivity industries in the EU and US (which include software manufacturers, electronics and technology-intensive manufacturing) are generally characterized by high levels of investment, not only in the form of physical capital but also R&D. R&D investments create new products and processes emphasized by Schumpeterian innovations and also enable workers to absorb these new processes and products; the learning by doing effects generate cumulative effects. The following two tables report the contributions of R&D per hour for several industrialized countries such

Table 2.5 Annual average levels of output per hour, investment per hour and R&D per hour in manufacturing (1990–98) at 1995 prices

	Output per hour	Investment per hour	R&D per hour
Canada			
low tech	21.0	2.80	0.15
high tech	24.9	3.45	1.69
total	22.9	3.12	0.91
Denmark			
low tech	25.1	4.24	0.20
high tech	27.4	4.75	2.12
total	26.3	4.50	1.20
France			
low tech	27.1	4.22	0.71
high tech	32.9	4.85	3.97
total	30.3	4.57	2.48
Germany			
low tech	20.7	3.64	0.18
high tech	25.8	3.81	2.69
total	24.1	3.75	1.82
Italy			
low tech	29.4	5.39	0.05
high tech	29.5	5.69	1.24
total	26.4	5.56	0.71
UK			
low tech	23.1	2.82	0.15
high tech	26.5	3.48	2.24
total	24.9	3.2	1.34
US			
low tech	27.6	2.91	0.31
high tech	35.5	4.68	4.21
total	32.3	3.86	2.62

See Corley et al. (2002 for details)

as Canada, Germany, Italy, Denmark, UK and US over the period 1990–98 (Table 2.5).

Table 2.7 summarizes the effect of tangible (physical) and intangible (R&D and human capital) investment on labor productivity in terms of the regression equation

$$LP_{i(1994-98)} = b_0 + b_1(RD/L)_{1990-93} + b_2(I/L)_{1994-98}$$

where $LP_{i(1994-98)}$ is the level of labor productivity in industry i averaged over four years (1994–98), $(RD/L)_{i1990-93}$ is the R&D spending per worker in industry i lagged four years (1990–93) and (I/L) is gross fixed capital formation per worker in industry i averaged over the four years (1994–98). *HK* is the share of R&D scientists and engineers in the labor force for the whole economy level averaged over 1994–98.

When this model is re-estimated using a fixed effects model with dummy variables to capture the country effects the result improves in terms of adjusted R^2 (Table 2.7).

Table 2.6   The regression results over 1990–98 (fixed effects model)

Industry	*I/L*	$(RD/L)_{t-u}$	Adj R^2
High tech	0.409**	0.152**	0.934
Low tech	0.469**	0.055	0.983
Total	0.421**	0.151**	0.943

Table 2.7   The elasticities of R&D per work hour (The regression of labor productivity on I/L, RD/L and HK (1994–98) for EU and US)

standardized coefficients (elasticities)	Constant	*I/L*	*RD/L*	*HK*	*N*	Adj R^2
Industry						
High tech	8.25	0.47**	0.30**	0.16	80	0.346
	(1.33)	(5.04)	(3.16)	(1.65)		
Low tech	8.17	0.91**	0.09	0.16	40	0.759
	(1.94)	(9.51)	(0.82)	(1.33)		
Total	8.06	0.54	0.34	0.14*	120	0.452
	(1.83)	(7.67)	(4.83)	(2.01)		

Note:
1. *t*-ratios are in parentheses; one and two asterisks denote significance at 5% and 1% respectively.
2. *N* is the number of observations
3. All coefficients of explanatory variables are standardized and represent elasticities.

Note the R&D investment has a statistically significant effect on productivity only in the high-tech industries. These are precisely the industries that compete in the international field with dynamic comparative advantage. As Table 2.5 shows, in terms of R&D per hour, high-tech industries in US and UK score about 14 times higher or more than the low-tech industries. A major strength of the US economy is the dynamic competitive advantage that enables the manufacturing sector to increase productivity while simultaneously increasing employment. If the EU countries and India have to close the competition gap with the US as measured by income per capita, they must increase productivity while maintaining or increasing employment levels.

Modern theories of growth developed by Romer (1990), Lucas (1993) and others have emphasized the endogenous forces in the form of knowledge capital. Knowledge capital, unlike physical capital, is assumed to be an input in the aggregate production function showing increasing marginal productivity. To the extent that knowledge capital may be viewed as external to the firm but internal to the industry, the competitive market model may still apply, but with endogenous technological change. In contrast to the models based on diminishing returns, growth rates in this new class of endogenous models can be increasing over time. In such a framework the effects of small random disturbances (i.e., shocks) can be applied by the actions of private business and large countries may grow faster than small ones, if they can keep up their dynamic efficiency over time. Romer and Lucas have provided long-run empirical evidence in support of this type of endogenous growth theory.

At the microeconomic level we have to ask: what makes a firm grow? What causes an industry to evolve and progress? From a broad standpoint two types of answers have been offered. One is managerial, the other economic. The managerial perspective is based on organization theory, which focuses on the cost competence as the primary source of growth. The economic perspective emphasizes productivity and efficiency as the basic source of growth. Economic efficiency of both physical and human capital including innovations through R&D have been stressed by the modern theory of endogenous growth.

Core competence, rather than market power, has been identified by Prahalad and Hamel (1994) as the basic cornerstone of success in the modern hypercompetitive world of today. Core competence has been defined as the collective learning of the organization, especially learning how to coordinate diverse production skills and integrate multiple streams of technologies. Four basic elements of core competence are: learn from own and outside research, coordinate, integrate so as to reduce unit costs and innovate so as to gain market share through price and cost reductions.

A company's own R&D expenditures help reduce its long-run unit costs and also yield spillover externalities. These spillovers yield increasing returns to scale as discussed before. Now we consider a dynamic model of industry evolution, where R&D investments tend to reduce unit costs and hence profitability. This profitability induces new entry and also increased market share by the incumbent firms who succeed in following the cost efficiency frontier.

In macroeconomic perspective, the spillover technology and externalities of R&D investments have played a critical role in the endogenous growth model due to Lucas. While emphasizing the point that Asian growth miracles cannot generally be explained only by physical capital accumulation alone, he discussed the productivity-enhancing role of human capital accumulation at school and on the job. This rate of expansion in knowledge in both forms transforms Solow's *level effect* into a growth effect. This knowledge capital is a non-rival input with other inputs like labor and physical capital since it has strong complementarities with other inputs. An important dimension of the learning by doing impact of spillover technology is that for such learning to continue on a long-run sustained basis, the workers, managers and entrepreneurs must work continually to improve the technology through what Grossman and Helpman (1993) called the 'quality ladder effect'. Finally, the spillover technology is closely associated with Schumpeterian innovation in its many forms, e.g., R&D spending, new processes, new products and services and new markets and networks. When the fruits of research are allowed to be exploited more openly and broadly by free global trade, such trade generates a scale effect helping to speed up the growth of trading countries. In many ways the spillover technology allows dynamic externalities, which generate dynamic gains from trade. Thus, declining computer prices and improved technology-based inputs have helped the NICs in Asia and China to reap the benefits of spillover technology. As an example of the productivity augmenting impact of externalities, consider the production function estimates of the manufacturing sector in South Korea (1985–94) reported by Sengupta (2005).

$$\ln Y = 4.92** - 0347 \ln R_1 + 0.16 \ln R_2 - 0357 \ln R_3 + 1.51** \ln N$$

(Adj $R^2 = 0.96$)

Here Y is total manufacturing output, R_1 through R_3 measure the three rival inputs such as physical capital, energy and materials and N is a proxy for non-rival input measured by labor employed in the export sector only. Two asterisks denote significant values of t at the 1% level. Clearing the non-rival input (N) has significant effect in terms of increasing returns, implying that a 10% increase in N generates a 15% increase in total manufacturing output. When our attention is shifted to the IT-related sector specializing in high-tech goods and services, the impact of non-rival inputs (N) is much higher than 1.51.

The experience of Taiwan among the growth miracle countries (i.e., NICs) in Asia is more striking. The scale economies of the IT sector have been diffused over the other sectors at a rapid rate. Indirectly it has helped to maintain a more or less equitable distribution of income through gains from global trade. Gort and Konakayama (1982) and Sengupta (2004) have analyzed dynamic models of diffusion in the production of innovation that aptly described the growth of the electronics industry and the IT sector in Taiwan. This diffusion model is of the form

$$\begin{aligned}
E_{it} &= \alpha(n_{it}^* - n_{i,t-1}), \quad 0 < \alpha < 1 \\
n_{it}^* &= TC(q_{it}^*)
\end{aligned} \tag{2.20}$$

where E_{it} is net entry in industry i (either the existing or the new industry) at time t, n_{it} equals the actual number of producers in industry i at t, n_{it}^* equals the expected cost minimizing number of producers and the total cost function TC(.) relates the expected equilibrium output q_{it}^* of the industry. As the cost efficiency improves in the industry i, it tends to generate the situation $n_{it}^* > n_{i,t-1}$ resulting in an increase in net entry. Likewise net exits increase when $n_{i,t-1} > n_{it}^*$. Gort and Konakayama (1982) have applied this simple model (2.19) to the manufacturing data (1947, 1954, 1958, 1963, 1967 and 1972) in US for seven firms and found that the phenomenon of diffusion of an innovation measured by the number of patents is very well explained by this model, when $n_{it}*$ is related to other explanatory variables such as the technical change, dynamic adjustment costs and the growth of transferable accumulated experience presumably through the transfer of personnel from existing to new firms.

The experience of Taiwan over the period 1995–2000 is summarized in Table 2.8. This table shows the most rapid growth of the export sector and the strong emphasis the state has placed on expanding education at the primary and secondary levels. Encouraging foreign direct investment from the EU and US also helped utilize the R&D externalities in high-tech products such as electronics and computer products and services.

As Table 2.8 shows the IT products and telecommunications equipment grew at an average annual rate of around 15.1% and 14.0% respectively. The Taiwanese Council for Economic Planning and Development prepared a ten-year plan (1980–89) that set up specific targets for R&D expenditures. Both the government and private entrepreneurs pursued an international technology policy by cutting costs through productive efficiency and transferring the results of research in government laboratories to the private sector. In terms of complementary human capital accumulation, a deliberate policy

Table 2.8 Economic growth indicators in Taiwan

	1995	1998	2000
Export/GDP (%)	42.03	41.32	47.66
Gross investment/GDP	24.93	24.72	22.57
Export growth rate (%)	20.0	−9.42	21.98
Literacy rate (%)	21.33	−8.53	26.49
Secondary school enrollment rate (%)	95.93	97.21	99.61
Higher education enrollment rate (%)	45.32	51.06	60.85
Output of electronics and IT sector			
Total (US $ bill)	15.4 (1990)	–	69.8 (2005)
Information products	6.9 (1990)	–	35 (2005)
Consumer electronics	2.3 (1990)		7.0 (2005)

Source: Sengupta (2004)

of sending trainees abroad and inviting foreign collaborators with lucrative incentives was deliberately pursued. All these show the importance of learning spillovers technology that was utilized by Taiwan at a rapid rate.

The recent experiences of India and China in the growth of the knowledge economy are remarkable. The most important factor that induced the new wave of investment in R&D in China and India is the large supply of highly skilled IT professionals. Thomas (2009) has reviewed this growth of the knowledge economy and has noted that both China and India are now ahead of the US with respect to enrollment in tertiary technical education. In China, science and technology was a major plank in the 'four modernizations' the government embarked on after 1978. Today the Chinese government promotes R&D through two major national initiatives: the national high-tech R&D program and the national program for basic research. The following Table 2.9 shows China's record in science and technology.

In January 2006 China announced the initiation of a new 15-year plan for development of science and technology. This plan calls for China, to become an innovation-oriented society by 2020 and a world leader in science and technology by the year 2050. Since the plan was announced, a variety of detailed policy measures have been initiated and major projects have been introduced as part of China's 11th five-year plan (2006–10). In spite of difficulties and challenges,

Table 2.9 Select indicators of China's science and technology Development

	1998	2004	2006
1. R&D expenditure			
gross exp (US & billion)	6.65	27.75	36.79
rates to GDP	0.69	1.23	1.42
2. R&D performance			
enterprise (%)	44.83	66.83	71.08
basic research (%)	5.25	5.96	5.19
3. Scientists & engineers			
employed in R&D	485.5	926.2	1224
(1000 person-year)			

Source: Statistical Yearbook on Science and Technology 2006 (Beijing & China Statistical Press, 2006)

China is forging ahead with its plan to build a world-class innovation efficient knowledge economy.

Sengupta and Neogi (2009) have discussed the growth of the knowledge economy in India and noted that India in the fourth largest software market in the APAC region (excluding Japan) with about 9.5% of the regional market and this software market is among the fastest growing in the APAC region with an expected compound annual growth rate of 15% through 2008. Thus both India and China have great potential for growth in the innovation-oriented sectors and high-tech industries. Their world prospects are most promising like other NICs in Southeast Asia.

2.5.   Innovations and hypercompetition

The recent surge in information technology and growth in industry productivity shows that economic efficiency has played a most dramatic role in the growth of nations in the world today. Two factors are most significant in this framework: one is technology and innovations; the other is hypercompetition and the role of competitive advantage. Technology involving dynamics of productivity improvement is not captured fully by Solow's residual denoted by the parameter A(t) in the production function $Y(t) = F(A(t), L(t), K(t))$. Besides allocative efficiency, Solow's residual ignores all efficiency gains through Schumpeterian innovations like new products, new managerial changes and various methods of network efficiency and cooperation in R&D ventures. Any method that helps to internalize the spillover benefits and achieve better coordination through agency efficiency could bring substantial economies of scope, which were ignored in the Solow approach.

Even innovations through R&D investments encourage industry growth through reducing average unit costs. This type of efficiency improvement can be easily modeled as

$$\dot{s} = a(\overline{c} - c(u))$$
$$\dot{c}(u) = b_0 - bk; \quad b_0, \quad b > 0 \tag{2.21}$$

Here s is market share of innovating firm with dot denoting time derivative and $\overline{c}, c(u)$ are the industry average cost and the unit cost of the firm with u as R&D effort; k is the long-run R&D capital which reduces unit costs in the long run, where spillover effects can be easily introduced through firms i and j, $i \neq j$, as

$$\dot{c}_i(u) = b_0 - b_1 k_i - b_2 k_j$$

The above cost reduction model (2.21) assumes that such R&D investments alone are critical in reducing costs. But there exist other processes. For example, initiation, ingenuity and improvement of existing information technology have helped Japan and the other NICs in Asia to learn and improve technology from abroad. The first-mover advantage has also helped immensely in the computer industry today.

In software and other high-tech fields, competitive pressure has been very strong. D'Aveni (1994) has called this state 'hypercompetition' and suggested that this vigorous competition leads to four types of dynamic efficiency: production efficiency, innovation efficiency, access efficiency and resource efficiency. The first two types are emphasized in economic theory, while the last two in managerial theory. The model (2.21) shows that when c(u) falls below the industry level unit cost $\bar{u}$, the market share of the innovating firm improves and the cost reduction over time $\dot{c}$ increases as the innovation capital k increases.

The access efficiency occurs when the innovating firm races up the escalation ladder and through mergers or buy-ups to keep new entrants out. Resource efficiency occurs when the companies seek to expand their resource base over the whole world. Hypercompetitive firms must use their fixed assets to build their next temporary competitive advantage. Thus IBM bet the company on the 360 series computers and the bet paid off in the 1960s. But its resource base could not sustain its position very long. Tiny competitors like Apple and Microsoft became giants by seizing this opportunity. Resource efficiency played its dramatic role.

Finally, we would like to emphasize the role of 'the market for research ideas' in the overall economic framework, which plays a crucial role in industry growth. 'Contagion effects' and 'linkage effects' have often been mentioned here. Teece (1986), a management scientist, observed that a new innovating firm's ability to gain competitive advantage from its investors depends on the presence of a 'market for idea' in the industry. Teece identifies two basic elements in the process that affects the market for ideas: (1) the technology is not easily expropriated by others and (2) specialized assets such as product capabilities or core competence exist that must be used in conjunction with the innovative product. The first emphasizes the point that if a technology is not well protected by patents the innovator can hardly expect to enjoy the monopoly returns. The second point emphasizes the benefits of developing specializations of the product and/or service so that winning the patent race may be easier.

Porter (1998) views the dynamic side of competition as an evolutionary process, where firms initially gain competitive advantage by altering the basis of static competition. They win not just by recognizing new markets or net technologies but also by moving aggressively to exploit them. They sustain their advantages by investing to improving the existing sources of advantages and to create new ones. These advantages form the basic element of the concept of 'core competence' of a firm so strongly emphasized by the modern experts on management. The economists have failed to emphasize these managerial aspects of dynamic efficiency behind the evolutionary principle of survival of the fittest.

3
Knowledge Diffusion and Learning by Doing

Economic growth based on innovation is stimulated by two major factors. The most important is learning by doing which has many facets. The other is the interaction effect through spillovers. Young (1991) discussed in detail the different aspects of learning by doing and how it brings about technical and managerial advances in knowledge economies, which spill over from one sector or product to another. The learning by doing may be simply characterized by an equation $C_n = AE_n^{-b}$, where C_n is the cost of production of the n-th unit, E_n is the cumulative output up to and including the n-th unit and A is the cost of the first unit and b is the elasticity of technical progress. In Arrow's (1962) learning by doing, E_n may denote cumulative experience that may be proxied by cumulative investment or total capital including both physical and knowledge capital. In this formulation $b>0$ and productivity gains from learning by doing are unbounded. Young (1991) argues that this may not hold empirically unless there comes a stream of new Schumpeterian innovations. The spillover or externality effect not only helps the development of new productive technologies but also stimulates the process of rapid learning by doing. Both the diffusion and the learning by doing methods of technology transfer have a stochastic component, since there are inherent uncertainties associated with R&D and the fact remains that producers using newly produced technologies rarely achieve commercial viability until after they experience a prolonged period of learning by doing.

We now discuss the theory of the learning process underlying the new endogenous theory of economic growth. Modeling the learning process in new growth theory involves an understanding of the stochastic sources implicit in the diffusion process of modem technology and its spillover across the global trade. Stochasticity of this diffusion process and its impact on instability are discussed here in a theoretical setup. The empirical relevance of this type of analysis is also discussed in relation to the rapid growth episodes of newly industrializing countries of Southeast Asia. Various aspects of the stochastic learning process as they affect economic growth are discussed and their economic implications analyzed both theoretically and empirically.

3.1.   New growth theory

New growth theory refers to the recent developments in endogenous models of economic growth, which purport to explain the rate of sustained growth of per capita income in the long run. From an applied perspective three types of forces have played an active dynamic role in this growth process. One is the technology and innovation as the engine of sustained growth. The endogeneity of technological progress is mostly due to the direct and intentional investment by profit-seeking entrepreneurs, who hold a forward-looking view of the state of the world. Schumpeter (1934), Solow (1994) and many others, e.g., Grossman and Helpman (1994) have emphasized this dynamic role of technology for future sustained growth. A second important factor is the dynamic externalities due to the international diffusion of *'knowledge capital'* and the rapid advance of information technology. According to Lucas (1993), this knowledge spillover effect may be the most significant factor explaining the large differences in marginal productivity of capital between a less developed and a fast developing or developed economy, when the concept of capital is broadened to include human capital. The third important source of endogenous growth, as evidenced by the rapid growth episodes of the newly industrializing countries (NICs) of Southeast Asia is the openness in trade and its impact on sectoral growth of output. Lucas (1993) has strongly emphasized that the diffusion of spillover research technology implies the strong connection we observe between rapid productivity growth and trade or openness. Consider, for example, two small economies like Korea and the Philippines in 1960. Suppose now, as Lucas argues, that

Korea shifts its workforce into producing new goods intended for the world market, but Philippines continues to produce the traditional goods. Then according to a learning-based growth theory, Korean production would grow more rapidly. Thus a large volume of trade is essential for this type of growth episode.

Modeling the learning process in the framework of new growth theory and empirically applying it over time series data has posed several challenges before researchers. Two basic reasons may be cited. One is that the learning process has a core component of stochasticity. This is evidenced both in the inception of R&D technology and its diffusion across industries and over international boundaries. The second is the adjustment process, linking future expectations and gradual policy adjustments in the short run. The gap between the myopic and the steady state optimal paths of the policy variables has several stochastic components, which are important in a policy framework.

Learning in growth models may take several forms. Here we restrict ourselves to three types of learning phenomena. One is called learning by doing in the capital goods industry, where the productive efficiency of each producer depends on the cumulative aggregate output of capital goods. Arrow's model exploited this aspect of learning, which is unrelated to both research and new inventions. The second view of learning involves adopting newer and more efficient technology. This leads to scale economies and a decline in the level of minimum average cost over time. In endogenous growth theory this comes about through different sources such as knowledge spillover across domestic sectors and through international trade by means of either final products embodying new technology, or intermediate inputs bearing the blueprints of more efficient technology. Romer (1990), Grossman and Helpman (1991) and Jovanovic (1997) have explored this type of learning as a source of persistent growth of an economy. Finally, learning involves a process of dynamic adjustment in producer behavior, which is influenced both by past history and future expectations. Whereas 'history' accounts for the initial resource endowments, preferences and the existing technology, the 'expectations' refer to the innovations and investments for newer technologies that have a future goal. Thus history emphasizes a backward looking view, whereas expectations presume a more active role by the forward looking entrepreneurs who take a global view of the world market in future much in the Schumpeterian tradition of a capitalist innovator. This type of learning phenomena has been explored by Kennan (1979), Krugman (1991) and Sengupta and Okamura (1996).

The impact of stochasticity of the learning process in growth is examined in this chapter by comparing two types of formulation as follows:

(a) deterministic and stochastic environment with learning, and
(b) the stochastic environment with and without learning.

Section 3.2 discusses the comparative formulations of the deterministic and stochastic framework of the Solow model, both under learning by doing. To emphasize endogeneity of this learning process this section starts from the formulation due to Nordhaus (1967) and others, where the savings rate and the rate of technical change are determined by the producer's optimizing objective. The risk averse attitude of the producer and its consequences for the optimal growth path of output are analyzed here in terms of the variance characteristics of the optimal trajectory. In general it is shown that the temporal fluctuations in variance tend to be positively correlated with the growth trend of mean output. For nonlinear dynamics this may give rise to a chaotic instability. A producer who is averse to the high rate of fluctuations in the variance process will tend to prefer a lower output trajectory in a stochastic environment than in a deterministic environment.

Section 3.3 discusses openness in international trade and its stochastic impact on overall growth under conditions of positive learning and no learning. Here knowledge spillover occurs through the interaction of two groups of sectors, one oriented to exports and international trade and the other to the domestic economy. Helpman (1997) analyzed the empirical data of about 100 countries over the period 1971–90 and found substantial R&D spillovers. For example, a developing country that has an import share of foreign machinery and equipment of about 7% enjoys total factor productivity (TFP) elasticity with respect to foreign R&D capital of about 0.06, which is quite substantial. Since the international transmission of knowledge capital and know-how occurs mainly through the human capital, it is useful here to empirically evaluate the role of human capital accumulation in the context of specific NICs in Asia, which exhibited rapid economic growth episodes. Hence Section 3.3 attempts to empirically estimate for South Korea the growth trend in human capital and the influence of past history and future expectations.

Finally, Section 3.4 presents the stochastic framework of a dynamic limit-pricing model, where risk aversion is directly incorporated into the objective function of a representative producer, who is competing in the international market. Here learning takes two forms: one is in the form of cost declines due to improved technology adoption and scale and the other in the form of new entry to an oligopolistic market which is sensitive to new technology and the persistence of high profits in the short run. Whereas the first type of learning emphasizes the role of first-time innovators in the Schumpeterian process of 'creative destruction', the second type shows in a direct fashion the impact of stochastic market growth on the two groups of Cournot producers. In the latter case the impact of increased or decreased risk aversion on the price and output trajectories can be directly evaluated. Hence one can more directly compare the optimal paths for deterministic and stochastic versions.

3.2. Stochastic Solow-type models

The earliest form of learning by doing is due to Arrow (1962), who modeled the technical innovation process in terms of the experience of the airframe industry. Here the experience is measured by cumulated gross investment $K(t)$:

$$K(t) = \sum_{-\infty}^{t} I(v)\,dv \tag{3.1}$$

and the production function is specified as

$$Y(t) = F[K(t), A(t)\,L(t)] \tag{3.2}$$

where the current efficiency of labor is measured by

$$A(t) = [K(t)]^{\gamma},\ 0 < \gamma < 1 \tag{3.3}$$

Note that even if the production function $F(K, AL)$ has constant returns to scale in the two inputs K and AL, as in the neoclassical model, the overall function exhibits homogeneity of degree greater than one, e.g., in the Cobb-Douglas case

$$F(K, AL) = K^\beta (AL)^{1-\beta} = K^{\beta+\gamma(1-\beta)} L^{1-\beta}, \quad 0 < \beta < 1 \tag{3.4}$$

Assume a constant ratio (s) of savings to output. Then the ratio $k(t)$ of output to augmented labor $(k(t) = Y(t)/AL(t))$ follows the differential equation:

$$\dot{k} = s (1 - \gamma) f(k) - nk \tag{3.5}$$

where $\dot{L}/L = n$ is the fixed growth rate of labor. Let k^0 be the capital-labor ratio defined by

$$f(k^0)/k^0 = n(s(1 - \gamma))^{-1} \tag{3.6}$$

then by the property of the production function $f(k) > 0$, $f'(k) > 0$, $f''(k) < 0$ for all $0 < k < \infty$ it follows that starting from any arbitrary initial stock of capital k_0 the unique solution of (3.5) tends to k^0, i.e., $\lim_{t\to\infty} k(t) = k^0$, where k^0 is the balanced growth capital–labor ratio corresponding to a fixed savings rate.

It is clear that in a state of balanced growth with fixed k and a fixed level of savings per capita, the process of learning by doing follows the following path:

$$\frac{\dot{A}}{A} = \gamma\left(\frac{\dot{K}}{K}\right) = \frac{\gamma}{1-\gamma}\left(\frac{\dot{k}}{k} + n\right)$$

$$\text{i.e., } A(t) = \left[k(t)\right]^{\frac{\gamma}{1-\lambda}} \exp\left[t\left(\frac{\gamma n}{1-\lambda}\right)\right] \tag{3.7}$$

Clearly, the higher the level of γ, the higher is the learning curve effect in raising output. This effect is enhanced by also increasing the level of $k(t)$ itself, i.e., capital augmenting.

A second approach to learning by doing is to allow this effect through both labor and capital, i.e.,

$$Y = F(\gamma K, \mu L)$$

where the rates of factor augmentation are assumed to follow the rule

$$\frac{\dot{\gamma}}{\gamma} = g\left(\frac{\dot{\mu}}{\mu}\right) \tag{3.8}$$

where $g' < 0$ and $g'' < 0$.

This approach is due to Kennedy (1964), who has interpreted the $g(\cdot)$ function as an innovation possibility curve. With a fixed savings ratio s and the following per capita variables $y = Y/L$, $k = K/L$ and $x = \gamma K/\mu L$. Nordhaus (1967) has analyzed the time path of capital labor ratio as follows:

$$\dot{k} = s\mu f(x) - nk \tag{3.9}$$

To determine the optimal trajectory of technical change, Nordhaus assumes a planning authority that controls the aggregate savings rate s and the direction of technical change $= \tau = \dot{\mu}/\mu$. The objective is to maximize the discounted stream of per capita consumption, i.e.,

$$\text{Max } J = \int_{0}^{\infty} \exp(-\rho t)\left[(1-s)\mu f(x)\right] dt \tag{3.10}$$

Forming the Hamiltonian

$$H = \exp(-\rho t)[(1-s)\,\mu f\left(\frac{\lambda k}{\mu}\right) + p_1\left\{s\mu f\left(\frac{\lambda k}{\mu}\right) - nk\right\} + p_2 e^{ht}\, g(\tau)\, \lambda + p_3 \tau \mu]$$

and applying Pontryagin principle, the optimal trajectories must satisfy the following conditions on the continuous adjoint variables $p_i(t)$ ($I = 1, 2, 3$) as follows:

$$\dot{p}_1 = (\rho + n)\, p_1 - f'(x)\, \gamma\lambda$$

$$\dot{p}_2 = (\rho - h - g(\tau))\, p_2 - f'(x)\, k\gamma e^{-ht}$$

$$\dot{p}_3 = (\rho - \tau)\, p_3 - \gamma[f(x) - xf'(x)] \tag{3.11}$$

where $\gamma = 1 - s + sp_1$, h is the solution to the equation $g(\tau) = 0$, prime denotes derivatives and a dot over a variable denotes its time derivative. In addition, the optimal trajectories of $s(t)$ and $\tau(t)$ must satisfy at each time point the conditions

$$s(t) \text{ maximizes } \{1 - s + sp_1(t)\} \tag{3.12}$$

and

$$\partial H/\partial \tau = 0 = p_2(t)\, g'(\tau)\, \lambda e^{ht} + p_3(t)\, \mu$$

$$\partial^2 H/\partial \tau^2 \leq 0 \text{ and } g(\tau) \text{ is concave in } \tau$$

It is clear that these optimizing conditions may be interpreted in two different ways. One is to view it as a central planner's problem, where knowledge capital is in the public domain and both the savings rate and the direction of the public innovation process are endogenously determined as an optimal choice problem. This is very different from the Solow model, where these two variables are more or less exogenous. Secondly, it may be viewed as a monopolistically competitive market equilibrium solution, where the private firms undertake research innovations in order to exploit the dynamic profits and rents over time until new entry occurs with improved innovations. Aghion and Howitt (1992) have analyzed this second aspect in a framework of vertical innovations, when the amount of research in any period depends upon the expected amount of research in the next period. Furthermore, the productivity of research or R&D investment is measured by a parameter indicating the effect of research on the Poisson arrival rate of innovation.

We discuss in section 3.3 an alternative formulation of a two-tier model of technical diffusion, where the productivity shock is reflected in terms of a stochastic parameter. Note that this model of optimal technical innovation has several flexible features. First of all, the innovation possibility function (3.8) links capital augmentation to the efficiency of labor or human capital and this is very much in line with the modern theory of 'knowledge capital'. Secondly, the use of $\tau = \dot{\mu}/\mu$ as the control variable by the planning authority suggests that R&D expenditures have to be optimally allocated, since the ratio μ/λ must satisfy the optimality rule given in (3.12):

$$\mu/\lambda = (-e^{ht}\, g'(\tau))\, p_2/p_3$$

where $-g'(\tau)$ is positive. However the condition $g''(\tau) < 0$ which is required for optimality may not hold if the production set is non-convex and the competitive market equilibrium has to obtain. Thus there is a direct conflict between the planned economy setup and the competitive equilibrium. In endogenous growth theory, this conflict is handled in two ways, e.g., either one replaces the competitive framework by monopolistic competition, or the objective function (3.10) is replaced by a discounted profit functional for a private producer. In the latter case a two-tier framework of directing technical innovation is of central importance. In the domestic front the producer acts jointly with state support like a large quasi-monopoly firm, which exploits all the scale economies, whereas in the international front it acts more like a price taker. This aspect will also be discussed later in Section 3.3. Finally, the steady state level of k determined by (3.9) yields

$$f(x^0)/x^0 = n(s\lambda) \tag{3.13}$$

This may be compared with equation (3.6) when learning by doing occurs only through labor augmentation. Clearly, when μ rises, τ falls and this leads to an increase in the output–capital ratio in efficiency units given by the left-hand side variable in (3.13). For the labor augmenting variety of learning by doing, a rise in γ in (3.6) leads to an increase in output–capital ratio. Binder and Pesaran (1996) have empirically investigated the degree to which stochasticity in technological progress and the labor input can contribute to differences in steady state capital output ratios across countries. In the framework of this model (3.8), the parameters λ and μ would be stochastic in character, which would affect the transient and the steady state behavior of the capital-output ratio in the extended Solow model. The sources of this stochasticity are two-fold. One is the uncertainty associated with the R&D investments, which not only generates new information embodied in new products or new services, but also enhances the firm's ability to exploit existing information. Cohen and Levinthal (1989) have empirically analyzed R&D investment data of 1302 business units representing 151 lines of business from the FTC's data file and found that learning or absorptive capacity represents an important part of a firm's ability to create new knowledge or a new product. This explains why firms may conduct basic research, e.g., for reasons that they are more able to identify and exploit useful science and technology, whereby they may gain a first-mover advantage in exploiting new technologies. A second source of uncertainty involves adjusting labor and capital stocks to their desired levels. For example, a firm which finds that its current stocks of capital and labor are inconsistent with the long-run equilibrium implied by current factor prices and their expected changes in future, will generally spread the planned adjustment to long-run equilibrium over time. This imparts stochasticity to the changes in labor and capital. Treadway (1974), Kennan (1979) and Gregory, Pagan and Smith (1993) have analyzed such problems.

So far we have discussed learning by doing through the labor and capital inputs. A third type arises through the Hicksian technical progress function, where the production function is specified as

$$Y(t) = F[K(t), L(t), t].$$

Here t on the right-hand side represents a time trend variable used as a proxy for neutral technological progress, e.g., a shift in production function. Norsworthy and Jang (1992) have discussed the disadvantages of this type of specification and suggested other types of explanatory variables such as 'cumulative output' that has a learning curve effect of economies of scale. Assuming a Cobb-Douglas form, the production function here takes the form

$$Y = \dot{Z} = AZ^{\theta}L^{a_1}K^{a_2}; \quad \alpha_i > 0, \, 0 < \theta < 1 \tag{3.14}$$

where $Z(t) = \int_0^t Y(\tau)d\tau$ is cumulative output representing the embodied form of all knowledge capital and cumulative experience. With the other assumptions of the Solow model, i.e., a fixed savings ratio s and the growth of labor as $n = \dot{L}/L$, one could easily derive the logistic equation in terms of the variable $u = \dot{Z}/Z$ as follows:

$$\frac{\dot{u}}{u} = n\alpha_1\left(1 - \theta - \frac{s\alpha_2 Z}{sZ + K_0}\right)$$

This yields the reduced form

$$\frac{\dot{u}}{u} = r(m - u) \tag{3.15}$$

where $r = 1 - \alpha_2 - \theta$, $m = n\alpha_1(1 - \theta - \alpha_2)^{-1}$ and K_0 is set to zero as a starting point. This can also be written in a convenient form as follows:

$$\frac{\dot{u}}{u} = b\left(1 - \frac{u}{\bar{u}}\right) \tag{3.16}$$

where b is a suitable positive parameter and $\bar{u}$ is the maximum level of u, e.g., $b = rm$ and $\bar{u} = 1/m$ in the case above.

Two important types of economic interpretation may be emphasized in terms of the learning capability parameter θ in (3.15), when one compares the deterministic version of this model with the stochastic version. One type of stochastic version assumes that the parameter $m = m(t)$ in (3.16) which incorporates the learning capability parameter θ follows a Gaussian process $m(t) = m_0 + \gamma W(t)$ with $W(t)$ being white noise, then the mean and variance processes take the simple forms

$$\mu(x) = x(\alpha - x), \quad \sigma^2(x) = \gamma^2 x^2$$

Clearly, $\partial\mu(x)/\partial\sigma^2(x) < 0$, which implies that increased volatility tends to lower the mean level of output growth in the long run. Thus the deterministic model (3.15) implies that countries with high learning ability will evidence high rate of growth, since $\partial(\dot{u}/u)/\partial\theta = u$ is positive. But the stochastic analogue of this model would imply in the long run that this process might not be self-sustained due to the negative correlation of the mean and the variance. Note also that the time varying propagation of the u-process would be markedly different in a stochastic framework from that of a deterministic framework, due to the existence of the variance process $\sigma^2(x)$. So long as this variance $\sigma^2(x)$ is positive for any time t, the mean of the $u(t)$ process would differ from the deterministic solution. This has the further implication for the risk-averse agents involved in the macrodynamic innovation and investment decisions. Since higher risk aversion implies more sensitivity to fluctuations measured by variance, these agents would prefer lower levels of mean growth rates in investment and hence output. Unlike consumption risk, this stochastic impact implies a high cost of economic fluctuations on the firms whose production technology entails commitments that are costly to reverse. Since most of these fluctuations are unanticipated, they cannot be incorporated into the firm's production plans, hence volatility due to variance $\sigma^2(x)$ leads to lower mean output as a consequence of ex post technological inefficiency. This issue also remains very important in econometric estimation of the output trajectory, since the specification of the deterministic model must incorporate some form of cost due to unanticipated fluctuations.

Now consider two types of stochasticity in the logistic process models (3.15) and (3.16). One arises through the variations in the random parameters m in (3.15) and b in (3.16). The sources of randomness may be due to the Hicksian technical progress function. A second type of stochasticity arises through interpreting $u(t)dt$ as a stochastic process satisfying a birth and death process for example. Here we consider the probability that $u(t)$ takes a particular value at time t, when the transitions to other states are Markovian.

Consider the first case and assume that the parameter m varies randomly, i.e., $m = m_0 + \gamma(t)$ around the mean value m_0 with $\gamma(t)$ as a white noise component with mean zero and variance σ^2. One can then derive the appropriate Fokker-Planck equation for the population probability distribution $f(u, t)$ by following the methods outlined in Bharucha-Reid (1960). The steady state probability distribution $f^*(u)$ then takes the limiting form

$$f^*(u) = c \, \exp(-2\mu/\sigma^2)$$

where c is the normalization constant, making the integrated probability unity. The mean $M = E(u)$ and the root mean square relative fluctuation R can be derived as

$$M = M_0[1 - (\sigma^2/2m_0)] \tag{3.17}$$

$$R = \frac{\sqrt{E(\mu - M)^2}}{M} = \left[\frac{\sigma^2/2m_0}{1-(\sigma^2/2m_0)}\right]^{1/2}$$

Note that relative fluctuations become increasingly severe as σ^2 increases toward $2m_0$, beyond which no equilibrium or steady state solution exists. Thus the mean variance ratio m_0/σ^2 taking the value 0.50 provides a critical level of volatility measured by the relative fluctuations.

Consider now the second form of the logistic equation (3.16) and assume that the parameter $b = b_0 + \sigma\xi(t)$ fluctuates like a Gaussian variable around the mean value b_0 with a variance σ^2 where $\xi(t)$ represents white noise. This yields a Gaussian delta continuous process for $u(t)$, which satisfies the Fokker-Planck equation

$$\partial P / \partial t = -\frac{\partial}{\partial u}[a(u)P] + \frac{1}{2}\frac{\partial^2}{\partial u^2}[c(u)P]$$

(3.18)

where $P = p[u|y,t]$ is the conditional probability that the random variable U will take the value u at time t given that it takes a value y at time zero and $a(u)$, $c(u)$ are defined as follows:

$$a(u) = \sigma(u) + \frac{1}{4}\frac{\partial}{\partial u}(\beta(u)^2); \quad \alpha(u) = b_0 u\left(1 - \frac{u}{\bar{u}}\right)$$

$$c(u) = [\beta(u)]^2; \quad \beta(u) = \sigma u\left(1 - \frac{u}{\bar{u}}\right) \quad \text{and} \quad du/dt = \alpha(u) + \beta(u)\,\xi(t).$$

Again one can show that such stochastic processes, which are completely determined by the coefficients $a(u)$ and $c(u)$ of the Fokker-Planck equation have unlimited state spaces if $c(u) > 0$ and $a(u)$ is infinite. In such cases the relative fluctuations enter an explosive phase as in (3.17). For the normalized variable $z = \exp(\sigma u)$ the mean Ez and variance $Varz$ can be derived as follows:

$$Ez = \exp\left(\frac{\sigma^2 t}{2}\right)\exp\left[\sigma\left(u_0 + \frac{b_0 t}{\sigma}\right)\right], \quad u_0 = u(t) \text{ at } t = 0$$

$$\text{var } z = (Ez)^2\left[e^{t\sigma^2} - 1\right]$$

$$\sqrt{\text{var } z}\,/\,Ez = \left(e^{t\sigma^2} - 1\right)^{1/2} \to \infty \text{ as } t \to \infty.$$

Note also that the deterministic model is

$$du/dt = b_0 u(1 - u/\bar{u})$$

which completely ignores the effects of $\beta(u)\,\xi(t)$, which combines the noise terms σ^2 and $\xi(t)$. Thus the effect of variance σ^2 may be stabilizing when it tends to reduce the mean level of u as t gets larger; or it may be destabilizing when it tends to make the u-process explosive. The zones of stability and chaotic instability are thus characterized by the stochastic interpretation of the growth model subject to the Hicksian type of neutral technological progress. The empirical estimation by Binder and Pesaran (1996) of the volatility of the capital–output ratio over 72 countries (1960–92) shows the importance of such issues for stochastic growth models. The steady state probability density function $p(u)$ of the process defined by (3.18) is of the form

$$p(u) = Cu^{(2b_0/\sigma^2)-1}(1 - u/\bar{u})^{-(2u/\sigma^2)-1} \qquad (3.19)$$

which shows that if $2b_0/\sigma^2$ is less than one, then the density function is U-shaped, indicating that it approaches zero or $\bar{u}$. But if $2b_0 > \sigma^2$ then the density is monotonically increasing in a J-shaped form; which suggests the existence of explosive regions where the steady state equilibrium may not exist at all.

There is an alternative way of looking at the deterministic growth equation (3.15) for $u(t)$. One can rewrite it with an additive error term $d\varepsilon$:

$$du = [(g\,u - h\,u^2)\,dt] + d\varepsilon \qquad (3.20)$$

where the first term under square bracket on the right-hand side represents the systematic part of the stochastic changes du and the error term $d\varepsilon$, has a mean zero in the limit with a variance $(g\,u - h\,u^2)dt$. Note that the parameters g and h are functions of the parameters r and m defined before in (3.15), i.e., the learning and experience effects in the R&D processes. Let μ be the asymptotic mean of the $u(t)$ process and $X(t) = u(t) - \mu$. Then

$$X(t + \Delta t) - X(t) = [gu(t) - hU^2(t)]\,dt + d\varepsilon(t).$$

This implies

$$E[X(t + \Delta t) - X(t)] = [g\,E(u(t)) - h\,E(u^2(t))]\,dt + E(d\varepsilon).$$

Letting $\Delta t \to 0$ this yields

$$(g/h)\,\mu - \mu^2 = \sigma_u^2 \qquad (3.21)$$

where σ_u^2 is the asymptotic variance of μ. This shows very clearly that

$$\frac{\partial \sigma_u^2}{\partial u} = \frac{g}{h} - \mu \overset{>}{\underset{<}{=}} 0, \text{ as } \mu \overset{<}{\underset{>}{=}} \frac{g}{h}$$

Hence $\partial \mu / \partial \sigma_u^2 < 0$ if $\mu > g/h$.

Thus as the mean income level μ increases above the level set by g/h, higher variance of u leads to a lower mean level of u, i.e., higher volatility tends to have lower means. But for the other case when $\mu < g/h$, the correlation between μ and σ_μ^2 is expected to be strongly positive.

Now we consider a stochastic birth and death process model for $u(t)$ and assume that the transition probability $p_u(t) = \text{Prob}[u(t) = u]$ for $u = 0, 1, 2, \ldots$ satisfies the standard Markovian assumptions, e.g., (i) assumption of stationary independent increments, i.e., the transition from u to $u + 1$ is given by $\lambda_u \, \Delta t + 0(\Delta t)$ and from u to $u - 1$ by $\mu \, \Delta t + 0(\Delta t)t)$, where $0(\Delta t)$ denotes infinitesimals of order two or higher which can be neglected for $\Delta t \to 0$ and (ii) the probability of no transition is $(1 - \lambda_u - \mu_u) \, \Delta t + 0(\Delta t)$ and (iii) the probability of transition to a value other than the neighboring value is $0(\Delta t)$. Under these assumptions the transition probability $p_u(t)$ of $u(t)$ taking a value u at time t satisfies the following Chapman-Kolmogorov equation (see, e.g., Tintner and Sengupta (1972):

$$\frac{dp_u}{dt} = \lambda_{u-1} p_{u-1}(t) + \mu_{u+1} p_{u+1}(t) - (\lambda_u + \mu_u) \, p_u(t) \tag{3.22}$$

where the parameters λ_u, μ_u which depend on the level of u are called birth and death rate parameters, since the former leads to positive growth (e.g., effect of experience) and the latter to decay (e.g., obsolescence due to the introduction of new technology). Now assume that the birth rate parameter λ_u declines with increasing u but the death rate parameter μ_u remains proportional to u^2, i.e.,

$$\lambda_u = u \, a_1(1 - u), \, \mu = a_2 \, u^2$$

where a_1, a_2 are positive constants. Then the mean value function $m(t) = E[u(t)]$ would follow the trajectory as follows:

$$\frac{dm(t)}{dt} = (a_1 + a_2) \left[\frac{a_1}{a_1 + a_2} m(t) - m^2(t) - v(t) \right] \tag{3.23}$$

where $v(t)$ is the variance function for the income process $u(t)$. For the deterministic growth model the differential equation (3.23) reduces to a simpler form

$$\dot{u}(t) = a_1\, u(t) - u^2(t) \tag{3.24}$$

if we normalize as $a_1 + a_2 = 1.0$. The stochastic case however is of the form

$$\dot{m}(t) = a_1\, m(t) - m^2(t) - v(t) \tag{3.25}$$

On comparing the deterministic and stochastic forms of the growth equations (3.24) and (3.25), one may derive some useful results. First of all, in the steady state one obtains

$$\partial m/\partial v < 0 \text{ if and only if } m > (\tfrac{1}{2})\, a_1$$

whereas $\dot{u}(t)$ is zero at the level $u(t) = a_1$ and positive for $u(t) < a_1$. Otherwise the higher variance would tend to be associated with a larger mean. Clearly, some countries would correspond with the latter case, as Goodwin (1990) has shown in his nonlinear model of economic growth. Secondly, the presence of a positive variance function in (3.25) implies that the deterministic trajectory $u(t)$ in (3.24) would tend to be shifted downward in the stochastic growth model. Due to this downward bias the steady state value of the mean m^0 would be less than the steady state deterministic value of u, i.e., $m^0 < a_1 = u^0$. Note that the shift in the mean value process $m(t)$ can be empirically analyzed through the econometric tests on the variance process $v(t)$, i.e., whether it follows random walk or other Arch processes. Sengupta and Zheng (1995) have empirically estimated mean variance models of stock market volatility, where chaotic behavior could not be ruled out. Finally, one may consider a discrete time variant of the logistic model (3.24) as $u_t = f(u_{t-1})$ and analyze the stability of the map $f(\cdot)$ given an initial point u_0. The sequence of points $u_0, f(u_0), f^2(u_0), \ldots$ is called the orbit of the map where the iterates $f^n(u_0)$ are defined by $f^{n+1}(u_0) = f[f^n(u_0)]$ and $f^0(u_0) = u_0$. The following classification for the stability of the map $f(\cdot)$ is often used in chaos theory:

$|f'| > 1$: linearly unstable

$|f'| \leq 1$: linearly stable

$|f'| < 1$: strongly stable

$|f'| = 1$: marginally stable

$f' = 0$: superstable

where f' is the slope of the map f at a fixed point with $|f'|$ denoting its absolute value. Note that the equation in discrete time form:

$$u_t/u_{t-1} = a(1 - u_{t-1})$$

has its critical parameter a acting as a bifurcation parameter in the sense that the qualitative behavior of u_t suddenly changes for different value of a. For example, the range $1 < a < 2$ defines monotonic growth of u_t converging to the steady state $u^0 = (1 - 1/a)$, but for $a > 3$ the steady state becomes unstable and a two-period cycle emerges. In fact the simulation studies by Lorenz (1963) showed that as a increases beyond $1 + \sqrt{6} = 3.45$, higher and higher even-order cycles emerge; beyond 3.57 he found that very higher odd-period cycles appear and so on. This type of chaotic behavior may sometimes be reduced or aggravated by the variance process in the stochastic process model.

3.3.   Trade and externality effects

The dynamic effects of openness in trade have been strongly emphasized in new growth theory. Export growth and the impact of the export-intensive sectors on the other sectors of the economy have played a very critical role in the rapid growth episode of countries like the NICs in Southeast Asia. In new growth theory openness in trade has been viewed as a catalytic mechanism that alleviates the bottlenecks that impede the steady growth of the less developed countries (LDCs). Empirical studies of the growth of exports have revealed two broad trends for the successful NICs. Thus Bradford (1987) examined empirical data for more than a dozen countries over 1965–80 covering the link between structural change and economic growth, where the index of structural change was derived from 16 manufacturing sectors and concluded that high rates of growth and rapid structural change are closely associated with those countries which are the successful NICs. Moreover for some countries like South Korea the pace of rapid structural change was also associated with a change in export-mix in response to world competition. The shift from traditional to R&D intensive products in export growth has been remarkable for the four successful NICs in Asia is given in Table 3.1.

This analysis by Kellman and Chow (1989) also showed another important characteristic, e.g., the traditional export items mainly from the primary sector were very dissimilar in pattern across the four countries above and also very insensitive to changes in relative prices but all the four countries were found to be very similar in the pattern of exports of certain sophisticated R&D intensive products such as electrical machinery, optical equipment and telecommunications and computer equipment and consumer electronics; also these R&D intensive products were found to be strongly responsive to international competition. In the more recent decade, 1986–1996, this tendency has intensified due to two main reasons, e.g., (a) the impact of innovation in the semiconductor industry and its spillover effects on other sectors and (b) the globalization of trade which has increased the competitive efficiency.

Several key channels have been identified in modern growth theory in order to explain the close association by the openness in trade via exports and the rapid overall growth. One channel is the 'trade-knowledge externality' which was originally emphasized by Alfred Marshall. The benefits of this trade-knowledge cannot be fully appropriated internally. As Caballero and Lyons (1992) have interpreted, the expression of 'trade-knowledge' includes according to Marshall not only R&D but also knowledge along the lines of process innov-

Table 3.1   Percentage distribution of exports to the US

Product-group	Hong Kong		Korea		Singapore		Taiwan	
	1966	1986	1966	1986	1966	1986	1966	1986
1. Traditional	67.9	62.2	56.5	52.7	44.6	49.1	73.6	13.9
2. R&D intensive (general)	9.8	23.8	2.0	19.2	15.8	22.3	0.0	58.2
3. R&D intensive (sophisticated)	17.5	29.5	3.9	29.6	20.3	29.2	0.20	78.1

ation and best practice technology in general. In Romer's (1990) endogenous growth theory, the capital input embodies this trade knowledge externality. The export sector's externality spills over to the other sectors and generates a feedback effect. A second channel of interaction of why the export sector plays a leading role is that it is more productive and more intensive in modern technological inputs. Hence the export sector exerts a strong positive influence on the rest of the economy. A direct empirical test of this dominance effect of the export sector may be made by means of a two-sector model with outputs X and N for the export and the non-export sector subject to two production functions:

$$N = F(K_N, L_N, X); \quad X = G(K_X, L_X, N) \tag{3.26}$$

where $K = K_N + K_X$ is total capital and $L = L_N + L_X$ is total labor. It follows therefore

$$\Delta N = F_K \, \Delta K_N + F_L \, \Delta L_N + F_X \, \Delta X \tag{3.27}$$

$$AX = G_K \, \Delta K_X + G_L \, \Delta L_X + G_N \, \Delta N$$

where the subscripts on F and G denote the marginal productivity of the two inputs in the two sectors. A direct empirical estimate of the two-sector model (3.27) from Korean national income statistics data produced the following results:

	1964–83	1964–86	1969–86	1970–90
FX	1.92	1.00	0.99	0.89
G_N	0.28	0.31	0.32	0.30
F_X/G_N	6.90	3.20	3.11	2.96

It is clear that the dynamic interdependence effect from the export to the non-export sector is roughly between three and seven times larger than the reverse effect from the non-export to the export sector. The estimates for other successful NICs in Asia analyzed by Sengupta (1993) confirm this dominance hypothesis for the export sector. Finally, Lucas (1993) has emphasized the knowledge spillover effect as the most significant factor that explains the difference in capital productivity between an LDC and a developed economy. Thus the external benefits of human capital in his theory can be captured by specifying the production function for sector i ($i = 1, 2$) as

$$y_i = A_i \; x_i^{\beta_i} h_i^{\gamma_i}; \quad \Delta h_i = h_i(1 - u_i)\, \theta_1 \qquad (3.28)$$

where the three variables y, x and h denote output, physical and human capital per effective worker. The term $h_i^{\gamma_i}$ is interpreted as an externality that multiplies the productivity of a worker at any skill level just as the shift factor A_i. For the export-intensive sector ($i = 1$, e.g.) we have higher h_1 and higher γ_1 than the other sector. Also h_1 tends to grow faster over time, since the proportion $(1 - u_1)$ devoted to human capital accumulation and its productivity effect (θ_1) is likely to be higher for the export sector ($I = 1$).

There is an alternative way of modeling the knowledge spillover effect through human capital in the global economy. This follows the approach of Grossman and Helpman (1991) and the learning models due to Jovanovic (1997), where endogenous quality increments follow the process of learning through research. Here there are invention costs but no adoption costs and the output of research is designs, which are sold by innovators to intermediate-goods producers. Specifically the use of the new intermediate good augments the productivity parameter A in (3.28). This formulation allows the direct introduction of the Schumpeterian innovation process which is sufficiently important to affect the entire economy, as has been shown by Aghion and Howitt (1992).

We now consider an empirical econometric application of the learning mechanism, as it influences the behavior of the representative producer as the dynamic agent. The model follows the formulations of Kennan (1979) and Gregory et al. (1993) and involves a two-step decision process. In the first step the producer decides on the optimal inputs given by the vector x_t^* say by minimizing a steady state cost function. The second step then postulates an optimal adjustment or learning rule toward the optimal target levels of input x_t^* and output $Y_t^* = F(X_t^*)$. The learning mechanism in the second step explicitly assumes a short-run adjustment behavior of the producer, who finds his current factor uses are inconsistent with the steady state equilibrium path (X_t^*, Y_t^*) determined in the first step by the relative factor prices and their expected changes in the future. In order to resolve or reduce the inconsistency problem the producer minimizes an intertemporal adjustment cost function, which includes the expected cost of deviations from the steady state equilibrium levels. Sengupta and Okamura (1996) have introduced a quadratic adjustment cost function involving two types of costs, e.g., disequilibrium costs due to deviation of X_t from X_t^* and risk aversion costs due to input fluctuations. Thus the two components of the expected adjustment costs illustrate the learning behavior through adaptivity. This dynamic adjustment model was applied to explain the trend of economic fluctuations in Japan over the period 1965–90 for the time series of input and output growth. The specific adjustment model minimizes the expected value of a quadratic loss function as follows:

$$\operatorname*{Min}_{x_t} E_t L \tag{3.29a}$$

where $L = \displaystyle\sum_{t=0}^{\infty} r^t[(x_t - x_t^*)'\Lambda(x_t - x_t^*) + (x_t - x_{t-1})' \psi(x_t - x_{t-1})]$

where $E_t(\cdot)$ is expectations of time t, $r = (1 + \rho)^{-1}$ is the exogenous rate of discount, $x_t = \ln X_t$, $x_t = \ln X_t^*$ and Λ, ψ are matrices of nonnegative weights. The first component of the cost function is an inefficiency cost due to deviations of short-run input levels from their optimal long-run levels. The second component reflects the cost of successive movement toward the optimal input combination. On applying the necessary condition for minimization of the expected loss function above, one could easily derive the optimal linear decision rule as follows:

$$[-(1/r)(P + (1 + r) I_m) Z + (1/r) Z^2 + I_m] E_t x_{t-1} = (-1/r) E_t x_t^* \tag{3.29b}$$

where $P = \psi^{-1} \Lambda$, I_m = identity matrix of order m for m inputs and Z is a backward lag operator. It is well known that the characteristic equation of this difference equation system (3.29b) will have half of the roots stable and half unstable. Let μ be the square matrix of stable roots of this system. Then one could define a long-run input demand vector as d_t:

$$d_t = (I_m - r\mu) \sum_{s=0}^{\infty} r^s \mu^s x_{t+s}^*$$

On the basis of this estimated demand vector, one could derive the partial adjustment rule as the final estimating equation. For example, with one input this would yield

$$\Delta x_t = \phi(d_t - x_{t-1}) + \varepsilon_t \tag{3.29c}$$

where $\phi = 1 - \mu_1$, $d_t = (1 - r\mu_1) E_t \left[\sum_{s=0}^{\infty} r^s \mu_1^s x_{t+s}^* \right]$ and it is assumed that the rational expectations (RE) hypothesis holds as

$$E_t(x_{t+1}) = x_{t+1} \tag{3.29d}$$

i.e., the expected value of the x_{t+1} equals the observed value.

If the error component ε_t is a white noise process and d_t estimated consistently by the instrument variable method as Kennan has done, then this dynamic adjustment equation (3.29d) which incorporates active learning by the producer can be estimated by a statistically consistent way.

Several important features of the learning mechanism are to be specifically noted. First, if there were no learning, the producer would have no adjustment, so that the observed input and output paths would exhibit more fluctuations due to the uncertainty in the exogenous variables and the various unanticipated externality effects of international trade. With some learning through the adjustment cost, the optimal producer behavior is more risk averse. As in portfolio theory it tends to reduce the variance of fluctuations around the selected decision rule. Secondly, the RE hypothesis implies that the estimated input demand turns out to be equal to the observed level on the average. This is the perfect foresight condition of the stochastic control model. If this condition is not fulfilled or fulfilled only partially, there would occur more divergence of the optimal from the actual trajectory. Finally, the objective function (3.29a) involves only the minimization of the expected loss function. A more general risk sensitive rule would be to minimize a weighted combination of mean and variance as follows:

$$\text{Min } E_t L + w \text{ Var } L$$

Risk-sensitive optimal decision rules of this type have been applied by Sengupta and Fanchon (1997).

Finally, the optimal linear decision rule equation (3.29b) may be directly used to test which of the two forces – past history or future expectations – played a more dominant role in the optimal capital expansion policies of the producers in Japan. Since future expectations are forward looking and hence more oriented to dynamic learning, its significance in an estimated equation would indicate the presence of active learning. The backward looking view represented by the past history and its trend would by comparison represent the less learning and less adjustment.

The detailed empirical model of dynamic adjustment was estimated by Sengupta and Okamura (1996) for Japan (1965–90) based on aggregate time series data. We report here two major findings that are relevant for learning-based growth of inputs. Based on a Cobb-Douglas production function

$$Q_t = B(A_t, V_t) K_t^a L_t^b$$

with the technical progress variable B as a function of export V_t and an external shock variable A_t for international transmission of knowledge, the linear decision rules for optimal demand for labor (L_t) and capital (K_t) appear as follows:

$$\Delta \ln L_t = \phi_L \left(d_t^L - \ln L_{t-1} \right) + \text{error}$$

$$\Delta \ln K_t = \phi_k \left(d_t^K - \ln K_{t-1} \right) + \text{error}$$

Note that we could derive here a relationship between the speed of adjustment parameter ϕ_i and the ratio θ_i of the weights on two cost components in (3.29a):

$$\theta_i = -\phi_i \, r + \phi_i (1 - \phi_i) - 1, \quad i = L, K$$

Since the target demand d_t^i can be estimated in terms of either the past lagged instrument variables (backward looking view), or the expected values of future instrument variables (forward looking view), we may derive two types as in Table 3.2.

Clearly, labor adjusts much faster than capital. Thus the ratio ϕ_L/ϕ_K varies from 6.6 to 10.2. The implications of a slow adjustment speed for capital are two-fold. First, the characteristic root for capital is very

Table 3.2 Estimate of the speed of adjustment parameters (ϕ_i) and the weight ratio $\theta_i = \Lambda_i/\psi_i$ ($i = K, L$)

Output (ln Y_t)	Input (ln X_{it})		ϕ_i	θ_i	Ch. root $\mu_i = 1 - \phi_i$
1. GNP	Backward looking	K	0.118*	0.016	0.882*
		L	0.898*	7.873	0.102
	Forward looking	K	0.082*	0.007	0.918*
		L	0.837*	4.281	0.163**
2. GDP	Backward looking	K	0.120	0.016	0.880
		L	0.924*	11.231	0.076*
	Forward looking	K	0.086*	0.008	0.914*
		L	0.569*	0.753	0.431

Note:
1. One and two asterisks denote significant *t*-values at 5% and 1% levels.
2. The stable characteristic roots μ_i are only reported.

close to unity. Secondly, much of capital expansion is in the form of capital deepening, thus reflecting a stronger role of future expectations. Also the forward looking estimates of the characteristic root $\mu_K = 1 - \phi_K$ are higher than the backward looking ones. A more direct estimate of the optimal demand equations produced the following results:

$$\Delta l_t = 2.241 - \underset{(t=-3.47)}{0.545}\ln_{t-1} + \underset{(2.53)}{0.432}\tilde{l}_{t+1} \quad R^2 = 0.372, \text{ DW} = 3.02$$

$$\Delta k_t = \underset{(-0.21)}{-0.026} - \underset{(-8.62)}{0.511}k_{t-1} + \underset{(8.00)}{0.512}k_{t+1} \quad R^2 = 0.893, \text{ DW} = 2.67$$

$$\Delta y_t = \underset{(0.21)}{0.039} - \underset{(-6.47)}{0.505}y_{t-1} + \underset{(5.45)}{0.500}\tilde{y}_{t+1} \quad R^2 = 0.735, \text{ DW} = 2.73$$

Here the lower case letters are in logs of labor, capital and output and the *t*-values are in parentheses. The tilda over a variable denotes its estimated value at $t + 1$ and this is used as a regressor in order to reduce the bias due to autocorrelation of errors. It is clear that the future variables $\tilde{l}_{t+1}$, $\tilde{k}_{t+1}$ and $\tilde{y}_{t+1}$ play a more dominant and significant role than the past denoted by l_{t-1}, k_{t-1} and y_{t-1}.

Similar estimates for South Korea over the period 1971–90 produced very similar results as follows:

$$\Delta l_t = \underset{(-4.58)}{0.099 - 0.510\, l_{t-1}} + \underset{(3.94)}{0.504\, \tilde{l}_{t+1}} \quad R^2 = 0.61,\ \text{DW} = 2.49$$

$$\Delta k_t = -0.110 - \underset{(-7.41)}{0.536\, k_{t-1}} + \underset{(6.79)}{0.544\, \tilde{k}_{t+1}} \quad R^2 = 0.86,\ \text{DW} = 1.64$$

$$\Delta y_t = -0.023 - \underset{(-5.13)}{0.504\, y_{t-1}} + \underset{(4.83)}{0.573\, y_{t+1}} \quad R^2 = 0.65,\ \text{DW} = 2.24$$

These results seem to support the hypothesis that learning-based future expectations play a more dynamic positive role in the growth of inputs and output in the Asian NICs.

Consider now the stochastic view of learning through the bivariate interaction of the two sectors in the growth process model in the form (3.26). Assume a bivariate birth and death process satisfying the Chapman-Kolmogorov equations as before. Then the system of differential equations for the transition probability $p_{x,n}(t)$ at time t can be written as

$$dp_{x,n}(t) = -(\lambda_x + \mu_x + \lambda_n + \mu_n)\, p_{x,n}(t) + \lambda_{x-1}\, p_{x-1,n}(t)$$
$$+ \mu_{x-1}\, p_{x+1,n}(t) + \lambda_{n-1}\, p_{x,n-1}(t) + \mu_{n+1}\, p_{x,n+1}(t) \tag{3.29}$$

for $x,\ n = 0,\ 1,\ 2\ldots.$ We now consider the application of the above system of differential equations to two special cases. The first case occurs when there is no death rate, i.e., $\mu_x = 0 = \mu_n$ and the deterministic system in $x(t)$ and $n(t)$ follows oneway interdependence as follows:

$$\frac{dx(t)}{dt} = \dot{x}(t) = b_1 v\, x(t)$$

$$\frac{dn(t)}{dt} = \dot{n}(t) = a_2 n(t) + b_2(1-v)\, x(t);\ 0 < v < 1.$$

Here $n(t)$ depends on $x(t)$ for its growth, whereas $x(t)$ grows due to the high proportion of total output $x(t) + n(t)$ devoted to human capital, i.e., high level of v which implies a low level allocated for the growth of the $n(t)$ sector. The means (M_x, M_n) and variances (V_x, V_n) may then be calculated as

$$M_x(t) = \exp(b_1 v t)$$

$$V_x(t) = v(2-v)^{-1} \exp(b_1 v t)[\exp(b_1 v t) - 1]$$

where the initial value $x(0)$ is set equal to one. However the non-export sector output follows a different mean variance structure. The mean is

$$M_n(t) = b_2(1 - v)(b_1v - a_2) -1 \exp(b_1vt) + \exp(a_2t)$$

but the variance is a more complicated function with a dominant term proportional to $\exp(2a_2t)$. It is clear from these mean variance relationships that

$$\partial M_x(t)/\partial V_x(t) < 0 \text{ as } M_x(t) < 1.0$$

i.e., countries with a higher volatility of export output would tend to have a lower mean export level, otherwise $\partial M_x/\partial V_x > 0$ as $M_x(t) > 1.0$. Secondly, the allocation ratio v can be used directly by public policy favoring the export sector. The national governments in NICs in Asia have always stressed these policy measures. For example, the government planners in Japan and Korea have consistently allocated a growing share of domestic and foreign resources through credit rationing and other export subsidy measures to capital-intensive industries and also consumer electronics. Finally, as $t \to \infty$, the coefficient of variation (CV) measuring the relative level of fluctuations tends to settle down in both sectors, $\text{CV}_x \sim (v/(2-v))^{1/2}$. This implies that the CV_x ratio increases as v rises.

A second case of the stochastic process model (3.28) occurs when the sectoral interdependence takes the following form

$$\lambda_x = \lambda_1 x, \ \mu_x = xf(x,n) = x(\mu_{11}x + \mu_{12}n)$$

$$\lambda_n = \lambda_2 n, \ \mu_n = nf(x,n) = n(\mu_{21}x + \mu_{22}n)$$

with $f(x,n) = \alpha_1 x + a_2 n$ denoting the interaction term. This form allows various types of interaction effects through the functions $f(\cdot)$ and $g(\cdot)$. One could derive from this system differential equations involving the first two moments of the stochastic process as follows:

$$\dot{m}_{11}(t) = \lambda_1 m_{11}(t) - \mu_{11}m_{12}(t) - \mu_{12}\bar{m}_{11}(t)$$

$$\dot{m}_{21}(t) = \lambda_2 m_{21}(t) - \mu_{21}\bar{m}_{11}(t) - \mu_{22}m_{22}(t) \tag{3.30}$$

Here $m_{11}(t) = E\{X(t)\}$, $m_{12}(t) = E\{X^2(t)\}$, $m_{21}(t) = E\{N(t)\}$, $m_{22}(t) = E\{N^2(t)\}$ and $\bar{m}_{11}(t) = E\{X(t) N(t)\}$ and the dot over a variable denotes its time derivative. Clearly, if there is no interaction between the sectors, then the two sectoral outputs $m_{11}(t)$ and $M_{21}(t)$ grow at the exponential rates λ_1 and λ_2 respectively. But if $\mu_{12} = 0 = \mu_{21}$, and both μ_{11} and μ_{22} are negative, then both sectoral outputs tend to grow exponentially. The deterministic system corresponding to (3.30) may be specified as

$$\dot{X}(t) = \lambda_1 X(t) - \mu_1 \alpha_1 X^2(t) - \mu_1 \alpha_2 X(t)\, N(t)$$

$$\dot{N}(t) = \lambda_2 N(t) - \mu_2 \alpha_1 X(t)\, N(t) - \mu_2 \alpha_2 N^2(t).$$

Note that this system has a logistic time profile for the export sector output if $\mu_1 \alpha_2$ is negligibly small, i.e.,

$$\dot{X}(t) = \lambda_1 X(t) - \mu_1 \alpha_1 X^2(t)$$

with steady state values

$$X^* = \frac{\lambda_1}{(\mu_1 \alpha_1)}, \quad N^* = \frac{\lambda_2}{\alpha_2 \mu_2} - \frac{\lambda_1}{\alpha_2 \mu_1}$$

The stability of these steady state values depends of course on the underlying characteristic roots. However the stability of the steady state values m_{11}^*, m_{21}^* of the stochastic system (3.30) depends on more restrictive conditions. As May (1973) has shown that the probability of unstable steady states is much higher and there exist biological systems where this type of instability phenomenon is persistent. For example, consider the second equation of the Lucas model (3.28) and assume a two-sector interacting framework as

$$\dot{h}_1 = h_1(t)\, f_1(h_1, h_2)$$

$$\dot{h}_2 = h_2(t)\, f_2(h_1, h_2) \tag{3.31}$$

Where

$$f_1(\cdot) = k_1 - h_1(t) - a\, h_2(t)$$
$$f_2(\cdot) = k_2 - h_2(t) - a\, h_1(t)$$

Here the coefficient a measures the symmetric competition between the two sectors for the common pool of human capital in the population and k_1, k_2 are the sector-specific parameters, which are constants in the deterministic case but random around a mean in a stochastic environment. In the steady state of the deterministic model the levels of h_1^* and h_2^* are found by putting the growth rates $\dot{h}_1 = \dot{h}_2$ to zero and then the linearized version around these steady states has the coefficient matrix

$$A = \begin{bmatrix} -h_1^* & -ah_2^* \\ -ah_1^* & -h_2^* \end{bmatrix}$$

Clearly, both the eigenvalues of this matrix are negative if and only if the coefficient $a < 1.0$. This is the well-known Gauss-Lotka-Volterra criterion for a stable bivariate population. Now let us consider a stochastic framework:

$$k_1 = k_0 + \gamma_1(t)$$

$$k_2 = k_0 + \gamma_2(t)$$

where the random parameters k_1, k_2 have a common mean value k_0 and two independent white noise random variables with zero mean and a common variance σ^2. Let R denote the root mean square measure of relative fluctuation as is used in (3.17) before. Then it holds approximately that

$$R^2 \sim \frac{\sigma^2}{k_0(1-a)}$$

This result derived by May (1973) has two important implications. One is that the system is stable so long as $a < 1.0$. But as soon as the magnitude of a increases up to 1.0 the interaction dynamics provide a weaker and weaker stabilizing influence and in the limit R^2 tends to be explosive. Secondly, the common parameter k_0 is only assumed for simplicity, the result would hold even if it were different for the two sectors. Clearly, as k_0 decreases to lower and lower values and satisfies the inequality $k_0(1 - a) < \sigma^2$, then the fluctuations measured by R^2 in (3.32) would tend to be higher and higher. This implies a tendency favoring increased random fluctuations in the $h_i(t)$ process and hence in the output process $y_i(t)$ defined in the Lucas model (3.28).

3.4.   Industry interactions and dynamic games

Rapid growth episodes in the NICs in Asia have been closely associated with some key trends in these countries. One is the persistence of scale economies that tends to produce oligopolistic firms even if there are no formal barriers to entry under competitive world trade. In this framework the output of each firm is given by Cournot-Nash equilibrium. Openness in world trade implying a larger market will tend to reduce the oligopolistic mark-up of price (p) over marginal cost (c). A second trend is the learning curve effect of cumulative experience of knowledge capital, which is undergoing an international spillover. For example, Norsworthy and Jang (1992) have empirically shown this effect to be substantial in Japan and other Asian NICs in microelectronics and semiconductor industries in particular. In a dynamic limit pricing model discussed, e.g., by Sengupta (1983) and more by Sengupta and Fanchon (1997) the entry into the market by other oligopolistic firms depends on the mark-up of price over marginal cost, where the actual price lies somewhere between the short-run monopoly price and the competitive price, the exact positioning depending on the barriers to entry, risk aversion and the impact on cost reduction through cumulative experience and learning. The third trend in the rapidly growing NICs in Asia is to capture the cost savings over time due to building capacity ahead of demand and to adopt flexible manufacturing practices. In this setup it is important to distinguish between current output ($\dot{y} = dy/dt$) and cumulative output $y(t)$ in the production function $F(y(t), x(t))$ where $x(t)$ denotes the variable inputs, e.g., the functional form

$$\dot{y}(t) = A \, y^{\delta} \, x(t)^{\frac{1}{\gamma}}$$

summarizes the dynamic process of producing the joint products of learning and output from resources and experiences. Assume now a duopolistic framework with two producers producing outputs $\dot{y}_1(t)$, $\dot{y}_2(t)$ at prices $p_1(t)$, $p_2(t)$. The NICs may represent one producer and the rest of the world as the second producer. The dynamic optimization model for the first producer may then take the form

$$\text{Max } J_1 = \int_0^{\infty} e^{-rt} (p_1(t) - c_1(t)) \, \dot{y}_1 dt \qquad (3.32)$$

s.t. $\dot{y}_i(t) = F_i(y_1(t), y_2(t), p_1(t), p_2(t)); \; i = 1, 2$

On using the current value Hamiltonian $H = e^{-rt} \{(p_1 - c_1 + \lambda_1) F_1 + (p_2 - c_2 + \lambda_2) F_2\}$ and assuming the regularity conditions for the existence of an optimal trajectory the Pontryagin maximum principle specifies the following necessary conditions for optimality (for $i = 1, 2$):

$$\dot{\lambda}_i = r\lambda_i - \frac{\partial H}{\partial y_i} \tag{3.33}$$

$$\dot{y}_i = F_i(y_1, y_2, p_1, p_2)$$

$$\partial H/\partial p_i = 0 \text{ for all } t$$

and $\lim e^{-rt} \lambda_i(t) = 0$ (transversality).

By using $[\mu_{ii} = (\partial F_i/\partial p_i)(p_i/F_i)$ and $\mu_{ji} = (\partial F_j/\partial p_i)(p_i/F_j)$ when $1 \neq j$ as the own price elasticity and cross elasticity of demand, the optimal price rule can be written as

$$p_1 = (1 + \mu_{11})^{-1} [\mu_{11}(c_1 - \lambda_1) - \lambda_2\mu_{21}] \tag{3.34}$$

with the optimal trajectory for $\lambda_1(t)$ as

$$\dot{\lambda}_1 = r\lambda_1 + (c_1 - \lambda_1) F_{1y_1} - p_1 F_{1y_1} + c_{1y} F_1$$

i.e.,

$$\lambda(t) = \int_t^\infty e^{-r(\tau-1)} \left[\left(\frac{p_1}{\mu_{11}} + \frac{\lambda_2\mu_{21}}{\mu_{11}} \right) F_{1y_1} + c_{1y_1} F \right] d\tau \tag{3.35}$$

where

$$F_{1y_1} = \frac{\partial F_1}{\partial y_1}$$

$$c_{1y_1} = \frac{\partial c_1}{\partial y_1} < 0, \text{ i.e., future cost decline}$$

$$\mu_{11} < 0, \mu_{21} > 0$$

Clearly, the optimal pricing rules involve the trajectories of both the current price $p_1(t)$ and the shadow prices $k_1(t)$. The current pricing rule (3.34) shows the price to be much lower than the monopoly price $(1 + \mu_{11})^{-1} \mu_{11}(c_1 - \lambda_1)$ since λ_2 is usually negative and since more competition hurts the market position of y_1 more. Secondly, the extent of future cost declines $(-c_{1y_1} > 0)$ tends to reduce the dynamic shadow price $\lambda_1(t)$. Thirdly, if the demand function in (3.33) is a function of prices alone, i.e., $\dot{y}_i = F(p_1 p_2)$ then the sign of $\dot{p} = dp/dt$ may be shown as

$$\text{sign}(\dot{p}) = \text{sign}(-r\lambda_1 + c_{1t} - \lambda_2\mu_{21})$$

where $c_{1t} = \partial c_1/\partial t$ is the decline of cost over time due to learning and experience since $c_{y_1} < 0$. This shows a strong pressure for price declines over time. This has happened exactly in the semi-conductor and R&D intensive industries such as electronics, telecommunications and personal computers. Helpman (1997) analyzed the empirical data of about 100 countries over the period 1971–90 and found substantial impact of R&D investment through foreign capital stock.

A simpler form of the decision model (3.32) results when we assume one average market price $p(t)$ for a homogenous product and a dynamic Cournot model with two outputs $\dot{y}_1$ and $\dot{y}_2$ as decision variables. In this case we reformulate the model as

$$\text{Max } J_1 = \int_0^{\infty} e^{-rt}(p(t) - c_1(t))\,\dot{y}_1\,dt$$

$$\text{s.t. } \dot{p}(t) = k(\tilde{p} - p), \quad \tilde{p} = a - b(\dot{y}_1 + \dot{y}_2) \tag{3.36}$$

where $\tilde{p} = \tilde{p}(t)$ is the demand price expected and p is the market price. Assuming quadratic cost functions, i.e., $c_1\dot{y}_1 = wu_1 + \tfrac{1}{2}u_1^2$ where $u_1 = \dot{y}_1$ and the parameter w declines over time due to learning and experience, the above is a linear quadratic control model and hence the optimal feedback strategies $u_i^*(t)$ can be easily calculated as

$$u_i^*(t) = [1 - bk\,h(t)]\,p(t) + bk\,m(t) - w \tag{3.37}$$

With

$$h(t) = (6k^2b^2)^{-1}\,[r + 4bk + 2k - \{(r + 4bk + 2k)^2 - 12k^2b^2)\}^{1/2}]$$

$$m(t) = (r - 3b^2k^2\,h(t) + k + 2bk)^{-1}\,[w - as\,h(t) - 2bkw\,h(t)]$$

Here zero conjectural variation on the part of each player is assumed. Clearly, this linear feedback form of the conjectural equilibrium output path in (3.36) yields a steady state price level p^* as

$$p^* = [2b(1 - bk\,h^* + 1]^{-1}\,[a + 2b(w - bk\,m^*)]$$

where h^*, m^* are the steady state values of $h(t)$ and $m(t)$ respectively.

Stochasticity in this framework may now be introduced in two simple ways. One is in the linear quadratic Gaussian (LQG) framework with the dynamic price equation rewritten as

$$dp(t) = k(\tilde{p} - p)\,dt + dv(t)$$

where $v(t)$ is a zero mean Gaussian process with stationary independent increments and a constant variance σ^2. The objective function now is to maximize the expected value of J_1 in (3.36). In this case the optimal $h(t)$ which is called the Kalman gain in filtering theory is directly influenced by the variances σ^2 of the error term and hence the steady state price level p^* changes due to σ^2. Generally the price level p^* gets higher with higher a. Secondly, the conjectural variation assumption that $\partial u_i/\partial u_j = 0$ for $i \neq j$ may not hold due to the presence of random noise in the market demand equation. In this case there may be stochastic instability in the convergence process and the steady state p^*, u_i^* may not be stable. In such cases the duopolists may see implicit cooperation by 'subjective random devices' as proposed by Aumann (1974). As Ohyama and Fukushima (1995) have shown, in dualistic market structures of the NICs in Asia, the Asian producers adopt a two-tier policy. In the domestic front they act more like a monopoly and tend to exploit all scale economies due to learning and experience, whereas in the international market they attempt to build up implicit cooperation with the US producers, since they do not have a large base in R&D investment.

Finally, one could directly introduce risk aversion into the objective function by rewriting it as:

$$\int_0^\infty e^{-rt}[E\pi(t) - \frac{1}{2}\operatorname{var}\pi(t)]dt$$

where $\pi(t) = \tilde{p}(t) - c_1(t)$ with E and V denoting the mean and variance of profits. Market growth can be postulated as $\tilde{p}(t) = ae^{nt} - b(\dot{y}_1 + \dot{y}_2)$. The stochastic model then would incorporate learning through risk adjustment and influencing market growth through knowledge spillover and uncertain entry. This type of model analyzed by Sengupta (1983) elsewhere compares the effects of learning on the steady state levels of optimal price, quantity and the market share. If S^* denotes the steady state optimal market share and p^* the optimal price, then the following results illustrate the impact of learning:

$$\frac{\partial S^*}{\partial n} > 0, \; \partial S^*/\partial k < 0$$

$$\frac{\partial S^*}{\partial r} < 0, \; \partial p^*/\partial n < 0, \text{ if } n > r/2$$

$$\frac{\partial P^*}{\partial r} > 0 \text{ and } \partial p^*/\partial k > 0, \text{ if } n > r$$

These results show that increased market growth increases the market share of the dominant firm and reduces the market price. An increase in risk aversion tends to increase the steady state optimal price and also reduce the market share of the dominant firm. But it imparts more stability to the optimal trajectories. Since a risk-averse optimal strategy tends to minimize variance of profits, it yields a more robust policy of price and output, when the conditions of entry are uncertain.

3.5.   Concluding remarks

The impact of learning by doing and the diffusion aspect of human capital in the modern endogenous growth theory have been mostly deterministic. Yet the stochastic aspects arise very naturally in this framework through learning about the future outcome of current R&D investment, expectations about future demand and even projecting a long-run state of the world market. Three basic sources of uncertainty and their economic implications for instability are briefly discussed here. First, we consider learning through the optimizing process of the producer deciding on the optimal direction of technical change. Stochastic versions of the Solow model are here compared with the new growth theory formulations. Secondly, we consider learning by knowledge spillovers through international trade and empirically estimate a linear decision rule for Japan, where learning-based expectations about the future play a more dynamic role than the past history. Finally, a dynamic limit-pricing model of uncertain entry is considered for a firm facing international competition and impact of learning through risk adjustment and uncertain market growth is analyzed.

4
Innovation Efficiency in Asia

Recent times have seen the emergence of endogenous growth theory which emphasizes several economic features, e.g., the increasing returns to scale, learning by doing, knowledge capital and the dynamic spillover effects from the growth of the export sector and foreign direct investment. This new growth theory has two profound implications. One is theoretical and the other empirical. Theoretically it implies a substantial modification, if not rejection of the neoclassical model of growth followed in the Solow-Swan type of model. Secondly, the last two decades (1997–2007) has seen a rapid rate of growth of the newly industrializing countries (NICs) of the East Asian Pacific Rim such as Hong Kong, Singapore, South Korea and Taiwan. Empirical data seem to show that growth in knowledge capital, openness in trade and outward looking policy measures in these countries have greatly contributed to their success rates. For example, Korea's export growth rate of 22.9% over the period 1965–87 accompanied the average per capita income growth rate of 6.4%. China's reform of its national innovation system started in the 1990s. In 2000, 60% of the country's R&D spending was funded and performed by the enterprise sector, comparable to that of most OECD countries. The majority of enterprise funded R&D was performed outside the state-owned enterprise sector. A good measure of R&D intensity is the ratio of R&D expenditure to GDP. By this measure, China's R&D intensity rose from 0.74 in 1991 to 1.23 in 2003. For Korea it rose from 1.92 to 2.96 while for Taiwan it rose from 0.82 to 2.16. Recent statistics for China have shown the R&D intensity to exceed 1.85. For China this level of R&D intensity is high, given its living standards. Among the world's low-income and middle-income countries, China has been the only country whose level of R&D intensity has increased beyond 1%.

Taiwan's contemporary knowledge-based economy has revealed more remarkable growth of the information technology (IT) sector than China and other NICs of Asia. From 1995 to 1999 Taiwan's information industry ranked third in the world after US and Japan. The state's strong leadership in R&D and other investment in the IT sector started in 1982, when the value of exports of IT products was only $106 million in US dollars. But by 1985 these exports climbed to $1.22 billion representing about 3.9% of all exports and some 1% of worldwide market share. In 1992, computer products accounted for 42% of the economy's exports. The overall R&D intensity rose from 1.78 in 1995 to 2.16 in 2003 and has exceeded 2.90 in 2008. The World Economic Forum (2004) has computed a growth competitiveness index (GCI) based on the infrastructure development, quality of public institutions and the adopting of best practice technology of the world. Its report for the period 2002–04 showed in Table 4.1.

Clearly Taiwan's record of performance in the IT sector is most impressive. In terms of the average number of annual US patents per million people, the top rankings in the world in 2004 are: 1 for the US, 2 for Japan and 3 for Taiwan. The number of patents is 301.48 (US), 273.40 (Japan) and 241.38 (Taiwan). Singapore ranks 10 and South Korea 14.

Table 4.1 GCI rankings

County	2002 Rank	2003 Rank	Technology Rank (2003)
Finland	1	1	2
US	2	2	1
Taiwan	6	5	3
Singapore	7	6	12
Japan	16	11	5
S. Korea	25	18	6
Hong Kong	22	22	37
Malaysia	30	27	20
Thailand	37	30	39
India	54	53	64
China	38	42	65

4.1.   Innovation dynamics in NICs

Two elements of innovation dynamics are most important for the rapid growth of NICs. One is the externality effect of world exports and openness in trade. The second is the learning effect of human capital in the form of education, skills and R&D expenditures. Two of the NICs are most important in this framework, e.g., South Korea and China including Hong Kong. These two countries differ in several ways. For example, Korea is democratic whereas China is not. Korea follows market capitalism with much less regulation by the state. Finally, Korea is more open in international trade than China and its exchange rate is determined in open markets like the US dollar. There are striking similarities however between these two countries, e.g., they both encourage foreign direct investment, openness in trade and heavy emphasis on exports. They both support strong state policies to foster R&D investments and science and engineering education. We will discuss some of these key elements of innovation dynamics here.

The linkage between exports, particularly exports of technology-intensive products and economic growth has been generally analyzed by two groups of methods. In the first, one takes export growth as a measure of openness in international trade and correlates this measure with per capita income growth. Chow (1987) carried out Granger-Sims causality tests and found a strong causal relationship from exports to income growth for a sample of 8 NICs. In the second method, Bradford (1987) and others looked at the composition of export products for 12 countries NICs or next-tier NICs for 1965–80 and found that high rates of income growth and rapid structural changes are strongly positively correlated, when structural change is measured by the share in GDP of 16 manufacturing branches that are technology intensive.

To consider the structural aspects of the growth process, consider a two-sector model:

$$E = G(L_E, K_E, A)$$

$$A = F(L_A, K_A, E)$$

$$L = L_A + L_E, K = K_A + K_E, Y = E + A \qquad (4.1)$$

with two outputs, E for the export sector and A for the rest produced by two inputs: labor (L) and capital (k). The presence of A in the export sector's production function measures the externality effect of the rest of the economy on the export sector. Thus the growth of output in the two sectors can be specified as

$$\dot{A} = F_K I_A + F_L \dot{L}_A + F_E \dot{E}$$

$$\dot{E} = G_K I_E + G_L \dot{L}_E + G_A \dot{A}$$

$$I_A = \dot{K}_A, I_E = \dot{K}_E \qquad\qquad (4.2)$$

where a dot over a variable denotes its time derivative and the subscripts K, L and E for F and G denote the respective marginal productivities for the export and the non-export sector. Note that the impact of the export sector on the non-export sector may be estimated by F_E and the ratio F_E/G_A may be used as a measure of the dominance of the export sector. The empirical estimates of these parameters for the Korean economy are as follows:

	1964–83	1964–86	1987–2006
F_E	1.92	1.0	2.30
G_A	0.28	0.31	0.33
F_E/G_A	6.9	3.2	6.96

Clearly, the externality effect of the export sector on the rest of the economy is most dominant in the sense that it is roughly 3–7 times the reverse effect.

An alternative interpretation of the externality effect may be given in terms of the aggregate production function

$$Y = H\,(K, L, E)$$

which implies

$$\dot{Y} = H_K I + H_L \dot{L} + H_E \dot{E} \qquad\qquad (4.3)$$

Empirical tests for the four variables Y, K, L and E show that they are non-stationary. Hence the standard least squares method is not appropriate. The first differences of the variables are however stationary. Hence the following least squares estimates for Korea (1967–86) are appropriate:

$$\Delta Y = -314.6 + \underset{(4.55)}{0.206^*}\, \Delta K + \underset{(2.24)}{0.029^*}\, \Delta L; \quad R^2 = 0.57$$

$$\Delta Y = -208.9 + \underset{(2.87)}{0.152^*}\, \Delta K + \underset{(1.92)}{0.024^*}\, \Delta L + 0.401^*\, \Delta E; \quad R^2 = 0.64$$

Here the *t*-values are in parenthesis and the asterisks denote the coefficient to be significant at 5% level. Clearly, the ratios $H_E/H_K = 2.65$ and $H_E/H_L = 16.71$ show the export sector as the leading sector for the diffusion of technological and managerial innovations. For the Asian NICs the Korean case is unique in that both export growth (30.6 on average) and the export share of GDP (16.1 on average) are very high and exports have grown at double the rate for the output growth for the period 1967–86 on the average. For later periods 1987–2006 this trend has continued. On reformulating equation (4.3) in another form

$$\Delta Y/Y = a_0 + a_1(I/Y) + a_2(\Delta L/L) + a_3(Eg_e/Y)$$

produces the following estimates for the period 1961–87, where Eg_e/Y is the product of export growth and export share representing the weighted impact of export growth:

a_0	a_1	a_2	a_3	Adjusted R^2	DW
−0.0002*	0.0005*	0.0011*	0.2508*	0.484	1.50
(−2.20)	(2.19)	(1.86)	(2.22)		

Clearly, the estimate of $a_3 = 0.2508$ is significant at 5% level of *t*-test and this is comparable to Feder's (1982) estimate of 0.302 based on 19 semi-industrialized countries for the period 1964–73. What is important in the Korean case is the relatively high magnitude of the externality coefficient a_3 compared to a_2. Another way to look at the externality or spillover effect of the export sector is through productivity growth in the form of technological progress. Thus if we assume that the externality effect of exports is embodied as Harrod-neutral technical progress associated with labor productivity, then the aggregate production function can be expressed as

$$Y = H(K,AL), \ A = A(E)$$

where AL is augmented labor with A depending on export growth, which allows learning by doing effects through spillover of knowledge and managerial skills from one industry to another by a diffusion process. Following new growth theory we now formulate an optimal growth path for an economy where the representative producer has the production function in per capita neoclassical form

$$y = f(k), \ k = K/AL, \ y = Y/AL$$

where $A = \exp(gt)$ and it is assumed that constant returns to scale prevails for the two inputs K and AL. The evolution of per capita capital is then

$$k = \alpha f(k) - (n + g + \delta)k - (c + e) \tag{4.4}$$

where $c = C/AL, eE/AL, \alpha = 1+m$, m being the import coefficient, n is the exogenous growth rate of labor force and δ is the constant rate of depreciation of capital. In this formulation the representative infinite horizon household seeks to maximize utility given by

$$U = \int_0^\infty u(\tilde{z})e^{-(\rho-n)t}dt$$

where $z = (C+X)/L$ is the per capita sum of consumption and exports and ρ is the constant rate of time preference. It is assumed that the momentary utility function $u(\tilde{z})$ is of the form

$$u(\tilde{z}) = (1-\theta)^{-1}(\tilde{z}^{1-\theta} - 1); \ \theta > 0$$

where marginal utility $u'(z)$ has the constant elasticity $-\theta$ with respect to z. As θ tends to one $u(z)$ tends to $\log(z)$. The optimal growth path is obtained by maximizing the utility function U by choosing the control variable $z = c+e$. As is well known, optimal growth satisfies the following first-order condition:

$$\frac{\dot{z}}{z} = \frac{1}{\theta}[\alpha f'(k) - \delta - \rho]$$
$$= \alpha f'(k) - \delta - \rho \ (\text{if } \theta = 1) \tag{4.5}$$

The maximization also requires a transversality condition that guarantees that the capital stock grows asymptotically at a rate less than the rate of return given by the marginal product of capital, i.e., this requires the condition $\rho > n + (1 - \theta)g$. This result (4.5) specifying the optimal trajectory of consumption-cum-exports has several fundamental implications for optimal growth. First of all, if the marginal product term $f'(k)$ does not decline over time or declines very slowly, the gap measured by $\alpha f'(k) - \delta - \rho$ would remain positive thus augmenting exports over time. One basic reason why the marginal product of capital may fail to decline is the presence of significant increasing returns to scale and the prevalence of non-rival inputs in the production of technology-intensive products. This aspect will be discussed in some detail in the next section. Secondly, in the steady state the per capita quantities y, k and z do not change and hence by equating $\dot{z}/z$ to the rate of technological progress g one obtains in the steady state

$$f'(k^*) = \delta + \rho + \theta g; \quad y^* = f(k^*)$$

where the asterisk denotes steady state values. This implies that technological progress has a favorable impact on marginal productivity of capital in the steady state and this explains why the export-mix for Korea shifted from traditional export to technology-intensive product in recent times. The empirical study of Asian NIC exports by Chow (1987) shows that traditional export items were very dissimilar in pattern across the four countries: Korea, Hong Kong, Taiwan and Singapore and also insensitive to changes in relative prices (e.g., real exchange rates); but similar and homogeneous patterns were found for exports of certain sophisticated R&D intensive products such as electrical machinery, optical equipment and tapes, telecommunications and computer equipment, which were also found to respond to international competition and the price signals. Table 4.2 from their estimates shows the upsurge of growth of exports and its shift from the traditional to R&D intensive products for the four successful NICs in Asia.

Thirdly, if we replace the control variable from z to e in the above optimal growth paths, we obtain

$$\frac{\dot{e}}{e} = \frac{1}{\theta}[\alpha f'(k) - \delta - \rho], \quad \alpha = 1 - a + m$$

Table 4.2 Percentage distribution of NIC exports to the US of selected product groups

	Hong Kong		Korea		Taiwan		Singapore	
	1966	1986	1966	1986	1966	1986	1966	1986
Traditional	67.9	62.2	56.5	52.7	44.6	49.1	73.6	13.9
R&D Intensive (general)	9.8	23.8	2.0	19.2	15.8	22.3	0.0	58.2
R&D intensive (more sophisticated)	17.5	29.5	3.9	29.6	20.3	29.2	0.2	78.1

where a has been redefined to incorporate the consumption coefficient $\alpha = c/f(k)$. It is now clear that marginal productivity of capital and its increase would have a strong positive multiplier effect on export growth if $0 < \alpha < 1$. Thus the link between high marginal productivity of capital and export growth is a two-way process when the marginal product of capital does not decline much due to increasing returns to scale: high marginal productivity in the export sector generates higher growth of exports and the latter induces more scale economies through investment in technology-intensive goods. Finally, the path of capital accumulation in (4.4) shows that the growth rates of per capita capital and income declines with k in some neighborhood of the steady state (k^*, y^*) but these growth rates need not however decline with k throughout the whole range of k. In particular if the saving rate $s = (f(k) - c)/f(k)$ rises substantially due to the income effect from an increase in k, then the growth rates of per capita capital and income may both rise. This clearly follows from (4.4) rewritten as:

$$k = (s+m)f(k) - (n+g+\delta)k - e$$

where $s = s(k)$ depending on k rises more so as to offset the income-reducing effect of k. It is quite striking that for the Korean economy this reversal effect has been very significant over the period 1967–86. Thus the savings ratio to GDP rose from 11.7% to 44.1% and the investment ratio rose from 20.2% to 37.5%. The growth of savings rate has roughly paralleled the exports ratio to GDP that rose from

8.5% to 48% during the same period. One consequence of this has been that the role of foreign savings F measured by the investment-savings gap (i.e., *F – I-S)* declined over those years as the level of domestic savings rose. This reversal effect has been very important for the other successful NICs in Asia also, but the magnitude has not been as spectacular as in Korea (see Table 4.3). Clearly, the gains in savings and investment rates were dramatic for Korea and to a lesser extent for Taiwan. Philippines showed a reduction along with the other two mature exporters Belgium and Germany. Japan showed a slight increase in the saving-investment ratios but it was much less than that of Korea and Taiwan.

Next to the externality effect of the export sector, increasing returns to scale has played a dynamic role in innovation efficiency in Korea and other NICs of Asia.

Increasing returns to scale has an important role to play in new growth theory. Three dimensions of scale economies have been emphasized in current theory. One is the presence of significant IRS in modern production, which involves non-rival inputs as semi-fixed inputs in Romer's terminology. Non-rival input is one for which subsequent units have a significantly lower unit cost of production than the first. In the extreme case, a non-rival input has a high cost of producing the first unit and a zero cost for subsequent units, e.g., a new design for a microprocessor which can be replicated at a negligible cost. The increasing use of such non-rival inputs has given a new dimension to commercial and non-basic R&D research thus intensifying the competitiveness in international trade.

The second dimension of IRS focuses on the knowledge spillover effects that improve labor productivity across the board. As Lucas

Table 4.3 Evolution of exports, savings and investment: an international comparison (1967–86)

	Initial	Final	Δ(E/Y)	Initial	Final	Δ(S/Y)	Initial	Final	Δ(I/Y)
Korea	8.5	48.1	39.6	11.7	44.1	32.4	20.2	37.5	17.3
Taiwan	24.4	84.0	59.6	18.2	47.0	28.8	23.3	25.1	1.8
Philippines	24.9	30.4	5.5	22.3	21.9	−0.4	21.5	12.9	−8.6
Japan	7.6	17.2	9.6	35.7	42.0	6.3	32.1	33.6	1.5
Germany	21.4	34.5	13.1	32.2	29.1	−3.1	28.3	22.4	−5.9
Belgium	40.5	76.4	35.9	28.4	23.2	−5.2	27.9	18.8	−9.1

(1990) pointed out this may be the most significant factor explaining the large difference in marginal productivity of capital between an LDC and a developed economy, when the concept of capital is broadened to include human capital. Thus, specifying the production function as follows can capture the external benefits of human capital:

$$y = Ax^{\beta}h^{\gamma} \tag{4.6}$$

where the three variables y, x and h denote output, physical and human capital per effective worker respectively. The term h^{γ} is interpreted as an external effect, which multiples the productivity of a worker at any skill level just as the intercept term A. It has also a spill-over effect on other workers.

The third dimension of IRS emphasizes the non-convexity of the total cost function associated with the modern technology-intensive products such as consumer electronics, personal computers and other mass consumption goods. We have already noted before the shift in NIC exports to sophisticated R&D intensive products, which also have significant scale economies reflected in the non-convexity of cost function. In such a situation it is more profitable to build capacity ahead of demand and the government planners in Korea have allocated a growing share of domestic and foreign resources through credit rationing and other measures to capital-intensive heavy and chemical industries and also electronics.

A direct empirical test of the existence of IRS can be obtained by estimating an aggregate production function with real GDP as the output variable (Y), capital stock (K) and employment (L) as the two aggregate input variables. Two major difficulties of this approach are that the aggregate function may involve significant heterogeneity in the way the variables are defined. Secondly, data on capital stock are not generally available in a reliable form from the official statistics. For the first difficulty we may consider separably a production function for the manufacturing sector in Korea for which Kwon's (1986) data are available. Secondly, we must construct a series of capital stocks (K_t) based on investment stream (I_{t-i}) and depreciation rate (δ) by following the method as follows:

$$K_t = \log 2 + \frac{1}{2}\log \sum_{i=0}^{t-1}(1-\delta)^i I_{t-i} + \frac{t}{2}\log(1-\delta) + \frac{1}{2}\log K_0$$

Table 4.4   Estimates of production function

	Constant	log K	log L	R^2	DW
Korea	2.599*	0.362*	1.563*	0.994	1.25
(1964–87)		(8.98)	(17.40)		
Japan	0.076	0.429*	1.663*	0.998	2.00
(1961–87)		(2.96)	(2.72)		
Taiwan	6.187	0.630*	1.825*	0.998	0.89
(1958–87)		(2.82)	(6.93)		
Singapore	1.420	0.501*	1.481*	0.989	0.95
(1960–80)		(2.01)	(3.84)		
Hong Kong	2.310*	0.381*	1.352*	0.994	1.21
(1959–82)		(7.42)	(5.81)		

t-Values in parenthesis, asterisk for 1% significance.

The results of fitting unconstrained Cobb-Douglas production for the successful NICs are given in Table 4.4.

It is clear that the evidence of IRS is overwhelming. Moreover, what is most striking is that the labor coefficient is about three to four times larger than the capital coefficient. This is definitely suggestive of the effect of 'learning by doing' or the spillover effects of human capital. These effects multiply the productivity of a worker at any given skill level by a positive multiple depending on the technology used. We may also mention the point that if each of the three variables – output, capital and labor – are first detrended and then the production functions re-estimated, the persistence of IRS is upheld. This suggests that scale economies are structural and not transitory and the high values of adjusted R^2 are indicative of the relative success of Cobb-Douglas production functions in capturing the process of overall output growth.

A more dis-aggregative way to estimate the scale effect is to concentrate on the manufacturing sector alone, which happens to be the most important sector in export growth performance of the successful NICs in Asia. For Korea, time series data on output, capital and labor are directly available from Kwon (1986) along with cost and price data over the period 1961–80. A direct way to estimate IRS in the export-intensive manufacturing sector in Korea is to fit a log linear cost function as follows:

$$\log C = 0.168^* + 0.797^* \log Y - 0.077 \log Z; \quad R^2 = 0921; \quad DW = 2.1$$
$${\scriptstyle (2.10)} \quad {\scriptstyle (4.57)}$$

where C is observed total costs, log C is its logarithmic value and Z is a proxy variable for measuring technical progress which is usually captured by a time trend. Clearly, the overall degree of IRS is 1.25, which is the reciprocal of the elasticity coefficient 0.797 for output *(Y)*. This implies that a 10% increase in inputs (scale) increases output by at least 12.50%. The realized output increase may be higher since technical progress and presence of non-rival inputs have additional cost-reducing impacts. Evidently, the manufacturing sector in the Korean economy has utilized scale economies most significantly over its growing phase and the high-income elasticity of world demand for Korean exports has helped its growth upsurge tremendously. One can empirically substantiate this further by estimating the impact of human capital in the form of equation (4.6) emphasized in the Lucas model. On the basis of Kwon's data for the more recent period (1970–86) the Cobb-Douglas production function estimates are as follows with log Y as the dependent variable:

	Constant	log x	log z	T	R^2	DW
Log *Y*:	−0.310	+0.166	1.030*	–	0.97	1.92
	(1.71)	(0.86)	(7.09)			
Log *Y*:	−3.856	+0.058	1.323*	1.321*	0.99	2.01
	(1.92)	(0.29)	(5.07)	(1.84)		

t-Values in parenthesis, asterisk for 1% significance.

Here z is a proxy variable for human capital h in the Lucas model measured by the lagged value of output per worker. Clearly the impact of the proxy variable z is highly significant and the estimate of IRS is 1.196 that is very close to the estimate 1.25 derived from the estimated cost function before. Furthermore, if we allow for the time trend separately (i.e., time t is very often used as a proxy for Hicksian type of technical progress), the coefficient for human capital (log z) increases from 1.030 to 1.323 thus increasing the degree of IRS from 1.196 to 1.381. Thus it is apparent that Korean economic growth has been significantly influenced by scale economies and the latter has been helped considerably by the sizable impact of human capital and the various skill levels associated with the labor force in Korea.

Now we consider the growth experience of China. China's export strategy encouraging FDI was started with the promulgation of the Chinese Foreign Venture Law in July 1979 with new provisions added in 1986. In the two decades since 1978 China became the largest recipient of FDI in the developing world and second only to the US globally since 1993. FDI flows were over $27 billion in US dollars in 1993 alone, which comprised 35% of total FDI in all developing countries. By the end of 2001 the FDI contracted value was $746 billion and total realized value was as high as $393 billion. During 1984–2002 the FDI inflows in China had recorded a persistent increase as given in Table 4.5.

Honglin (2004) estimates the impact of several economic determinants of FDI inflows into China by means of the model

$$FDI_{it} = \beta_{.i} + \delta X_{it} + \varepsilon_{it}$$

where $i = 1, ..., 29$ are the provinces, $t = 1, ..., 12$ for the year 1987–98 and X_{it} denotes various independent variables such as market size (M), labor cost (W), labor quality in terms of school enrollment (S), transportation services (T), incentives (I) and openness (O). The panel estimates as in Table 4.6.

Clearly FDI inflows into China, which provide the key engine of growth in China, had the major determinants represented by its

Table 4.5   FDI inflows in China 1979–2002

Year	FDI inflows (US $ billions)	Share of FDI in developing countries (%)	Share of FDI flows in world (%)
1979	1.8	11.48	3.88
1990	3.5	11.64	1.74
1998	45.4	27.40	7.06
1999	40.3	19.42	4.66
2000	40.7	16.9	3.20
2001	46.8	20.82	6.16
2002	52.7	32.50	8.10

Source: Honglin (2004).

Table 4.6 Panel estimates (1987–98) of the FDI regression

Regressors	Panel estimates
Market (*M*)	0.15**
Wage (*W*)	−0.03
School (*S*)	0.30**
Trans (*T*)	0.21**
Incentive (*I*)	1.31***
Openness (*O*)	1.95***
Adj. R^2	0.95
F Statistics	69.13

Note: Two and three asterisks denote significance of *t* values at 5% and 1% respectively.

liberalized trade policies (incentives, subsidies and openness) and the huge market size (*M*). The school enrollment, measured here by the proportion of secondary school students, also played a role in raising the labor quality.

The quantitative impact of exports on total industrial production was econometrically analyzed by Hung-gay et al. (2004) in two steps. In the first step they applied the cointegration test for the three variables: exports, imports and industrial production and found the single cointegration vector at the 5% level. At the second step they performed Granger-Sims type causality tests. Taken as a group, the imports and industrial production both affect exports significantly at 5%. This result is consistent with China's import policy, where imports are primarily for reprocessing and then for export. Granger-causality tests report the following results:

Dependent variable	Causality variable	*F*-value
Industrial Production	1. Imports conditional on exports	3.708**
	2. Exports conditional on imports	1.838*
	3. Both imports and exports	2.290*
Exports	1. Ind. production conditional on imports	1.966
	2. Both-imports ind. production	2.221*

Clearly exports and imports play a dynamic causal role in boosting industrial production in China, which helps the process of rapid growth of GDP in China.

In this connection we may refer to the hypothesis put forward by Jones (1995) that the growth experiences of advanced economies like the OECD countries do not show any positive time trend in the growth data. According to endogenous growth theory and R&D-based models, permanent changes in capital accumulation have permanent effects on the rate of economic growth of output. Nandi (2009) considers a model that takes output as a linear function of capital (which is broadly defined so as to include both physical and human capital) and estimates it for 112 widely diverse countries for the period 1950–2004. She finds that the rates of investment, especially for equipment have risen persistently over time, while GDP growth rates have not. The major exception is China. It is the only country for which extraordinary growth and capital accumulation have both followed similar positive trends. Using sophisticated unit root tests with multiple structural breaks she has shown that there exists a strong stable positive correlation between investment rates and growth rates and the direction of causality runs strongly from high past investment share of GDP per capita to current growth rates of total output per capita.

4.2.   Experiences of China and Taiwan

Over the last two decades China has maintained a very high growth rate of its GDP and competed very successfully in the world market. The World Bank Report (1996) has summarized China's economic progress as follows:

> Consider the period 1985 to 1994 when average GDP growth in China was 10.2%. Two-thirds of the growth rate was the result of capital accumulation, supported by an extraordinarily high savings rate that has come to depend increasingly on China's thrifty households. Less important but significant nonetheless have been increasing labor force participation rates. One third of growth was the result of productivity improvements in the use of inputs, due to structural change across sectors and efficiency improvements within production units. The most striking feature of structural

change in industry is the extraordinary growth of 'private' firms i.e., privately and individually owned enterprises, foreign joint ventures and foreign funded enterprises. This group increased its share of industrial value added from 1% in 1984 to 24% in 1994, much of it in the past five years. (World Bank 1996: 89)

The empirical estimates of GDP growth of 10.2% during 1985–94 can be decomposed into four major sources as: (1) factor accumulation – 6.69%, (2) agricultural reallocation – 1.0%, (3) ownership reallocation – 0.4% and (4) total factor productivity growth (TFP) growth – 2.2%. For the recent period 1990–94 the GDP growth rate of 10.5% has the following decomposition: (1) factor accumulation – 6.1%, (2) agricultural reallocation – 0.6%, (3) ownership reallocation – 0.9% and (4) TFP growth – 2.9%.

The most striking feature is the TFP growth, which is the Solow-type measure of technical progress. This resulted in significant productivity gains all across the industrial economy. Sengupta (2005) has discussed in some detail the sources of these productivity gains in China and compared these with India and other NICs in Asia. Recently Wu (2004) applied a frontier production function model to estimate the growth of productive efficiency in China over the period 1982–97. He extended Solow's (1957) measure of TFP growth by adding the dimension of technical efficiency.

Denoting actual and frontier output by y_{it} and $y_{it}^F = f(x_{it}, t)$ where x_{it} are the various inputs one could write the observed output as a fraction of frontier or optimal output

$$y_{it} = y_{it}^F \mathrm{TE}_{it}$$

Here technical efficiency (TE) denotes technical efficiency. It measures increase in production efficiency when the observed production function is shifted to the best practice or optimal function. From this equation one may derive the percentage changes as

$$\frac{\Delta y_{it}}{y_{it}} = \sum_i f_{x_i}\left(\frac{\Delta x_{it}}{x_{it}}\right) + f_t + \left(\frac{\Delta \mathrm{TE}_{it}}{\mathrm{TE}_{it}}\right)$$

where the first term on the RHS is output growth due to the various inputs, the second is Solow's technological progress and the third is the growth of technical efficiency. Here f_x and f_t represent output elasticities with respect to x and t. According to Solow, TFP is defined as the growth in total output not explained by input growth and is the sum of technological progress (TP) and changes in TE, i.e.,

$$\frac{\Delta TFP}{TFP} = \frac{\Delta TP}{TP} + \frac{\Delta TE}{TE}$$

(4.7)

Wu (2004) estimated this equation for China from a frontier production function. The estimates are reported in Table 4.7, using panel data of 27 provinces during the period 1982–97. TE, TP and TFP represent technical efficiency, technical progress and total factor productivity respectively. During this period the Chinese economy attained an average growth rate of 10.4%. Capital stock grew at about 11.6% whereas the growth rate of employment declined.

Several implications of Table 4.7 have to be noted. First, TFP has recorded an average growth-rate of 1.41% during 1982–97 and this growth is dominated by technological progress. The long-run growth-effect measured by TP averaged 1.28% during 1982–97. The US achieved a TFP growth rate of 1.5% during 40 years 1909–49 as estimated by Solow, whereas China achieved a growth rate of 1.41% per annum during only 15 years 1982–97.

Table 4.7 Estimated TP, TE and TFP growth in percentage in China 1982–97

Year	TE	TP	TFP
1982	0.39	1.23	1.62
1984	2.17	1.25	3.42
1986	−1.13	1.26	0.13
1988	0.79	1.26	2.06
1990	−0.40	1.29	0.89
1992	1.90	1.30	3.20
1994	0.42	1.30	1.72
1996	−1.53	1.30	−0.22
1997	0.27	1.31	1.58
Average rates			
1982–85	1.11	1.24	2.35
1986–91	−0.84	1.27	0.43
1992–97	0.45	1.30	1.75
1982–97	0.13	1.28	1.41

Secondly, TE growth is most remarkable in the early 1980s, i.e., the year after the reforms of economic policy. It was 1.11% during 1982–85 but it suffered a major downturn during 1992–97 when it was 0.45%. Thirdly, the efficiency decomposition formula (4.7) neglects a very important component of productivity growth due to allocative efficiency (AE). This type of efficiency results from optimal input substitutions when factor prices change in the market. It also results from output transformation when the market prices of output change. Also, these estimates are empirically obtained by econometric methods assuming a particular error structure. A more general method is the nonparametric technique also called data envelopment analysis (DEA), which does not assume any specific error structure. Sengupta (2000) and others have applied this DEA method to estimate TE, AE and TFP for industries like computers, power industry and the banking sector. These estimates are known to be more robust, but they broadly agree with the parametric estimates in most cases.

An important element of China's growth experience is its spread across regions and provinces. Decentralization of growth in China was much less than in Taiwan, but it was still very significant. This may be analyzed in terms of efficiency gains in some prosperous regions of China like Hong Kong, Guandong and Fujian and compared with that of Taiwan. Table 4.8 reports these estimates of TFE, TP and TE in terms of indexes. These estimates show significant growth in TFP for the four economies: Hong Kong, Guandong, Fujian provinces and Taiwan. In the past two decades these four economies have fostered rapid integration, where Guandong and Fujian have shown rapid catch-up with their neighbors. This is the result of significant spillover effects. Note that the estimates of technical efficiency show that Hong Kong and Taiwan were producing closer to their best-practice inputs in the 1980s. The TFP performance over time has been relatively stable in Taiwan but has been rising dramatically in Guandong and Fujian. This pattern of change has led to productivity catch-up and hence convergence among the four economies considered.

A study of the growth performance of Taiwan is important for two reasons. One is that its success record is very significant over the last two decades. Unlike China it follows democratic principles of market capitalism. Secondly its growth has been significantly decentralized

Table 4.8 TFP, TP and TE indexes

Index/Region	1979	1983	1993	1997
TFP				
Hong Kong	1.022	1.020	1.017	1.016
Guandong	0.999	1.013	1.047	1.060
Fujian	1.014	1.023	1.045	1.053
Taiwan	1.030	1.029	1.028	1.027
TP				
Hong Kong	1.010	1.015	1.028	1.033
Guandong	1.021	1.026	1.038	1.042
Fujian	1.020	1.026	1.039	1.043
Taiwan	1.013	1.019	1.032	1.037
TE				
Hong Kong	1.012	1.005	0.989	0.983
Guandong	0.979	0.987	1.009	1.018
Fujian	0.993	0.997	1.006	1.0095
Taiwan	1.016	1.010	0.996	0.990

Note: The figures indicate indexes relative to preceding values. Thus a number greater than one implies a positive growth, while a number smaller than one implies a decline in growth.

across the country, resulting in more equalitarian distribution of personal incomes. Thirdly, Taiwan did not adopt a heavy industry-oriented development strategy or a full-scale import-substitution strategy. Taiwan relied on the development of the labor-intensive characteristics of her resource endowments. For example, in 1953–60 the average annual growth rate of industrial output was 11% and the fastest growing industries were farm product processing, textiles, plywood, glass and so on. Due to the development of labor-intensive industries the industrial share of GDP rose from 17.7% to 24.9% during 1953–60 and the share of industrial products in total exports increased from 8.4% to 32.2%. This development laid a solid foundation for the subsequent economic takeoff. Finally, the government adopted a sustained policy of providing significant economic incentives to the agents, so that the private economy could earn large profits and achieve rapid accumulation of physical and human capital. The incentives to exploit the economy's comparative advantage depends on the relative prices in the economy and the state policy fostered the market mechanism to get the relative prices right. This

Table 4.9   US Patent awards (1995) to foreign countries: top 11 countries

Country	Invention	Design
Japan	21,925	1149
Germany	7311	258
France	3029	234
UK	2425	194
Canada	1964	240
Italy	1271	172
Switzerland	1196	93
Taiwan	1000	250
Netherlands	855	66
Sweden	627	98
S. Korea	538	48

Source: US Bureau of the Census: Statistical Abstract of the US (1995).

strategy secures significant degrees of allocative and technical efficiency, much greater than that of China and other NICs.

The state also took significant initiatives encouraging the high-technology firms to incur R&D expenditures including special zones such as the Hsinchu Research Park where agglomeration and skill complementarities were utilized. One measure of inventiveness in Taiwan is its record of US patent awards. The following estimates show that in inventions, Taiwan exceeds South Korea, Sweden and Netherlands. In terms of design however, Taiwan performs better than UK, Canada, France and Italy. It is clear that Taiwan has been a markedly successful learner of new ideas borrowed from abroad. In more recent times, Taiwan has improved its record much farther. For example, in 2003 Taiwan had the average annual number of US patents per million people as 241 with rank 3, whereas US and Japan had 301 and 273 with ranks 1 and 2, respectively.

A comprehensive measure of innovative capacity may be indicated by the growth competitiveness index (GCI) reported by Porter and Stern (2004). This index comprises three broad economic indicators such as the macroeconomic flexibility, the quality of public institutions and technology or innovations. Here the core GCI = ½ technology index + ¼ public institutions + ¼ macroeconomic environment. Table 4.10 reports their findings.

Table 4.10 National innovative capacity index (2002–03)

	2002	2003	Change
US	37.21	36.60	−0.61
Singapore	32.45	34.19	1.74
Taiwan	32.34	32.84	0.50
S. Korea	30.59	31.13	0.54
China	26.06	25.86	0.20
Malaysia	26.20	26.85	0.65
India	25.24	25.52	0.28
Japan	33.98	34.62	0.64

Clearly Taiwan's rank is higher than China, Korea and Malaysia and comparable to Japan. What are the sources of this significant innovative potential for Taiwan? First of all, electronics has been a major driving force in Taiwan's economic development. In 2002 the total value of production of IT hardware was $17.4 billion in US dollars, excluding semiconductor production and Internet appliances production. This made Taiwan the world's fourth largest producer of IT hardware after the US, China and Japan. The value of semiconductor production in 2002 was $19.2 billion and Internet appliances accounted for another $3.4 billion. This Taiwanese model of electronics industry development has been extraordinarily effective in increasing economic output and technological sophistication. In more recent times 2004–07 the Taiwanese industry, in multiple areas beside electronics, has become more R&D intensive with both foreign and domestic firms participating in R&D efforts. New areas are developing in which Taiwan appears to be rapidly approaching the cutting edge of technology such as wireless integrated circuits (IC) design. Secondly, if we measure innovative capabilities by the amount of industrial patenting and use the number of patents granted in the US as the metric, Taiwan looks very strong. Taiwan and Israel are the only two emerging economies to close the gap with the G7 countries in terms of the patent per capita ratio, with Taiwan being next after the US and Japan. Note that public policy has played a most dynamic role here. Public laboratories like the Industrial Technology Research Institute (ITRI) continue to be the major source of patents. Besides branding and innovation several other strategies were followed by

Taiwanese companies. For companies that are good at incremental innovation, diversification and decentralization often became a promising move at a minimum. Also, these companies often enter into partnership with China but their object has also been to keep ahead of the Chinese. Thirdly, Taiwan has recently developed and continues to develop other engines of innovation besides the ITRI model. It makes intensified efforts to develop critical masses of leading researchers in universities and laboratories capable of making fundamental advances in science and engineering. It strengthens closer direct links between universities and industry by linking Taiwan's microelectronics, computer and communications sectors with its traditional industries both in manufacturing and services.

4.3.   Innovation strategies and challenges

Both China and Taiwan have made consistent attempts to follow market capitalism, where the private industry is strongly encouraged. There exist however several differences. In Taiwan public research through ITRI and universities is initiated but transferred to the private sector by deliberate state policy. Also, the restrictions and legal limitations on private industry are much lower in Taiwan. Secondly, Taiwan's development in the past three decades may be regarded as a process toward western-style modernization. The private sector-based market economy directed by a strong Party-state proved to be quite successful in Taiwan, though more legal changes are needed to sustain rapid growth. A critical role played by education in the construction of a knowledge economy is innovation, which comes largely from the research end of higher education and from R&D departments of various industries. The state's role in encouraging this research has been very significant. The most important factor in the emergence of Taiwan's knowledge economy has been the state's heavy investment in human resource development through science education and implementation of multi-tiered strategies to reverse the brain drain. All these strategies were ultimately implemented by the state and conformed very closely to the development strategies proposed by UNESCO and US AID in the 1960s. Thirdly, Taiwan achieved much better allocative and production efficiency than China through regional arbitrageurship. By relocating or subcontracting activities to other low-cost regions such as Mainland China, while keeping offices in Taiwan as coordinating centers, manufacturing firms in Taiwan exploited their scale economies and gradually evolved into trading firms. Finally, in the recent trend toward the knowledge economy, innovation is the most valuable asset and the main source of an industry's competitiveness. Continuous improvement (CI) is thought to be the core of this innovation process. The goals of CI can be summarized as follows: (i) a company-wide focus to improve process performance, (ii) a gradual improvement through step-by-step innovation, (iii) organizational activities with the involvement of all people in the company from top managers to workers and (iv) create a learning and growing environment. Taiwan has succeeded in all these areas.

Taiwan's industry growth model is very close to the model of cost reduction developed by Spence (1984). The Spence model assumes a competitive market system where the criterion for determining the value of cost reducing R&D is profitability or revenues. Since revenues may understate the social benefits, the private free market system may not yield optimal levels of R&D. Secondly, the R&D investments largely represent fixed cost and hence the market structures are likely to be concentrated and imperfectly competitive. Taiwan attempted to solve these problems and achieved remarkable success. For the first problem, it developed a state subsidy policy. For the second problem, it developed a policy of widespread decentralization and multi-layered development process. In the Spence model, R&D investments can be written as

$$R\&D = zn/[1+\theta(n-1)]$$

where z is the accumulated knowledge of firms, n is the number of firms and θ lying between zero and one captures the spillover effects. If $\theta = 0$ there are no spillover effects or externalities but if $\theta = 1.0$ the benefits of each firm's R&D are shared completely. With $\theta > 0$ the unit costs have an upper limit of $1/\theta$ as n increases. Thus while spillovers reduce the incentives for cost reduction, they also reduce the costs at the industry level of achieving a given level of cost reduction. But the incentives can be restored through state subsidies and Taiwan's R&D policy precisely attempted to do this.

The decentralization process in Taiwan is much more vigorous than in China and this resulted in a more equalitarian distribution of personal income in Taiwan while China has still to face the problem of income equality. Yao (2005) used household incomes at 1990 prices to estimate Gini coefficients for rural and urban incomes in China as follows:

Year	Rural income	Urban income	Total GDP
1981	23.9	18.2	19.9
1985	25.8	20.1	19.2
1990	29.4	22.5	20.9
1993	33.0	27.1	23.7
1995	34.8	27.5	24.9

The Gini coefficients measure income inequality, higher values denoting more inequality. Taiwan's average Gini coefficient in the recent period 1990–95 is less than 13.0 for the total GDP combing all the sectors. It is clear that the higher income inequality in the rural sector will be a significant impediment to the economic growth in China and other NICs and also India and Indonesia. This means a greater challenge for the state welfare policy.

4.4.   Concluding remarks

The growth miracle in the Asian economies can be explained by their capital investments in both physical and human capital. Innovation in the form of small incremental improvement and technology imports from the advanced industrial countries played a most dynamic role. In China over 50% of the large and medium state-owned enterprises have imported technology, equipment and technical services through various channels such as joint ventures, FDI and so on to improve their technical level and management skills. In terms of the R&D intensity measured by the ratio of total R&D spending to GDP, the comparative record of China is very significant as may be seen from Table 4.11. It is clear that China's R&D intensity rose sharply during 1995–2000 and continued to rise in 2003. Growth of R&D intensity in China over the period 1995–2006 was 1.4%. By comparison the R&D intensity of most OECD countries and Taiwan lay in the range of 2–3% for China this level of R&D intensity is high given its living standards.

Table 4.11 Comparative measures of R&D intensity (1991–2003)

	1991	1995	2000	2003
China	0.74	0.60	1.00	1.23
US	2.72	2.51	2.76	2.62
Germany	2.52	2.25	2.49	2.50
Japan	2.93	2.89	2.99	3.12
S. Korea	1.92	2.50	2.65	2.96
Taiwan	–	1.78	2.05	2.16
France	2.37	2.31	2.18	2.20
Italy	1.23	1.00	1.07	–
Brazil	0.46	0.69	1.05	–
India	0.85	0.77	0.86	–

Source: National Bureau of Statistics: Comprehensive Statistical Data (2005). China Statistics Press, Beijing.

Table 4.12 High-technology exports as percent of exports of manufacturing in 2002

	China	India	Thailand	Brazil
Low to middle income countries (17%)	23	5	31	19
Upper middle income (21%)	Malaysia 58	Hungary 25	Mexico 84	Argentina 7
High income (23%)	US 32	Japan 24	S. Korea 32	Taiwan 42

Source: World Bank Report (2005).
Note that Taiwan exceeds both US and Japan and China is very close to Japan.

Among the world's low and low- to middle-income countries, China has been the only country whose R&D intensity has risen beyond 1%. Compare the records of India and Brazil, which are lower than that of China, although Brazil's per capita income is approximately three times that of China. Evidence of this high R&D intensity is the technology-intensiveness of Chinese exports. Table 4.12 reports the statistics.

New Asian innovation dynamics show evidence of most of the growth feature outlines of the recent theory of endogenous growth. Many Asian countries have taken the innovation challenge very seriously. For example, the long-term plan for the development of science and technology (2006–20) has been introduced by the Chinese government in 2006 to turn China into an innovation-oriented society by the year 2020. This plan commits China to the development of capabilities for indigenous innovation and to leapfrogging into leading positions in new science-based industries by the end of the plan period. Other NICs in Asia such as India and Malaysia have started adopting more innovative polices for improving their technological performance in exports and international trade.

5
Efficiency Dynamics and Industry Growth

Growth of economic efficiency and productivity are the keys to industry growth. Cost reduction resulting from efficiency growth provides the dynamic strategy in both competitive and monopolistic markets. Solow characterized the long-run growth of the US economy as due to technological progress. Innovation in various forms, such as R&D, knowledge capital and inventive activity, comprises technological progress. Recent endogenous models of growth have emphasized learning by doing and knowledge capital as crucial to long-run sustained growth. We discuss in this chapter two aspects of efficiency dynamics and industry growth. First, we discuss the various theoretical and empirical models that analyze industry growth due to efficiency changes. We discuss here the role of technology and innovations in productivity growth. The impact of R&D and its externalities are also discussed. Secondly, we discuss the innovation dynamics in Asia with reference to China and India, since these countries are likely to emerge as leading players in future growth episodes in Asia.

5.1. Models of innovation

In recent times competition has been most intense in modern high-tech industries such as microelectronics, computers and telecommunications. Product and process innovations, economies of scale and learning by doing have intensified the competitive pressure leading to declining unit costs and prices. Thus Norsworthy and Jang (1992) in their measurement of technological change in these industries over the last decade noted the high degree of cost efficiency due to learning by doing and R&D investment. Also the empirical study by Jorgenson and Stiroh (2000) noted the significant impact of the growth of computer power on the overall US economy. As the computer technology improved, more computing efficiency was generated from the same inputs like skilled labor. Thus the average industry productivity growth (i.e., TFP growth in a specific industry) achieved a rate of 2% per year over the period 1958–96 for electronic equipment, which includes semiconductors and communications equipment. High productivity growth led to falling unit cost and price. For instance, the average computer prices have declined by 18% per year from 1960 to 1995 and by 27.6% per year over 1995–98. More recent estimates for 2000–05 exceed 30% per year. R&D investments and learning by doing have contributed significantly to this trend of decline in unit costs and prices.

The increase in productivity due to innovations leads to increased market shares for the technology-intensive firms. Through falling prices it can help expand the market and product innovations can even create new markets, e.g., the iPod and iPhone. Corley, Michie and Oughton (2002) analyzed the average annual rates of growth of labor productivity over the period 1990–98 in the manufacturing sector and the contributions of R&D and gross fixed capital formation per worker for eight OECD countries. The regression equation is of the form:

$$y = b_0 + b_1 x_1 + b_2 x_2 + b_3 x_3 + \text{error} \qquad (5.1)$$

where

y = level of labor productivity in industry i averaged over four years 1994–98

x_1 = R&D expenditure per worker averaged over four years

x_2 = gross fixed capital formation per worker in industry i averaged over 1994–98

x_3 = share of R&D scientist and engineers in the labor force averaged over 1994–98.

All the variables are taken in logarithms so that the coefficients b_1 to b_3 denote elasticities. The estimates are as given in Table 5.1

Table 5.1   Elasticities of manufacturing labor productivity per worker in OECD countries (1994–98)

	Elasticity coefficients					
Industry	b_0	b_1	b_2	b_3	**Adj. R^2**	n
Total	8.065*	0.339***	0.540***	0.143**	0.45	120
High-tech	8.255	0.299***	0.466***	0.156*	0.35	80
Low tech	8.166*	0.089	0.909***	0.156	0.76	40

Note: One, two and three asterisks denote significant *t* values at 10%, 5% and 1% respectively.

The results show very clearly that all three forms of investment denoted by x_1 to x_3 have significant effect on labor productivity in the manufacturing sector. Thus a 1% increase in physical investment to labor ratio raises the labor productivity level by 0.54%, followed by R&D where the effect on productivity is 0.34% and human capital investment where the effect is 0.14%. It is remarkable that the R&D elasticity coefficient for the high-tech manufacturing sector is more than three times the value for the low-tech manufacturing sector. Physical investment is found to be the dominant determinant of labor productivity in both high- and low-tech industries in the manufacturing sector. In this respect the NICs in Asia have similar growth experiences.

We now consider a class of semiparametric models where efficiency gains provide the key to growth of firms and industries. The impact of innovations as R&D or knowledge capital is analyzed here in terms of three types of models. One emphasizes the unit cost reducing impact of R&D as we discussed before in connection with the Spence model. Second, the impact on output growth (TFP growth) through input growth including R&D inputs is formalized through a growth efficiency model. Here a distinction is drawn between *level* and *growth* efficiency, where the former specifies a static production frontier and the latter a dynamic frontier. Finally, the overall cost efficiency is decomposed into technical (TE) or production efficiency and allocative efficiency (AE). Thus the three components of efficiency growth, i.e., ΔTFP, ΔTE and ΔAE may completely measure the firm and efficiency growth.

Denote unit cost by $c_j = C_j/y_j$, where total cost C_j excludes R&D cost denoted by r_j for firm $j = 1,2,...,n$. Then we set up the non-parametric model also known as a data envelopment analysis (DEA) model as

$$\text{Min } \theta$$

$$\text{s.t. } \sum_{j=1}^{n} c_j \lambda_j \leq \theta c_h, \sum_{j=1}^{n} r_j \lambda_j \leq r_h, \sum_{j=1}^{n} y_j \lambda_j \geq y_h$$

$$\sum_{j} \lambda_j = 1, \lambda_j \geq 0, j \in I_n = \{1,2,...,n\} \tag{5.2}$$

On using the dual variable $\beta_1, \beta_2, \alpha, \beta_0$ and solving the linear program (5.2) we obtain for an efficient firm h, $\theta^* = 1$ and all slack zero the following average cost frontier

$$c_h^* = \beta_0^* - \beta_2^* r_h + \alpha^* y_h$$

since $\beta_1^* = 1$ if $\theta^* > 0$. Here y_j is output and r_j is R&D spending. If we replace r_h by cumulative R&D knowledge capital R_h as in Arrow's learning by doing model, then the AC frontier becomes

$$c_h^* = \beta_0^* - \beta_2^* R_h + \alpha^* y_h$$

A quadratic constraint as

$$\sum_{j=1}^{n} r_j^2 \lambda_j = r_h^2 \tag{5.3}$$

may also be added to the LP model (5.2), where the equality constraint is added so that the dual variable β_3^* may be free of sign. So long as the coefficient β_3^* is positive r_h or R_h may be optimally chosen as r^* or R^* if we extend the objective function in (5.2) as $\text{Min } \theta + r$ or, $\text{Min } \theta + R$ and replace r_h or R_h by r or R. In this quadratic case (5.3) if the coefficient β_3^* is positive, r_h may be optimally chosen as r^*:

$$r^* = \frac{1 + \beta_2^*}{2\beta_3^*}$$

Clearly, if $\theta^* < 1$ in (5.2) the firm h is not efficient since then $\sum_{j=1}^{n} c_j \lambda_j^* < c_h$, so that other firms, or a convex combination of them, have lower average costs. Thus an innovating firm gains market share by reducing unit costs, i.e., as r_h or R_h rises, it reduces unit costs c_h^* when $\beta_2^* > 0$.

Now consider growth-efficiency measured in a nonparametric way. Consider a firm j producing a single composite output y_j with m inputs x_{ij} by means of a log linear production function:

$$y_j = \beta_0 \prod_{i=1}^{m} e^{B_i} x_{ij}^{\beta_i}; \quad j = 1, 2, ..., N$$

where the term e^{B_i} represents the industry effect or a proxy for the share in total industry R&D. On taking logs and time derivates one can derive the production function

$$Y_j = \sum_{i=0}^{m} b_i X_{ij} + \sum_{i=1}^{m} \phi_i \hat{X}_i$$

where

$$Y_j = \sum_{i=0}^{m} b_i X_{ij} + \sum_{i=1}^{m} \phi_i \hat{X}_i$$

$$b_i = \beta_i, b_0 = \frac{\dot{\beta}_0}{\beta_0}, X_{0j} = 1, j = 1, 2, ..., N$$

$$e^{B_i} = \phi_i \hat{X}_i, X_{ij} = \frac{\dot{x}_{ij}}{x_{ij}}, Y_j = \frac{\dot{y}_j}{y_j}, \hat{X}_i = \frac{\sum_{j=1}^{N} \dot{x}_{ij}}{\sum_{j=1}^{N} x_{ij}}$$

and dot denotes time derivative. Note that b_0 here denotes technical progress in the sense of Solow (representing long-run TFP growth) and ϕ_i denotes the industry efficiency parameter.

We now consider how to empirically test the relative efficiency of firm h in an industry of N firms with observed input–output data (x_{ij}, y_{ij}). We use the nonparametric DEA model as and LP model:

$$\text{Min } C_h = \sum_{i=0}^{m} (b_j X_{ih} + \phi_i \hat{X}_i)$$

$$\text{s.t. } \sum_{i=0}^{m} (b_j X_{ij} + \phi_i \hat{X}_i) \geq Y_j, \quad j = 1, 2, ..., N$$

$$b_i \geq 0, \phi_i \geq 0 \tag{5.4}$$

and b_0 is free in sign. Denote the optimal solutions by b^* and ϕ^*. Then the firm h is growth efficient if

$$Y_h = b_0^* + \sum_{i=1}^{m}(b_i^* X_{ih} + \phi_i^* \hat{X}_i)$$

If instead of equality it is a 'less than' sign, the h-th firm is not growth efficient – observed output growth is less than the optimal output growth. Note that this nonparametric DEA model has several flexible features. First of all, one could group the firms into two subsets, one growth efficient, the other less efficient. The successful innovating firms are necessarily growth efficient. Their technical progress parameter b_0 may also be compared. By measuring $b_0^*(t), \phi_j^*(t)$ and $b_i^*(t)$ over sub-periods one could estimate if there is efficiency persistence over time. Secondly, if the innovation efficiency is not input specific, i.e., $e^{B_i} = \phi.t$, then one could combine the two measures of dynamic efficiency as say $b_0^* + \phi^* = \tilde{b}_0^*$. In this case the dual problem for (5.4) as

Max u

$$\text{s.t.} \sum_{j=1}^{N} \lambda_j X_{ij} \leq X_{ih}; \quad i = 0,1,...,m$$

$$\sum_{j=1}^{N} \lambda_j Y_j \geq u Y_h; \quad \sum_{j=1}^{N} \lambda_j = 1, \quad \lambda_j \geq 0$$

If the optimal value u^* is one, then firm h is growth efficient, otherwise it is inefficient. Finally, we note that the growth-efficiency model can be compared with the level efficiency of firm h by running the LP model as

$$\text{Min } C_h = \tilde{\beta}_0 + \sum_{i=1}^{m}[\tilde{\beta}_i \ln x_{ih} + \tilde{\phi}_i x_i]$$

$$\text{s.t.} \tilde{\beta}_0 + \sum_{i=1}^{m}[\tilde{\beta}_i \ln x_{ij} + \tilde{\phi}_i \ln x_i] \geq 0$$

$$x_i = \sum_{j=1}^{N} x_{ij}; \quad \tilde{\beta}_i, \tilde{\phi}_i \geq 0$$

and $\tilde{\beta}_0$ is free in sign.

We now consider an empirical application of growth efficiency to the US computer industry. The data is from Standard and Poor's Compustat database, where on economic grounds a set of 40 firms over a 16-year period 1984–99 is selected. The companies included here comprise such well-known firms as Apple, Compaq, Dell, IBM, HP, Toshiba and also less well-known firms such as AST Research and so on. For measuring growth efficiency we use a simpler cost-based model where any observed variable $\tilde{z}$ denotes $\dot{z}/z$ or the percentage growth in z.

$$\text{Min } \theta(t)$$

$$\text{s.t.} \sum_{j=1}^{N} \tilde{C}_j(t)\mu_j(t) \leq \theta(t)\tilde{C}_h(t)$$

$$\sum_{j=1}^{N} \tilde{y}_j(t)\mu_j(t) \geq \tilde{y}_h(t), \quad \sum_{j=1}^{N} \mu_j(t) = 1$$

$$\sum_{j=1}^{N} \tilde{y}_j^2(t)\mu_j(t) = \tilde{y}_h^2, \quad \mu_j \geq 0, j \in I_n$$

where $C_j(t)$ and $y_j(t)$ denote total cost and total output of firm j and the quadratic output constraint is written as an equality, so that the cost frontier may turn out to be strictly convex if the data permits it. The dynamic cost frontier showing growth efficiency may then be written as

$$\tilde{C}_h(t) = \dot{C}_h(t)/C_h(t) = g_0^* + g_1^*\tilde{y}_h(t) + g_2\tilde{y}_h^2$$

If one excludes R&D spending from total costs C_h and denote it by $R_h(t)$, then the dynamic cost frontier can be specified in finite growth form as

$$\Delta C_h(t)/C_h(t) = \beta_0^* + \beta_1^*(\Delta y_h(t)/y_h(t)) - \beta_2^*(\Delta R_h(t)/R_h(t))$$

here β_1^*, β_2^* are nonnegative optimal values and β_0^* is free in sign. Here the elasticity coefficients β_2^* estimates in the DEA framework the influence of the growth of R&D spending on reducing costs. The estimates for the selected firms in the computer industry are given in Table 5.2.

Consider now a regression approach to specify the impact of R&D inputs on output measured by net sales. Here x_1 to x_3 are three inputs comprising R&D inputs, net capital expenditure and all other direct production inputs. The production function turns out to be

$$y = 70.8^* + 3.621^{**}x_1 + 0.291^{**}x_2 + 1.17^*x_3; R^2 = 0.981$$

Table 5.2 Impact of R&D on growth efficiency based on the cost-oriented model

	1985–89		1990–94		1995–2000	
	θ^*	β_2^*	θ^*	β_2^*	θ^*	β_2^*
Dell	1.00	2.71	1.00	0.15	0.75	0.08
Compaq	0.97	0.03	1.00	0.002	0.95	0.001
HP	1.00	1.89	0.93	0.10	0.88	0.002
Sun	1.00	0.001	1.00	0.13	0.97	1.79
Toshiba	0.93	1.56	1.00	0.13	0.97	1.79
Silicon Groups	0.99	0.02	0.95	1.41	0.87	0.001
Sequent	0.72	0.80	0.92	0.001	0.84	0.002
Hitachi	0.88	0.07	0.98	0.21	0.55	0.001
Apple	1.00	1.21	0.87	0.92	0.68	0.001
Data General	0.90	0.92	0.62	0.54	0.81	0.65

where one and two asterisks denote significant *t*-values at 5% and 1% respectively. When the regressions are run separately for the DEA growth efficient and inefficient firms, the impact of R&D inputs is about 12% higher for the efficient firms, while the other coefficients are about the same. When each variable is taken in incremental form the estimates are

$$\Delta y = -6.41 + 2.65^{**}\Delta x_1 + 1.05^{**}\Delta x_2 + 1.17^*\Delta x_3; R^2 = 0.994$$

It is clear that the R&D input has the highest marginal contribution to output in the level form and incremental form.

Technical progress measured by TFP growth in the Solow model does not consider however the growth of technical (TE) and allocative efficiency (AE) which we found to be quite significant in the rapid growth of the Chinese economy.

We now consider these two efficiencies in terms of the non-parametric DEA model. Consider now the standard input-oriented DEA model with observed input X_j and output Y_j vectors with m and n elements and N firms. To test the relative efficiency of the k-th firm we set up the LP model

Min θ

s.t. $\sum_{j=1}^{n} X_j\lambda_j \leq \theta X_k, \ \sum_{j=1}^{n} Y_j\lambda_j \geq Y_k, \lambda'e = 1, \ \lambda \geq 0$

where e is a column vector with each element unity and prime denotes a transpose of a vector. Let λ^* and θ^* be the optimal solution of the above LP model. Then the reference firm k is technically efficient if $\theta^* = 1$ and all the slack variables are zero. Thus θ^* provides a measure of technical efficiency (TE). If $0 < \theta^* < 1.0$, then it is not technically efficient at the 100% level. Overall efficiency (OE) however combines both TE and AE, i.e., $OE_k = TE_k * AE_k$; $k = 1,2,...,N$.

To characterize overall efficiency of firm k one sets up the LP model

$$\operatorname*{Min}_{x,\lambda} q'x = \sum_{i=1}^{m} q_i x_i$$

$$\text{s.t.} \sum_{j=1}^{N} X_j \lambda_j \leq x, \sum_{j=1}^{N} Y_j \lambda_j \geq Y_k, \lambda'e = 1, \lambda, x \geq 0, k = 1,2,...,N$$

Here q is an m-element vector of unit prices observed in the market and x is an input vector to be optimally decided by the firm. Here X_j and Y_j are the observed input and output vectors of firm j. Let λ^* and x^* be the optimal solutions. Then the minimal input cost of firm k is given by $c_k^* = q'x^*$, whereas the observant unit cost is $c_k = q'X_k$. Hence the three efficiency measure are defined as

$$TE_k = \theta^*, OE_k = c_k^*, AE_k = OE_k / TE_k = c_k^* / \theta$$

The role of R&D inputs and the spillover effects may also be characterized in a more generalized version of the DEA model. This has been discussed in some detail by Sengupta and Sahoo (2006) who showed several sources of efficiency, e.g., (1) unit cost reduction due to the complementary effect of R&D inputs, (2) the scale effect due to learning by doing, (3) the spillover effect of knowledge capital and (4) Solow type TFP or technological progress. The innovating firm can utilize all these efficiency sources to grow and gain in market share. The NICs in Asia made systematic attempts to utilize these efficiency sources to achieve such significant growth rates over the last two decades.

5.2.   A Cournot model of growth

Schumpeter maintained the hypothesis that when a new firm succeeds in introducing a new innovation at a significant level, it tends to enjoy quasi-monopoly profits till others catch up. An example of such a model is due to Cellini and Lambertini (2008), who considered the strategy of reducing unit costs over time through R&D and knowledge capital as instrumental to gaining market share and to enjoying quasi-monopoly profits. When the strategy is successful, the Cournot firm may achieve dominance in the market either as the leader or as a dominant player in a cartel-like framework.

The Cournot model of growth assumes a duopoly with a homogeneous good with a market demand function

$$p(t) = A - q_1(t) - q_2(t)$$

and a cost function $C_i(c_i, q_i) = c_i(t)q_i(t)$ where firm $i = 1, 2$ produces output $q_i(t)$ at time t with a marginal cost $c_i(t)$ which declines over time as

$$\frac{dc_i(t)}{dt} = \dot{c}_i(t) = c_i(t)[\delta - k_i(t) - \beta k_j(t)]$$

where $i \neq j$ and $k_i(t)$ is the R&D effort of firm and δ is the constant rate of depreciation. The cost of setting up a single R&D laboratory or knowledge capital is

$$G(k(t)) = b(k(t))^2, \quad b > 0$$

or, if each firm undertakes independent ventures then the cost is

$$G_i(k_i(t)) = b(k_i(t))^2, \quad b > 0$$

Two cases are considered independent ventures or joint ventures. In the former case each firm chooses output level and R&D efforts independently and maximizes the profit function.

$$\operatorname*{Max}_{k_i(t),\, q_i(t)} \pi_i = \int_0^\infty e^{-rt} \pi_i(t)\, dt$$

where $\pi_i = [A - q_i(t) - q_j(t) - c_i(t)]q_i(t) - b(k_i(t))^2$ \hfill (5.5)

subject to

$$\frac{\dot{c}_i(t)}{c_i(t)} = -k_i(t) - \beta k_j(t) + \delta$$

$$\frac{\dot{c}_j(t)}{c_j(t)} = -k_j(t) - \beta k_i(t) + \delta$$

On using the Hamiltonian function $H_i(t)$ for firm i as

$$H_i = \exp(-rt)\{[A - q_i(t) - q_j(t) - c_i(t)]q_i(t) - b(k_i(t))^2$$
$$- \lambda_{ii}(t)c_i(t)[k_i(t) - \beta k_j(t) + \delta] - \lambda_{ij}(t)c_j(t)[k_j(t) - \beta k_i(t) + \delta]\}$$

where $\lambda_{ij}(t) = \mu_{ij}e^{-rt}$ is the co-state variable associated with the state variable $c_j(t)$ we may derive the first-order optimality conditions

$$\frac{\delta H_i}{\delta q_i(t)} = A - 2q_i(t) - q_j(t) - c_i(t) = 0$$

$$\frac{\delta H_i}{\delta k_i(t)} = -2bk_i(t) - \lambda_{ii}(t)c_i(t) - \beta\lambda_{ij}(t)c_j(t) = 0$$

These conditions must hold with the initial conditions $c_i(0) = c_{0i}$ and the transversality conditions

$$\lim_{t \to \infty} e^{-rt}\lambda_{ij}(t)c_j(t) = 0; \quad i, j = 1, 2$$

The optimal levels of output and knowledge capital (R&D capital) can then be derived as

$$q^*_i(t) = \frac{1}{2}(A - q_j(t) - c_i(t))$$
$$k^*_i(t) = -(2b)^{-1}[\lambda_{ii}(t)c_i(t) + \beta\lambda_{ij}(t)c_j(t)] \tag{5.6}$$

These are the best reply functions of the dynamic Cournot model. From (5.6) the growth of knowledge capital may be computed as

$$\dot{k}_i(t) = -(2b)^{-1}[\dot{\lambda}_{ii}c_i(t) + \lambda_{ii}(t)\dot{c}_i(t) + \beta\{\dot{\lambda}_{ij}c_j(t) + \lambda_{ij}(t)\dot{c}_j\}]$$

By imposing the symmetry condition $c_i(t) = c_j(t) = c(t)$ and the steady state condition $\dot{k}_i = 0$ we obtain the steady state optimal capital $\bar{k}_I = (6rb)^{-1}c(A - c)$, I denotes independent ventures. This is derived from the dynamic equation

$$\dot{k}_i(t) = rk_i(t) - (6b)^{-1}[c(t)(A - c(t))]$$

Note that the technological spillover parameter β affects the level of marginal cost as

$$\frac{\delta \bar{k}_I}{\delta \beta} = \frac{\delta \bar{k}_I}{\delta c}\frac{\delta c}{\delta \beta} = (6rb)^{-1}[A - 2c]\frac{\delta c}{\delta \beta}$$

The steady state marginal cost can be derived from the dynamic cost equation

$$\dot{c}(t) = -c(t)[\overline{k}_I(t)(1+\beta) - \delta] = 0$$

yielding the steady state level of unit costs

$$\overline{c} = (2(1+\beta))^{-1}[A(1+\beta) \pm \{(1+\beta)[A^2(1+\beta) - 24br\delta\}^{1/2}$$

The solutions are real if $\delta.r \le A^2(1+\beta)/24b$.
In this case we obtain the unique saddle point equilibria as

$$\overline{c}_I = [2(1+\beta)]^{-1}[A(1+\beta) - \{(1+\beta)[A^2(1+\beta) - 24br\delta]\}^{1/2}$$
$$\overline{k}_I = \delta(1+\beta)^{-1}$$

Clearly, this shows that

$$\frac{\delta\overline{k}_I}{\delta\beta} = -\delta(1+\beta)^{-2} < 0$$

i.e., as the spillover effect increases the incentive to invest in process innovation declines.

In case of cartel the firms combine their efforts to maximize joint profits. With the symmetry conditions $c_i(t) = c_j(t) = c(t)$ and $k_i(t) = k_j(t) = k(t)$ when

$$\frac{\dot{c}(t)}{c(t)} = -k(t)(1+\beta) + \delta$$

The joint profit function in this case is

$$\text{Max } \overline{\pi}_i = \int_0^\infty e^{-rt}\{[A - q_i(t) - q_j(t) - c(t)]q_i(t) - b(k(t))^2\}dt$$

We can derive the growth equation of R&D capital as

$$\dot{k}(t) = -\frac{(1+\beta)}{2b}[\lambda(t)c(t) + \lambda(t)\dot{c}(t)]$$

where $\lambda(t) = -2bk(t)/[(1+\beta)c(t)]$

This yields

$$\dot{k}(t) = rk(t) - (6b)^{-1}\{c(t)[A - c(t)](1+\beta)\}$$

On setting $\dot{k}(t) = 0$ the steady state value of innovation capital becomes

$$\bar{k}_c = (6rb)^{-1}\{c[A - c](1 + \beta)\}$$

where the subscript c on $\bar{k}$ denotes the case of a cartel.

On comparing the two steady states we see that $\bar{k}_c > \bar{k}_I$, i.e., in the case of cartel the optimal steady state capital is higher. It can be checked that the steady state marginal cost in the case of cartel is the same as in the case of joint ventures.

Cellini and Lambertini (2008) also compared the welfare performance of the two frameworks in the steady state and found that the private and social incentives toward R&D cooperation coincide for all admissible levels of technology spillovers. This result differs from the conclusions of the Spence model we considered earlier. In the Spence model there are no additional costs of setting up the R&D laboratory as the convex cost function in the Cournot growth model. In the Spence model the unit (or average) cost $c_i(t) = F(z_i(t))$ depends on the accumulated effects of the investment by firm i, where z_i is the accumulated knowledge of firm i where it is assumed that

$$\frac{dz_i(t)}{dt} = \dot{z}_i(t) = m_i(t) + \theta \sum_{j=1}^{n} m_j(t)$$

Here there are n symmetric firms with $m_i(t)$ as the current expenditure on R&D by firm i and θ captures the spillover effect. If $\theta = 0$ there are no spillovers or externalities and if $\theta = 1$, the benefits of each firm's R&D are shared completely. In this Spence model, which assumes a Cournot-Nash framework, the optimal R&D costs at the industry level turns out to be

$$R\&D = (nz)[1 + \theta(n - 1)]^{-1}$$

Thus spillovers reduce the incentives for cost reduction but they also reduce the costs at the industry level of achieving a given level of cost reduction. The state subsidies can help the incentives for cost reduction in this model.

Some comments on the Cournot growth model are in order now. First of all, the optimal output growth for firm i can be derived from the first-order condition

$$q_i(t) = \frac{1}{3}[A - 2c_i(t) + c_j(t)]$$

$$\dot{q}_i(t) = \frac{1}{3}[-2\dot{c}_i(t) + \dot{c}_j(t)]$$

Thus the two rivalrous firms in the Cournot framework of independent ventures face competition for cost reduction. If $\dot{c}_j(t)$ falls, the output $\dot{q}_i(t)$ falls. But any reduction $\dot{c}_i(t)$ over time increases the output growth $\dot{q}_i(t)$. Secondly, the saddle point equilibrium solution provides a type of stability characterized by two real eigenvalues with different signs. This implies that there is a stable manifold along which the firms converge to their steady state equilibrium values. Finally, one has to point out that if $\dot{c}_i(t)$ falls much more than $\dot{c}_j(t)$ or if $\dot{c}_i(t) > 0$ with $\dot{c}_j(t) = 0$ then the firm i attempts to capture the market by increasing its market share and in the Schumpeterian framework this provides additional incentives for investing large sums in R&D. The lure of monopoly profits provides a significant incentive for firms to invest in R&D and innovation.

5.3.   Innovation dynamics in Asia

Asia has strengths and potential to make it a leading center of technological innovation in the twenty-first century. These strengths are substantial and durable. Human capital and the capacity for learning by doing have played a key role in these strengths. Technological innovation provides the basic foundation, since the centers of technological innovation become centers of innovation across a broad economic spectrum. This occurs through the spillover effect and externalities, and the re-gearing of a society for innovation of any kind spreads its impact on capital, learning by doing and the level of industrial culture that spill across boundaries. The two forces of technology push and the market pull have significant dynamic impacts on the growth of innovation dynamics in China, India, Taiwan and other Asian countries. Our objective here is to discuss this framework and evaluate its potential.

One of the most robust indicators of change in the distribution of innovation potential is a change in the distribution of corporate research laboratories. In software and electronics, NEC, Hitachi,

Sony, IBM and Microsoft all have established R&D centers in China. Multinational companies are opening new labs or expanding the existing ones at an astounding rate. In the pharmaceutical industry, companies such as Roche, Pfizer, AstraZeneca and Eli Lily all have established large R&D centers in China. More recently, in 2009 Exxon Mobil chemical has started building a $70 million research center in the Zizhu Science-based Industrial Park in Shanghai, China. The trends, the durable fundamentals and the leading indicators all suggest that Asia, led by China, India and Taiwan, will be a leading force in the innovations that transform the world in the twenty-first century. The stronger the global integration becomes, the better the odds of a smooth and broadly beneficial outcome.

In global markets today, economic efficiency and its improvement over time holds the key to success. The most important aspect of competitiveness in world markets is national productivity especially in sectors like IT and software services. Porter (1990) studied the growth process of several important countries such as Denmark, Germany, Japan, South Korea, Singapore, Sweden, Switzerland, UK and USA and reached three important conclusions. First, the sustained growth at the firm and industry level requires that an economy continually upgrade itself through improving human capital and developing the capability of competitive success in entirely new and sophisticated industries like software and communications. Secondly, the competitive advantage principle requires that a country take advantage of the comparative advantage dynamics emphasized by modern theory of international trade and specialize in those sectors and industries where firms are relatively more productive. Note that firms can gain competitive advantage from conceiving new ways of doing business, new technologies and new product lines. For instance, Makita in Japan adopted this strategy and emerged as a leading world competitor in power tools. Finally, one must note that governments cannot create competitive industries but they can encourage them by providing incentives and initial support. Again the best example is of Japan, where the government encourages early demand, develops cooperative R&D and other policies for adopting frontier up-to-date technologies and speeds up the process of upgrading the old innovations. This provides a remarkable application of the Schumpeterian principle of creative destruction. The Japanese model is successfully followed up by Taiwan, South Korea and Singapore.

China's technology policy in recent years has attempted to apply a most progressive strategy for productivity growth and competitive efficiency. The 1997 National Conference on Technological Innovation promoted the role of private enterprises in the nation's R&D activities. At the 1999 conference the government further demanded that high-tech enterprises spend at least 5% of their annual sales on R&D. The most recent policy measures have emphasized the implementation of a technology standardization framework and a patent-focused strategy in enterprise innovation behavior. In 2000, R&D spending by Chinese enterprises exceeded 60% for the first time, implying that the enterprises in the private sector had become a more important player in research and innovation. Over the period 2000–03 the top 100 domestic electronics and IT enterprises spent about 3% or more of annual sales revenues with some companies like Datang Telecommunications spending about 10% of sales revenue to R&D. For more than 10 million medium- and small-sized firms, about 150 thousand allocated more than 5% of sales to technological development.

In China a firm can register as 'high-tech' only if it satisfies the following requirements: at least 30% of its employees have college education, more than 5% of its sales are spent on R&D and more than 60% of its sales revenue are related to technology services and high-tech products. Thus high-tech industries in China's trade statistics include computers and telecommunications, life sciences, aerospace, electronics, biotechnology and so on. China's national system of science and technology has undergone drastic transformation in the reform era. The pre-reform system of central planning and control has given way to a hybrid system comprising both state-patronage and a market-driven incentive structure.

Enterprises have become the most critical element in the technological innovation. As a result the proportion of R&D patents and R&D expenditures have steadily increased. The ratio of R&D to GDP has risen from 0.74 in 1991 to 0.90 in 2000, 1.23 in 2004 and 1.42 in 2006. Lu and Hu (2008) estimated a patent production function in the form

$$E(P_{it}) = \exp(\alpha + \beta \log R_{it}) + \lambda_f(f_{it} \log R_{it}) + \lambda_m(m_{it} \log R_{it}) + \theta D_t)$$

for the period 1990–2003 with yearly dummies (D_t) where P_{it} is the patent count in region i and year t, R_{it} is the region's R&D stock where the Poisson regression equation is of the form:

$$E(P_{it}) = \exp(\alpha + \gamma \log R_{it})$$

with $\gamma = \beta + \lambda_f f_{it} + \lambda_m m_{it}$.

Here γ is the elasticity of patent production with respect to R&D stock; f denotes the large- and medium-sized firm's share of research fund use. The extent of market-based technology transfer is measured by m. The estimated coefficients of the patent production function are as follows:

	$\log R_{it}$	$f_{it} \log R_{it}$	$m_{it} \log R_{it}$	R^2	N
1. With year Dummies only	0.7997**	0.430**	0.2900**	0.78	361
2. With both year and provincial Dummies	0.5970**	0.1310**	0.1195*	0.97	361

Note: One and two asterisks denote significant z-statistics at 5% and 1% respectively.

This estimation follows the Poisson regression approach developed by Griliches (1984) and others.

The estimated result of Poisson regression above with the high Pseudo R^2 seem to validate two major hypotheses:

H_1: Participation of enterprises raises the elasticity of patent production with respect to knowledge stock, i.e., $\lambda_f > 0$ significantly.

H_2: Development of the technology market also raises the elasticity of patent production with respect to knowledge stock, i.e., $\lambda_m > 0$ significantly.

The accession of China to WTO in 2001 apparently has been a great stimulus to patent application for this period.

The above estimates of the Poisson regression model of the patent production function have two implications that need to be commented on. First, the role of R&D in knowledge stock has been very significant in the innovation process that is embodied in the patents. The push given to science and technology education and the market incentives provided by state policy have played significant roles. Secondly, the high elasticity coefficients of the patent production function in China have been sustained over the later years. Note that the percentage growth of R&D spending in China over the period 1999–2004 has been about 21.1, which exceeds both Japan (4.8%), Europe (6.2%) and US (6.6%).

In January 2006, China announced a 15-year medium- to long-term plan (MLP) of science and technology to become a world leader in science and technology by 2050. One of the interesting aspects of the MLP implementation is the encouragement of China's wealthy local governments to invest more in science and technology. Spending on science and technology by provincial governments constituted about 39% of total government expenditure on science and technology in 2005. This is up from 29% in 1995 and has been rapidly rising since. This surge in local government spending is leading to major new funding sources for R&D and to new cooperative ventures between the central and the local governments.

Taiwan is another example that shows how a small country emphasized science and technology in its human capital and strongly supported the growth of R&D efforts in its national innovation process. The production of IT output fueled Taiwan's impressive growth record for the past two decades. Its IT output grew from US $100 million in 1980 to more than $5 billion in 1989 reaching $21 billion in 1999 and if Taiwan's manufacturing enterprise in China is included the total IT output exceeds $35 billion in 1999. And it is steadily rising. One basic indicator of Taiwan's technological achievements is its ranking among US patent recipients. In 1980 it ranked twenty first, by 1990 it reached eleventh and in 1995 it ranked seventh. Today Taiwan receives more patents per capita than the other Asian NICs and ranks ahead of all the G7 countries except US and Japan.

There exist several factors for this rapid growth. First, the agglomeration and scale economies flowing from the large infusion of managerial and entrepreneurial resources from the US, which provided important linkages to technology and markets in Silicon Valley. These occurred in areas such as manufacturing of integrated circuits (ICs), PCs and related components. Secondly, two separate clusters of entrepreneurship, one in the Taipei area comprising small and medium companies and the other in the Hsinchu Science Park took advantage of supportive state policies that affected a rapid research of public R&D. The creation of a domestic VC industry was influenced greatly by the Silicon Valley model in California. Finally, Taiwan did not adopt the high-volume assembly strategy of large vertically integrated Korean agglomerates. Instead it developed an extensive supplier and subcontracting infrastructure that produced an ongoing stream of innovation-intensive small- and medium-sized enterprises (SMEs).

As an example of how Taiwan sustained its productivity and efficiency at the industry level while staying on the technology frontier one may refer to the study by Wang and Tsai (2002) who estimated the effect of R&D investment in Taiwan's manufacturing firms on output growth. They estimated the Cobb-Douglas production function

$$Q_{it} = A_0 e^{\lambda t} L_{it}^{\alpha} K_{it}^{1-\alpha} R_{it}^{\beta}$$

where Q, L, K and K denote the value added, labor, physical capital and R&D capital. The R&D capital is measured by the stock of knowledge of the firm in the form of skill level and technology level of the firm and A_0 is a constant. A data set of 136 firms over a seven-year period 1994–2000 yielded the estimates as shown in Table 5.3 after correcting for serial correlation.

They estimated the average rates of return on R&D capital in manufacturing and found it to be around 35% for the high-tech firms such as electronics. They also estimated the average annual rates of TFP growth as given in Table 5.4.

Table 5.3 Production function estimates for Taiwan's manufacturing sector

		α	β	λ	R^2
All firms	($n=136$)	0.485**	0.187**	0.037*	0.352
High-tech firms	($n=43$)	0.305**	0.297**	0.125**	0.468
Other firms	($n=93$)	0.674**	0.055	0.021	0.326

Note: One and two asterisks denote significant *t*-values at 5% and 1% respectively.

Table 5.4 Average annual rates of TFP growth (%)

Industry	1996	2000
Ford	5.14**	5.73*
Chemicals	2.31*	5.46
Textiles	1.24*	7.39*
Machinery	4.12*	8.33*
Metals	2.78	−1.49*
Electronics	6.39*	13.21*

Note: One and two asterisks denote significant *t*-values at 5% and 1% respectively.

It is clear that the impact of R&D capital on productivity growth has been very significant. The growth rates of Taiwan's computer software products are equally impressive. It rose from 18.34% in 1997 to 24.4% in 2000 on an overall basis. But its three component branches grew at different rates as follows:

	1997	2000
Product market	11.94	16.95
Project market	31.39	25.00
Services	14.07	42.00
Overall	18.34	24.40

The details of the IT sector data analyzed by Sengupta (2005) show that almost all R&D expenditure in Taiwan is for applied research and technology development, e.g., the electronic machinery industry allocates about 75% of total R&D spending to technology development and 25% to applied research.

Many researchers have predicted that new Asian innovation dynamics will be led by China and India. D'Costa and Parayil (2009) have analyzed this trend, where China's high-technology exports and India's software exports play key roles in the world market today and in the future. We have already analyzed the key characteristics of China's technology-intensive growth. We may now discuss some characteristics of the growth process in India. The strength of India and China and other Asian economies is in its human capital endowments. D'Costa and Parayil (2009) discuss several features of human capital development in India. First of all, Indian universities and technical institutes unlike their Chinese counterparts cannot legally initiate commercial enterprise. Indian firms have been quite successful and entrepreneurial but rarely collaborative with public research institutions. Secondly, Indian companies have remained very risk averse. For example, the IT industry in India has found it convenient to stay with customized and contract services for US and Europe. Similarly, in biotechnology and pharmaceuticals India has been very risk averse in securing contract research and less innovative R&D services. Table 5.5 reports some statistics on the performance of R&D activities in India, China and US. Clearly India lags behind China and US. Sengupta (2005) reviewed the comparative performance of India in the context of NICs in Asia, using statistical data on an R&D index comprising, several components such as high-tech exports share of total manufacturing export, the number of scientist and engineers in R&D as a proportion of total industrial employment and average annual number of patents.

Selected rankings are as follows: Japan (1), US (3), Singapore (6), South Korea (13), China (20) and India (22). This ranking indicates how far India has to improve on the R&D front.

Table 5.5   Select indicators of performance in R&D in India, China and US

	India	China	US
1. R&D expenditure (billions of US $ at 2002 prices)	3.7	15.6	276.2
2. R&D expenditure of % of GDP 2000–05	0.8	1.4	2.7
3. No. Of researchers in R&D per million people 1990–2005	119	708	4605
4. High-tech exports as % of total manufacturing exports 2005	4.9	30.6	31.8
5. Patents granted to residents per million people 2000–05	1	10	244

Source: UNDP Reports and UNCTAD (2005).

Two important points about India's growth potential need be mentioned here. First, India's growing middle class and its potential for educational skills as human capital is a strong source of future growth. India's emergence as the world's fifth largest consumer economy will bring significant benefits to the country and the world. Growth will pull hundreds of millions of people out of poverty. For the world's business India thus represents one of the largest consumer market opportunities for the next two decades. Secondly, India's growth potential in the IT sector is enormous. Software and IT services accounted for 1.98% of India's GDP in 2002 and it exceeded 8% by 2006 according to some estimates. But most of these software services exported abroad are in terms of human services. Patents and R&D components are very low. Hence there exists ample scope for reforms in the IT sector. Currently India is the fourth largest software market to the APAC region (excluding Japan) with about 9.5% of the regional market and India's software market is among the fastest growing in the APAC region with an expected compound annual growth rate of 15% or more from now through 2012. Thus India's new knowledge economy shows a dynamism and challenge: the dynamism due to innovation needs and challenge due to the need to improve core competence and economic efficiency in the IT sector. Key players like China and India can significantly dominate the trend in innovation dynamics in Asia in the next two decades.

5.4.   Innovation and market dynamics

The dynamics of technology, industry growth and globalization have a dramatic impact on the current economic growth of nations, significantly changing the market structure and world trade. These developments have challenged the competitive equilibrium models and their guiding principles. In the world of high technology, innovations and spillover effects of R&D, various forms of non-competitive markets structures have evolved in recent times. We discuss here briefly some of these non-competitive models, some of which have been analyzed before in earlier chapters. Three types of models are discussed here. One is an industry growth model in a Cournot-Nash framework. The second model is based on a quality ladder model, where a firm that innovates first and succeeds wins the quality leadership. The third model discusses a cooperative pricing model, where the oligopolistic firms may avoid rivalrous pricing strategies by facilitating coordination through traditions and conventions that stabilize the competitive environment.

Consider now a model of industry growth activated by the innovation efficiency of a firm. In industry evolution, a firm's growth is critically dependent on innovations that may be broadly conceived in Schumpeterian terms, which include R&D investment and other technical and organizational improvements. In this framework innovations tend to provide several channels of potential market power that may deter future entry. Assume a Cournot type model where each firm j seeks to maximize profits.

$$\pi_j = p(y_j + Y_{-j})y_j - C(y_j) \tag{5.7}$$

where y_j is the output of firm j, Y_{-j} is the total output of all its rivals, $C(y_j)$ is the total cost of production with marginal cost $\hat{c}_j$. The optimal mark up μ can be easily derived as

$$\mu = \frac{p - \hat{c}_j}{p} = \frac{(1 + a_j)s_j}{e}$$

$$s_j = \frac{y_j}{Y}, a_j = \frac{\delta Y_{-j}}{\delta y_j}$$

where s_j is the market share of firm j, a_j and e is the price elasticity of demand. To arrive at the industry average mark up ($\bar{\mu}$) we weight the above equation by market shares and derive

$$\bar{\mu} = \frac{p - \bar{c}}{p} = (1 + a)H \tag{5.8}$$

where $\bar{c} = \sum_{j=1}^{r} s_j \hat{c}_j$ and H is the Herfindahl index measuring concentration and it is assumed that the symmetry condition holds, i.e., $a_j = a$. The Schumpeterian theory of innovations assumes a stream of innovations whereby a successful innovator produces a newly invented good or service and continues to dominate the market (sometimes under the protection of patent rights) until driven out by the next innovator. Thus the relative success of the new entrant in driving out (or reducing the market share of) the incumbent depends on his ability to reduce unit cost. Since the rate of change in market share s_j can be viewed as proportional to the cost differential,

$$\frac{\dot{s}_j}{s_j} = \lambda(\bar{c} - c_j)$$

where λ is the speed of selection at which firm shares react to their efficiency differences. On assuming λ, a_j and e to be fixed, the mark-up equation reduces to

$$\dot{\mu} = \lambda_\mu = [(1/e)\{\lambda(1+a_j)s_j(\bar{c} - c_j)] \tag{5.9}$$

Note that as an industry-specific parameter, a high λ would characterize an industry with a strong competitive adjustment mechanism much like the Walrasian process, while a low λ would imply a monopolistically competitive adjustment. In the latter case, excess profits are competed away more slowly due to the higher concentration ratio. Kessides (1990) has established empirically that for US manufacturing industries the following tendencies persist:

$$\frac{\delta\lambda}{\delta H} > 0, \frac{\delta\lambda}{\delta g} > 0, \frac{\delta\lambda}{\delta\text{MES}} > 0, \frac{\delta\lambda}{\delta K} > 0 \tag{5.10}$$

where g is the growth rate of total industry demand, minimum efficient scale (MES) is a measure of minimum efficient scale of output and K represents total capital required for the MES level.

Sengupta (2004) has discussed three types of efficiency in this context: technological, access and resource (stronghold) efficiency. Resource efficiency is emphasized by the contribution of K in (5.10), technological efficiency by MES and the access efficiency by H and g. By building barriers around a stronghold, the firm can reap monopoly profits. Access to distribution channels and low-cost supply sources in the supply chain and dynamic economies of scale may provide major barriers to trade by which the successful innovator firms may sustain a stronghold.

Since increased market share may be viewed as a proxy variable for entry, it is clear from (5.9) that potential entry could be increased by reducing unit cost c_j below the industry average level $\bar{c}$, i.e., by increasing efficiency. In this context, Cabral and Riordan (1994) have considered a game-theoretical model that posed the question: once ahead, what does the leading firm have to do to stay ahead? Here it is assumed that a firm's unit cost $c(s)$ is a decreasing function of cumulative past sales s. It is assumed that each firm's strategy depends only on the state of the game. Clearly the market dominance of the leading firm would depend on two dynamic effects: a cost effect and strategy effect. Thus a firm at the very bottom of its learning curve maintains a strategic advantage as long as its rival has a higher cost. The strategic or prize effect refers to the potential prize from winning the lagging firm. Thus, if the lagging firm has a sufficiently larger prize, then the prize effect could dominate the cost effect. In equilibrium the price difference of two firms would be proportional to the cost difference, i.e., $p_2 - p_1 = a(c_2 - c_1)$ where a is a positive constant, its higher value indicating a larger market dominance by the leading firm. Sutton (1998) has discussed these strategies in a more general context where each firm invests in one or more R&D programs of varying quality and conditions for a dynamic entry equilibrium to be established.

The Cournot-type market game models are intended to explain the two processes at work. One is the set of actions of firms intended to affect the current conduct of rivals and the other by alternating the market structures in such ways that constrain the rival's subsequent strategies in the future. Of several types of investment that the incumbent firms can make, limit pricing has been one of the major strategies which are invoked so as to discipline pricing decisions in the short run. The simplest limit pricing model which advances the proposition that potential competition disciplines short-run pricing decisions assumes homogeneous goods and scale economies, uses price alone as a strategic weapon and invokes the *Sylos postulate*, i.e., the entrant believes that incumbent will maintain the same output after entry to establish the entrant's conjecture about the post-entry equilibrium. An alternative view allows existing firms to tolerate entry if that is in their best interests and thus puts a lower bound on the limit price that one is likely to observe. Encaoua, Geroski and Jacquemin (1990) have emphasized that the Sylos postulate is not a credible belief for large-scale entrants. This means one has to consider other weapons that can be used to discourage entry, for example, advertising and investment in learning and R&D strategies. An R&D

strategy could create entry difficulties if a competitor's costs of product development lagged behind those of an early mover.

Thus large firms can adopt several types of non-pricing strategies to deter new entry and sustain their dominance, e.g., (1) large capital cost in R&D, (2) preserve early mover advantages, (3) maintaining access and network efficiency and (4) increasing the costs of potential entry through large advertisement expenditure.

Now consider the second type of model due to Folster and Trofimow (1997) who have developed a dynamic model of industry evolution with R&D externalities. In this model the entry of new firms denoted by $\dot{n} = dn/dt$ depends on the net present value from entry $(v - z)$, i.e.,

$$\dot{n} = \alpha(v - z) \tag{5.11}$$

where z is the cost of entry, $v(t)$ is the discounted sum of future profits, i.e.,

$$v(t) = \int_0^\infty e^{-r(s-t)}\pi(n,\, u)dt$$

On differentiation one obtains

$$\dot{v} = \frac{dv}{dt} = rv - \pi(n,\, u) \tag{5.12}$$

where u is the R&D effort and the profit function $\pi(n, u)$ is assumed to be strictly concave. Foster and Trofimov (1997) assume that the good produced by the firms has a number of qualities j ranked by an exponential function $\exp[(\lambda - 1)j]$ where $\lambda > 1$ denotes the extent of quality improvement. At each time point t the homogenous firms are engaged in R&D competition toward the next quality level. A firm that innovates first wins quality leadership in the industry and enjoys a temporary monopoly position until another entrant brings out a new innovation and drives out the incumbent. There is no winner during the period dt if no firm is successful in the quality game. In this case all firms are involved in Bertrand-type price competition.

The profit function $\pi(n, u)$ is the difference of expected monopoly profit uh/n and the cost of R&D effort $c_i + u^b/b$ where c_i is the fixed

R&D costs and the convex function $u^b/b; b > 0$ denotes the variable cost:

$$\pi(n, u) = \frac{uh}{n} - c_i - \frac{u^b}{b} \tag{5.13}$$

Here the expected monopoly profit for the successful firm from the quality improvement race is the product of h and the probability that the firm succeeds in innovation. It is assumed that successful innovations arise as a result of a Poisson process with an intensity u. Since firms have equal chances of winning the game, the probability that any particular firm becomes a winner is $(u/n)dt$. Note that the position parameter h here denotes the extra price gain is due to the quality improvement obtained by the successful innovator.

We may add several comments on this interesting dynamic model, where product quality improvement through successful innovation drives the long-run evolution of a high-tech industry. First of all, if we maximize short-run profits $\pi(n, u)$ in (5.13) and obtain optimal profit as $\pi(n)$ then the dynamics of industry evolution may be written as

$$\dot{n} = \alpha(v - z)$$

$$\dot{v} = rV - \pi(n) \tag{5.14}$$

The characteristic equation for the system (5.14) is

$$\mu^2 - r\mu + \alpha\pi'(n) = 0$$

where $\pi'(n) = \delta\pi / \delta n$ denotes the marginal impact on static profits $\pi(n)$ when n increases. The evolution of the number of firms and hence total industry profits depends on the shape of the profit function. Their empirical estimates found the profit function $\pi(n)$ to be S-shaped. This means that the profit function is increasing for some interval as n is increasing from level zero and decreasing otherwise. This positive effect on incumbent profits is explained by R&D externalities such as externalities and technological spillovers.

The steady state equilibria of the dynamic system (5.14) are given by $\dot{n} = \dot{v} = 0$ yielding

$$v^* = z, \pi(n^*) = rz$$

When $\pi'(n^*) < 0$ we obtain a pair of real eigenvalues μ_1, μ_2 with different signs and the steady state in this case is a saddle point. Since $\pi'(n^*) < 0$ is more plausible in empirical estimates, the saddle point equilibrium is more plausible. In case $\pi'(n^*) > 0$ we obtain two positive eigenvalues implying that the equilibrium is an unstable focus.

A second point to note about this model is that it does not incorporate the effect of increasing returns to scale when the R&D investments tend to reduce unit costs. One way to see this is to consider an alternative model, where we use the concept of MES at which a firm's average cost (AC) is close to the minimum, say within 10% of the minimum. Writing total cost of production as $TC = F + cy$ with average cost $AC = F/y + c$, it follows that the minimum average cost is given by $c > 0$. Let the MES correspond to average cost c^0. Then on equating AC to c^0 we obtain the optimal output level

$$y = F(c^0 - c) = \text{MES}$$

It is natural to interpret changes in MES as changes in the value of fixed cost F, i.e., an increase in F by a factor λ implies an increase in MES by the same factor. Thus if MES increases by a factor of 4, then the number of firms decreases by a factor of $\sqrt{4} = 2$. Since a large part of R&D costs (about 40% or more) is fixed cost, the increase in MES is mainly an increase in F. Thus if we consider two industries that differ in the value of F, then the industry with the greatest degree of scale economies is more concentrated. Thus, the size of a firm is the key to the market dominance by medium to large firms. Finally most large firms are self-financed due to imperfect capital markets and besides scale economies, the economies of scope in performing R&D and the spread of risks help large firms to innovate more in R&D. The incentives for mergers largely depend on these cost-reducing scale economies and scope economies.

The third model discusses a model of implicit cooperation in pricing, when explicit collusion is not allowed legally. The starting point in this analysis is the premise that *ceteris paribus* firms would prefer prices to be closer to their monopoly levels than to the levels reached under Bertrand or Cournot competition. Let (P_0, π_0) be the industry price and profits in the prevailing period and (P_M, π_M) be the price and profit when all firms charge the monopoly price P_M. The industry as a whole would be better off for the firms at the monopoly price, so $\pi_M > \pi_0$. Assume now that each of the N firms in this industry faces a prisoners' dilemma. Thus if an individual firm expects its competitors to raise their prices to the monopoly level, that firm gets a larger profit by sticking to a price P_0. If it matched the price increase it would have obtained 1/N-th of monopoly profits. A firm's one period move from refusing to cooperate with others is thus $E = \pi_0 - (1/N)\pi_M$. If $E>0$ then it has no incentive to cooperate.

Now consider an infinite horizon when each firm discounts future profits using a discount rate of r per period. If each firm believes that its competition will raise the price from P_0 to P_M in the current period and thereafter will follow a rivalrous strategy, then each firm will find it optimal to charge the monopoly price as long as

$$\frac{(1/N)(\pi_M - \pi_0)}{[\pi_0 - (1/N)\pi_M]} \geq r$$

This formula has been derived by Besanko et al. (2010). Its numerator on the left-hand side is the simple period benefit to an individual firm from cooperating. The denominator is the extra profit the firm could have earned in the current period if it had refused to cooperate. The inequality above states that the cooperative pricing will be sustainable when this ratio exceeds the prevailing discount rate r. The formula above is a special case of what game theorists have called the *folk theorem* for infinitely repeated prisoners' dilemma games. The folk theorem says that for sufficiently low discount rates any price between P_M and marginal cost can be sustained as equilibrium in the infinitely repeated prisoners' dilemma game. Two comments are in order. First, the cooperative pricing strategies are more difficult to achieve when the firms are asymmetrical due to product differentiation. Secondly, this type of pricing strategy may not be legally permissible. Hence the firms have to depend on customs and traditions. Game theorists have used the concept of correlated strategies to arrive at such cooperative schemes.

To conclude this chapter we may refer to some ideas of Schumpeter on innovation and the concept of 'creative destruction'. In Schumpeter's view the process of creative destruction means that static efficiency associated with competitive equilibria is less important than dynamic efficiency, i.e., the achievement of long-term growth and technological improvement. There is no end to the list of new technologies that established new markets and their dominant firms, e.g., quartz watches, cellular communications, computer flash memory and so on.

One important point to note is that the efficiency effect due to R&D innovation makes an incumbent dominant firm's incentive to innovate stronger than a potential entrant's incentive. The reason is that the incumbent can lose its monopoly power if it does not innovate, whereas the entrant will become at best a duopolist if it successfully innovates.

This chapter has emphasized the role of noncompetitive market structures in a world where innovations and learning by doing tend to create disruptive technologies which replace the old technologies. Growth under new technology and innovations create paradigms of industry evolution over time.

6
Time Series Tests of the AK Model of Endogenous Growth*

6.1. Introduction

In the AK model of growth, a country's output per capita grows linearly with investment as a percentage of GDP. The model predicts that changes in policies that affect the investment rate should in turn affect growth rates, given a fixed capital–output ratio and depreciation, allowing an endogenous form of growth. The theory thus requires fundamental similarity in the dynamics of economic growth and investment rates for an economy.

A much-cited publication that tests the AK model of growth is Jones (1995). He found little empirical support for the AK model in a sample of developed nations. His tests showed that persistent increases in investment have not been matched by persistent growth of income. In particular, he found that economic growth rates were generally mean-reverting whereas investment rates were not.

Several other studies that empirically test the AK model are available, each with different conclusions regarding the applicability of the theory. These studies again looked at only OECD nations for short time spans.

Here, we re-evaluate the AK model of growth using a relatively longer time frame (1950–2004) and a more comprehensive set of 112 developed and developing economies. We screen the data and ask

*Contributed by Dr. Ishita Nandi, Department of Economics, University of California, Santa Barbara

whether the growth and investment rate time series in any of these countries exhibit properties consistent with the AK model. Our testing strategy, similar to Jones (1995), is based on stationarity analyses to determine fundamental trends of the time series for each country. Similarities in the dynamic properties of the two series indicate necessary consistency with the AK model's predictions: growth rates should exhibit persistent upward movements if and only if investment rates exhibit persistent upward movements over time.

Our econometric method supports Jones' findings, revealing evidence that appears to run contrary to the general prediction of AK-type models. Of the 112 countries studied, only 10 (<9%) satisfy the AK model's predictions according to our screening criteria. Output growth is generally mean stationary while investment rates in total physical capital and producer durables are non-stationary. Thus, the AK model may not provide a good description of the historical economic growth process in most of the economies considered. More interestingly, of the ten countries that appear consistent with the AK theory, only China stands out with trends in growth and capital accumulation over the past half-century that are strongly consistent with the basic dynamic requirements of the AK model. Both growth and investment rate series are trend stationary processes for China, with trends in the same (positive) direction.

Further tests using Chinese data reveal that growth and investment rates (at the aggregate level and industrial level) are both segmented trend stationary, have trends in the same direction and experience structural breaks in approximately the same years. We also find a stable positive correlation between China's investment and growth rates, and establish that the direction of causality runs strongly from high past investment shares of GDP to current growth.

This is the first time a time series study of the AK model has revealed the critical role of physical capital accumulation in historically promoting growth in this large and significant world economy.

The chapter is arranged as follows. In the next section, we describe a simple AK model of growth and outline previous investigative findings regarding the model in the empirical literature. Section 6.3 describes economic data of the over one hundred world economies we consider during the period 1950–2004. It also outlines the econometric method and results of our preliminary empirical screening tests. In Section 6.4, we take a closer look at the unique case of China and outline the data and econometric tests used to critically examine its growth and investment patterns, finding that the data are not inconsistent with the AK model of growth. Section 6.5 concludes.

6.2. The AK model of endogenous growth: literature review

The benchmark 'AK model of endogenous growth' is a classic economic model in which capital accumulation directly determines future growth. The model is derived from the standard neoclassical production function:

$$Y = AK^{\alpha}L^{1-\alpha} \tag{6.1}$$

where Y denotes output, K denotes broad capital, L denotes labor and A reflects the level of technology. If the output elasticity with respect to capital, α, is assumed to be equal to one (constant and non-diminishing returns to capital, due to either surplus labor, or, positive externalities linked to capital accumulation) then:

$$Y = AK \tag{6.2}$$

which is the basis for the name 'AK model'. Given the underlying assumption on returns to capital, doubling broad capital, given a fixed stock of knowledge, will double output. Doubling both capital and knowledge will more than double output.

With a constant rate of depreciation of capital (δ) and investment-GDP ratio i, the capital accumulation equation can be written as

$$\dot{K} = iY - \delta K = iAK - \delta K \tag{6.3}$$

The growth rate of capital, g_K, is therefore:

$$g_K = \frac{\dot{K}}{K} = i\frac{Y}{K} - \delta = iA - \delta \tag{6.4}$$

which is independent of capital. In addition, the growth rate of output, g_Y, is equal to the growth rate of capital, g_K, if A is assumed constant over time:

$$g_Y = \frac{\dot{Y}}{Y} = \frac{\dot{K}}{K} = iA - \delta \tag{6.5}$$

The growth equation above requires similarity in the dynamic natures of the g_y and i time series. It defines a simple linear relationship between the economic variables: Growth is positively linked to savings or investment rates. As an illustration, according to the AK model a country with a capital–output ratio of 5 needs an additional 5% of GDP to go to investment to lift growth by 1%, ignoring depreciation. If the country targets a 5% growth rate, it will need to increase the investment rate to 25% of GDP.[1]

Jones (1995) conducted Augmented Dickey Fuller (ADF) (Dickey and Fuller 1979) unit root tests and time trend tests for 15 OECD countries from 1950–88 to examine whether the growth and investment rate series had similar time series properties. He found little support for the AK model. His tests showed that persistent increases in investment have not been matched by persistent growth of income in most developed nations – growth rates were generally mean reverting whereas investment rates were not. He found that investment rates influenced growth rates for at most eight to ten years. He also argued, 'the process of industrialization and development is likely to be different from the process generating sustained growth of the countries that have already industrialized' and did not consider Asian or other developing economies in his paper.

Romero-Avila (2006) tested the validity of the AK model for a sample of 26 OECD countries over the period 1950–92. It is likely that output growth and investment rates experienced some structural change over the postwar era (Ben David and Papell 1995) and so Romero-Avila improved upon Jones' method by using unit root tests developed by Ng and Perron (2001) that prevent the non-rejection of the unit root hypothesis when the series is actually stationary but with a structural break. This kind of unit root test allowed for an unknown change in the intercept and slope of the series. He concluded that there was little support for the AK model in these countries' experiences. Romero-Avila also estimated autoregressive distributed lag growth models. The estimation delivered insignificant long-run coefficients on the investment rates, casting further doubt on the AK model.

Some authors have found support for the AK model in advanced economies. McGrattan (1998) used data from 1870 to 1989 for OECD countries and for three non-OECD Asian countries (India, Taiwan and Korea). She used simple time series graphs to demonstrate that the key prediction of standard AK theory was consistent with the data over a long time horizon – periods of high investment rates roughly coincided with periods of high growth rates. Looking at data before the World Wars (1870–1914), during the Wars (1914–49), and after the Wars (1950–89), she found that the average growth rates are two or three times higher in the postwar period than in the prewar period (1870–1950). The investment rates were highest in the postwar period: for France and the United Kingdom, the investment rates were approximately twice as high after the wars as before them. Periods of time during which investment rates rose while growth rates remained constant or fell were short lived and not persistent. She argued that this graphical evidence contradicts Jones' negative conclusion about the usefulness of the AK model: in 11 countries over the last century, the AK models' prediction of simultaneous long-run movements in investment and growth were confirmed. Next, using cross-country averages of data for the period 1960–85 for 125 countries with varied development experiences, she illustrated a positive correlation between investment rates and growth rates. The slowest growing countries had an average investment rate around 7%, whereas the fastest growing countries had an average rate almost four times higher, approximately 25%. Thus, she claimed that higher investment rates coincided with higher growth rates, both across time and across countries. However, McGrattan did not investigate the stochastic properties of output growth and investment rates. She based her conclusions solely on the presence or absence of deterministic trends in economic growth and investment rates.

D. Li (2002) extended the analysis of Jones (1995). The author looked at a sample of 24 OECD countries from 1950 to 1992 and examined long-run patterns in investment rate data from 1870 to 1987 for five major industrialized countries. D. Li argued that the *total* physical investment share is relevant for testing the AK models, not the share of producer durables investment (the sum of machinery and transportation equipment). He found that the case against AK-type models is weaker when the deterministic trends of total investment shares and economic growth are compared. He also estimated distributed lag growth models and found a positive long-run effect of total investment on growth for most countries. D. Li and Jones' conclusions regarding the success of the AK model diverge, and this may have been caused by their use of different definitions of investment and D. Li's consideration of autoregressive terms in the growth regressions that helped control for adjustment dynamics characteristic of Solow-type models. D. Li (2002) did not test the stationarity properties in his series and his conclusions, like McGrattan's (1998), were based only on the presence or absence of non-stochastic trends in growth and the total investment rate.

Bond et al. (2004) used annual and five-year pooled data for 98 countries over the period 1960–98 and found that a higher share of investment in GDP predicted a higher level of output per worker in steady state, and that an increase in the share of investment resulted in a higher growth rate of output per worker, both in the short run and in the steady state. The long-run effect on growth rates was quantitatively and statistically significant, consistent with the AK model.

Here, we re-evaluate the AK model using a longer time frame than either D. Li (2002) or Romero-Avila (2006) and with a much larger set of countries. We ask whether this model of endogenous growth is able to describe the growth processes of our sample throughout 1950–2004. This is the first time so many economies have been considered in an evaluation of the AK model. It is of particular interest to study whether the AK model stands up to scrutiny in East Asian countries where rapid accumulation of physical and human capital and great progress in innovation potential is a well-documented fact. Our data, econometric method and findings are described below.

6.3. Data, method and results

6.3.1. Data

We have data on a total of 112 countries from around the world including all the OECD member countries. We look at South America, Africa, the four East Asian Tigers (Hong Kong, Singapore, South Korea and Taiwan), developing Asia including all of South East Asia and most of South Asia and finally a few economies given 'developed nation' status by the International Monetary Fund (Bermuda, Cyprus, Israel and Malta). We exclude Central American, Eastern European and small island nations due to their sparse and sometimes unreliable data. We also exclude Middle Eastern countries from this study as we believe the dependence on the production and export of oil renders their economic processes and development experience unique, justifying a careful and separate study of the region beyond the scope of this chapter.

The data we use is extracted from the Penn World Tables Mark 6.2 (PWT 6.2; data range 1950–2004)[2] in 2000 constant prices. The variables considered are the growth rate of Real GDP per capita in constant prices and the investment share of Real GDP in constant prices. We have derived producer durables investment (machinery plus transportation equipment) as a share of GDP using preliminary PWT 6.2 data sent to us by request from the Center for International Comparisons of Production, Income and Prices at the University of Pennsylvania.

6.3.2. Econometric method

Unit root tests are tools that help determine the stationarity of a series. If the test reveals that there are only deterministic time trends present, we understand that the series is generated by a predetermined non-random function of time with a random error component – the series will closely oscillate around the trend and will exhibit mean (trend) reversion. Such processes are called 'trend stationary processes' (TSPs). If the test indicates that only a stochastic trend is present, then the series is persistent and is described by a starting value and successive random occurrences with zero mean and constant variance – each present observation depends on its history of random innovations. Such processes are described as 'difference stationary processes' (DSPs), since a process of 'differencing' may be able to convert the non-stationary series into a stationary one. To study the AK model, we are interested in testing whether the growth and investment rate series (for total investment as well as producer durables investment definitions) are TSPs or DSPs for any economy.

To examine time trends we regress the economic series on a constant and a time trend variable. If the coefficient of the trend term is significant, it implies that (based upon the sign of the coefficient) the series grew or contracted significantly over time. Formally, we estimate

$$g_{y,t} = \alpha + \beta t + \varepsilon_t \tag{6.6}$$

$$i_t = \lambda + \pi t + \varepsilon_t \tag{6.7}$$

where t is time. The test statistics are the t-statistics corresponding to the Newey-West corrected standard errors and test the significance of the trends.

We also conduct the standard ADF unit root test on g_y and i. This tests the null:

$$H_0 : \rho = 1, \eta = 0$$

against the alternative:

$$H_1 : \rho < 1, \eta \neq 0$$

using estimates from the individual regressions,

$$g_{y,t} = \alpha + \rho g_{y,t-1} + B(L)\Delta g_{y,t-1} + \eta t + \varepsilon_t \tag{6.8}$$

$$i_t = \mu + \rho.i_{t-1} + B(L)\Delta i_{t-1} + \eta t + \varepsilon_t \tag{6.9}$$

Both series allow for a linear deterministic trend. The lag length of $B(L)$ is chosen using the Schwarz information criterion.[3] Here Δ is the first difference operator and ε_t is a white noise disturbance term. We use the ADF t-statistic as it has more power compared to an F-test of the joint null hypothesis (Elder and Kennedy 2001). The null implies that there is a unit root but no linear trend in the variable. The alternative hypothesis implies that the variable is stationary around a linear deterministic trend.[4] Approximate critical values are from MacKinnon (1991).

Finally, we construct 'screening criteria' to identify countries with growth experiences empirically consistent with the conventional AK model (Table 6.1). Theory requires similarity in the dynamic natures of the g_y and i time series. If investment rates exhibit persistent upward movements, growth rates should exhibit similar persistent movements over time as well. Thus, the **joint non-stationarity** of these series is necessary for consistency with the AK model. Such joint non-stationarity could take two forms. Either:

(a) Both series have stochastic trends and are cointegrated, or
(b) Both trend deterministically in the same direction

If, for both series, the ADF test fails to reject the unit root hypothesis and the variables are cointegrated, the country in question will be labeled 'strong, case (a)' in the Appendix, to indicate that the data are consistent with the AK theory. If, for both series, unit roots are rejected on the strength of the ADF test and significant deterministic time trends of the same sign are found, the country will be labeled 'strong: case (b)' in the Appendix, for the same reason – data are again consistent with AK theory using our definition of investment. If investment rates and growth rates are both stationary, the data are consistent with the AK model. However such consistency is only 'weak' evidence validating the theory, as the country's experience does not provide any helpful or interesting information regarding the evolution of growth and investment rates. The country will then be labeled 'weak' in the Appendix. All other combinations of time trend and unit root results are inconsistent with the AK model. This

Table 6.1   Where does the AK model hold?

Results from time series tests					
Presence of trend		**Presence of unit root**		**Conclusion from the test results**	**Consistency with theory?**
g_y	**i**	**g_y**	**i**		
✓	✓	✕	✕	Joint *deterministic* non-stationarity of series	**Strong: Case (a)**
✕	✕	✓	✓	Joint *stochastic* non-stationarity of series	**Strong: Case (b)**
✕	✕	✕	✕	Joint stationarity of series	**Weak**

method will therefore roughly screen our candidates and reveal whether or not there exist similar evolutionary time patterns in physical capital accumulation activity and output.

6.3.3. Econometric findings

In Tables 6.2(a)–6.2(d), we summarize the test results for our full set of 112 countries,[5] with cases of interest in bold. In Table 6.2(a) we describe the results of the time trend tests. The 37 countries along the diagonal have growth and investment data that trend similarly. Table 6.2(b) describes the results of the stationarity test. Across the diagonal of the table there are 32 countries that are potentially ('strongly') consistent with the AK model. In these countries, either both series reject the unit root hypothesis (23 countries), implying possible trend stationarity in both series, or, both series fail to reject

Table 6.2(a)   Results of the time series tests for the entire sample

| | | | *Growth rate trend* | | |
	# Countries	Negative, Significant	Insignificant	Positive, Significant	Total
Investment Rate trend Negative, Significant		7	28	1	36
Insignificant		8	24	0	32
Positive, Significant		6	32	6	44
Total		21	84	7	112

Table 6.2(b)   Results of the time series tests for the entire sample

| | | *Growth rate* | | |
	Countries	Reject unit root	Fail to reject unit root	Total
Investment rate	Reject unit root	23	2	25
	Fail to reject unit root	78	9	87
	Total	101	11	112

Table 6.2(c)   Results of the time series tests for the entire sample

Where the *unit root is rejected* in both series (entries are the number of countries):

		Growth rate trend			
		Negative, Significant	Insignificant	Positive, Significant	Total
Investment Rate trend	**Negative, Significant**	**2** (Gabon, Ecuador)	5	0	7
	Insignificant	2	**5** (New Zealand, (New Zealand, (New Zealand, Bolivia, Colombia)	0	7
	Positive, Significant	2	6	**1** (China)	9
	Total	6	16	1	23

Table 6.2(d)   Results of the time series tests for the entire sample

Countries where the unit root is rejected in both series

		Growth Rate Trend			
	# Countries	Negative Significant	Insignificant	Positive Significant	Total
Investment Rate Trend **Negative, Significant**		2 (Gabon, Ecuador)	5	0	7
Insignificant		2	5 (New Zealand, Cape Verde, Mali, Bolivia, Colombia)	0	7
Positive, Significant		2	6	1 (China)	9
Total		6	16	1	23

the unit root null (9 countries), in which case we check for cointegration. The growth experiences in the remaining 80 countries do not appear consistent with the AK model. In Table 6.2(c), we focus on the 23 countries for which the unit root null was rejected for both series, and note the nature and significance of their trends. The 8 countries along the diagonal satisfy the necessary time series criteria for consistency with the AK model with trends in the same direction for both series. Finally, in Table 6.2(d), we look at the 9 countries where we fail to reject the unit root null for both series. Of these 9, Engle-Granger (1987) cointegration tests indicate that only one country has cointegrated growth and investment rate series over the sample period and is consistent with the AK model.

These results can be interpreted as reasonably strong support for the view that, for a large set of countries and a long time range, investment rates generally contain large and persistent movements unlike growth rates of output which are characterized by little or no persistence and which revert to a constant mean. The investment and growth rate series are clearly dissimilar. Of the 112 countries studied, only 9 (~8%) satisfy the AK model's basic predictions according to our empirical criteria.

We tabulate the exceptional cases that are consistent with the AK model in Table 6.3. We include the case of Germany where the data are weakly consistent with the model using the 'durables investment'

Table 6.3   Consistency with the AK model of growth

Country category	Strong consistency with AK model	Weak consistency with AK model
OECD	Slovak Republic	Germany (only for **producer durables** investment share of GDP) New Zealand
Africa	Gabon	Cape Verde Mali
South America	Ecuador	Bolivia Colombia
Asia	**China**	

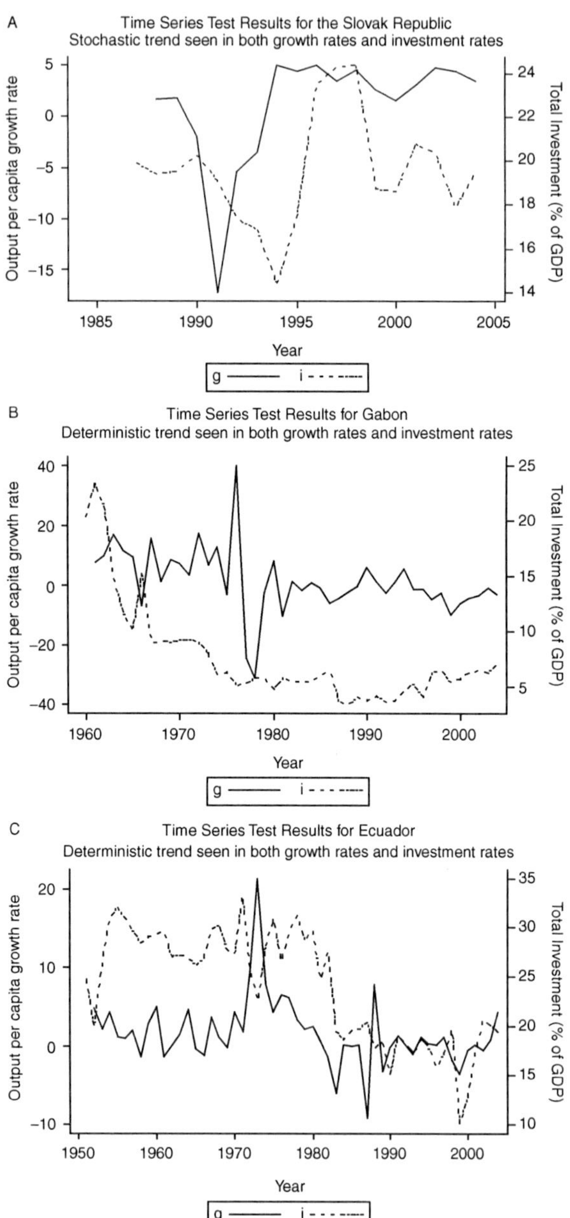

Figure 6.1 Time series graphs for countries consistent with the AK theory of growth (except China)

definition. In the Slovak Republic (Figure 6.1(a)), the growth and investment rate data are cointegrated indicating consistency with the AK model. In Gabon and Ecuador, both series have (negative) deterministic trends and no unit root (Figures 6.1(b), 6.1(c)). Finally, in China, the unit root hypothesis for both series is rejected and simultaneously there are significant positive time trends (Figure 6.2). It appears that the data are consistent with the AK model for China. The finding is interesting in the sense that the two series follow each other very clearly over time. This case is considered to be the most exciting find, and one that warrants further study.

6.4. China

The evidence in support of investment-driven growth for China is considerable (see, for instance, Chow 1993; Krugman 1994; Yu 1998; Kwan, Wu and Zhang 1999; Heytens and Zebregs 2003; Zhang 2003; Kuijs and Wang 2005; and Kuijs 2006). This part of the chapter is aimed at getting a clearer view of whether the experience of

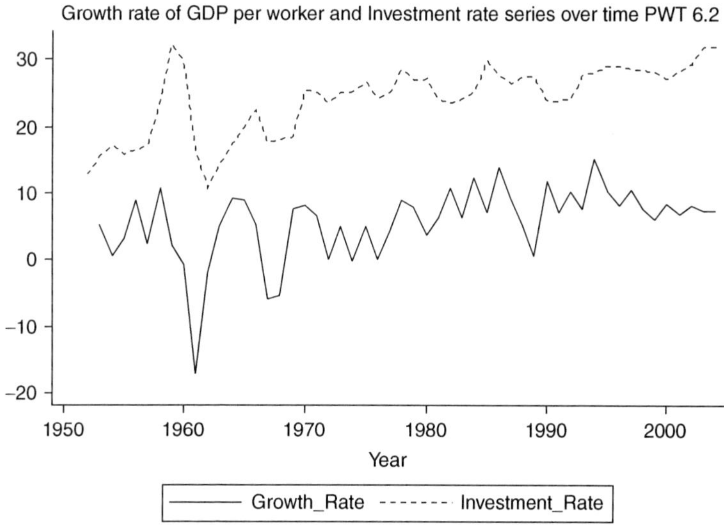

Figure 6.2 Time series properties of growth rate and investment rate in China

China, over the period 1950–2004, is consistent with the bench-mark AK model at the aggregate and sectoral levels of economy. We use structural break unit root tests to reassess whether both the series of interest are trend stationary processes. These sophisticated unit root tests prevent the non-rejection of the unit root hypothesis when a series is actually stationary but has a structural break. We also check for correlation and causality between growth and invest-ment rates. In our knowledge, this would be the first attempt at a rigorous study of the AK theory based on a comparative examina-tion of aggregate and sectoral investment and growth rates for China.

6.4.1. Data for China

The data used to study the AK model for the aggregate economy is again from the Penn World Tables Mark 6.2 (PWT 6.2; data range 1950–2004) in 2000 constant prices. Table 6.4 describes the PWT data on RGDP per capita, growth rates of RGDP per capita and invest-ment as a share of RGDP. For the analysis of China by sector, the data is derived from Dekle and Vandenbroucke (2006)[6] and is described in Table 6.5 and Figures 6.3 and 6.4.

Table 6.4   Five-year averages of RGDP per capita (level and growth rates), investment/RGDP (%)

China	RGDP per capita	RGDP per capita growth rates	Investment/ RGDP	Producer durables/ RGDP
1950–54	344.86	3.02	15.25	2.73
1955–59	407.54	5.53	21.12	3.78
1960–64	402.09	−1.04	17.68	3.17
1965–69	460.73	2.15	19.40	3.48
1970–74	538.74	3.98	24.94	4.48
1975–79	637.60	5.27	26.37	5.08
1980–84	889.55	7.91	24.85	5.65
1985–89	1365.39	7.31	27.80	7.22
1990–94	2008.65	10.45	25.62	7.56
1995–99	3204.34	8.54	28.68	9.40
2000–04	4643.41	7.64	29.77	10.76

Source: PWT 6.2.

Table 6.5   Disaggregated data on growth and investment/RGDP (%)

China	Growth in RGDP per worker (%)			Investment/sectoral RGDP per worker (%)		
Year	Total	Agriculture	Non-agriculture	Total	Agriculture	Non-agriculture
1978	1.92	0.17	−0.10	37.71	21.12	44.07
1979	6.14	-0.91	6.22	39.26	18.97	46.77
1980	2.30	4.84	−0.47	31.81	13.30	37.92
1981	4.13	7.55	3.03	33.87	13.04	40.91
1982	8.39	5.59	5.96	36.09	11.21	44.88
1983	14.45	13.66	7.01	36.92	10.89	45.62
1984	12.75	1.30	11.65	36.87	7.89	45.89
1985	5.59	1.55	3.59	31.19	7.83	37.30
1986	5.55	2.21	4.15	28.55	7.97	33.54
1987	5.16	-4.31	6.12	30.29	8.80	35.20
1988	−6.89	-6.92	−5.83	29.57	10.00	33.50
1989	−13.85	3.97	−17.64	29.81	11.13	33.62
1990	9.99	7.02	10.20	34.86	10.65	41.08
1991	15.68	7.16	14.81	31.70	8.29	37.46
1992	7.56	7.41	3.02	40.46	8.97	47.34
1993	7.38	1.18	4.90	46.73	14.05	53.55
1994	6.05	9.04	1.30	48.83	20.57	54.07
1995	8.02	13.01	4.39	51.35	7.49	59.37
1996	5.79	7.49	4.48	49.52	8.23	57.18
1997	5.50	10.04	4.07	47.83	7.97	55.26
1998	5.18	11.36	4.73	46.49	9.60	53.72
1999	4.21	4.27	4.14	45.42	7.72	53.39
2000	8.17	3.91	8.89	50.34	9.28	58.98
2001	8.95	3.13	9.95	52.12	8.71	60.84
2002	8.83	2.69	8.48	56.70	8.94	65.70

Source: Dekle and Vandenbroucke (2006).

6.4.2. Tests and findings using aggregate Chinese data

Unit Root Tests: In addition to the time trend and ADF tests of Section 6.3, we report Phillip-Perron (PP) unit root tests and the Dickey–Fuller Generalized Least Squares (DF-GLS)[7] tests on growth and investment shares of GDP for the entire Chinese economy in Table 6.6 and Table 6.7. In the case of China, the time trend tests with Newey West standard errors indicate the presence of significant

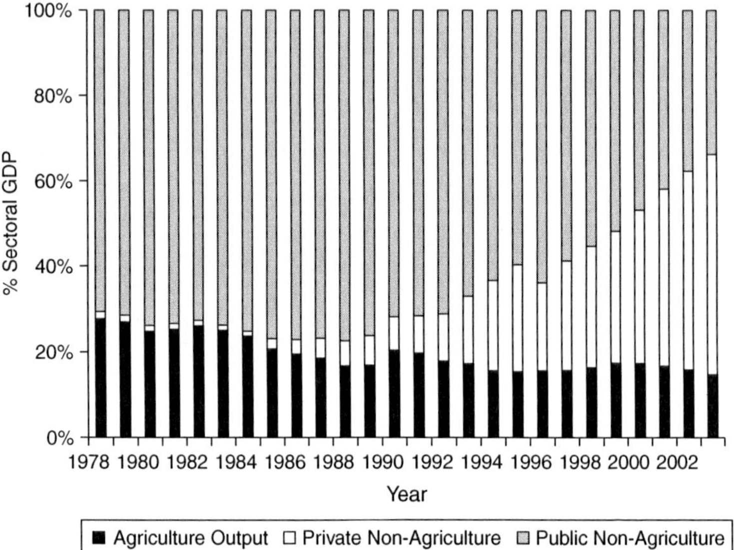

Figure 6.3   Sectoral distribution of output, China

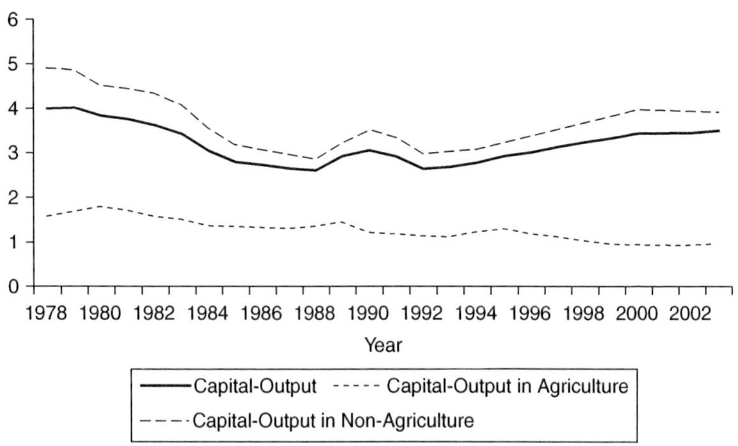

Figure 6.4   Capital output ratio

Source: Dekle and Vandenbroucke (2006)

Table 6.6   Time trend tests of RGDP per capita growth and investment/RGDP China (1950–2004)

	Time trend test
Growth rate	0.163***
	(0.054)
Investment/RGDP	0.254***
	(0.046)

Note: The time trend test reports the coefficient of the trend variable in regressions of gdp per capita growth rate (%) and investment shares (%) on a constant and a trend. The test statistic is the *t*-statistic corresponding to the Newey West corrected standard error and tests whether the above coefficient is 0. Figures in parentheses represent Newey West standard errors. A lag length of 2 is chosen in this annual time series analysis. *** implies significant at the 1% level.

Table 6.7   Unit root tests without breaks of RGDP growth and investment/RGDP China (1950–2004)

	Augmented Dickey-Fuller			Phillip-Perron	DF-GLS	
	Test statistic	Lags	P value	Test statistic	Test statistic	Lags
Growth rate	−5.640***	2	0.0000	−5.275***	−4.986***	2
Investment/ RGDP	−5.885***	1	0.0000	−3.728**	−3.875***	1

Note: Min SC for lag length selection. *P* value refers to the approximate Mackinnon *P* value associated with the test statistic. (***) and (*) denote the 1% and 5% levels of significance respectively.

positive deterministic trends in both series for the aggregate economy and the Augmented Dickey-Fuller (ADF), Phillip-Perron (PP) and DF-GLS test statistics all reject the null which indicates absence of a unit root in both series at 5% significance or higher. We can conclude from these general results that both growth and investment rates are trend stationary processes and that they share the same dynamic natures.

To verify these results we conduct unit root tests with breaks. Any time series study of China would need to take China's tumultuous history and continuous structural change into account.[8] Structural breaks in a time series can also severely reduce the power of Dickey-Fuller tests (Perron 1989; Perron and Vogelsang 1992).

Treating the possible breaks as endogenous, we use the Zivot and Andrews (1992) sequential trend break model Model C and the Lumsdaine and Papell (1997) Model CC to test the unit root hypotheses for real GDP growth and investment shares. These 'crash-and-growth' models allow for a single change in both intercept and slope at the break dates and take the following forms for Models C and CC respectively:

$$\Delta y_{it} = \mu_i + \alpha_i y_{it-1} + \beta_i t + \theta_i DU_t + \gamma_i DT_t + \sum_{j=1}^{k} c_{ij}\Delta y_{it-j} + \varepsilon_{it} \tag{6.10}$$

$$\Delta y_{it} = \mu_i + \alpha_i y_{it-1} + \beta_i t + \theta_i DU1_t + \gamma_i DT1_t + \varpi_i DU2_t \tag{6.11}$$
$$+ \psi_i DT2_t + \sum_{j=1}^{k} c_{ij}\Delta y_{it-j} + \varepsilon_{it}$$

where y represents the time series of interest.[9] The null hypothesis that the series $\{y_t\}$ is an integrated process without a structural break is tested against the alternative hypothesis that $\{y_t\}$ is trend stationary with one (or two) structural break(s) in the trend function. The observation-specific finite sample critical values for the t-statistics are obtained from Zivot and Andrews (1992). The lag length (k) is selected using the 't-sig' approach developed by Hall (1994).

The results of the unit root tests using Model C and Model CC are in Table 6.8. We find that unit root null hypothesis is rejected at 1%

Table 6.8   Aggregate economy

China (1950–2004)	**Model**	**Break date(s)**	**tα**	**Lags, k**
Growth rate	C	1963	−6.60***	2
	CC	1963, 1977	−7.18***	2
Investment/	C	1969	−6.56***	1
RGDP	CC	1963, 1969	−6.76**	1

Note: *** implies significant at the 1% level.
t_α is the test statistic of the coefficient of the lagged dependent variable.

significance for both growth and investment rate variables under Model C and Model CC. This indicates that the variables of interest are trend stationary with breaks in the sample period.[10]

Lee and Strazicich (2003, 2004) demonstrated that when utilizing these endogenous break unit root tests, researchers might conclude that the time series is trend stationary when in fact the series is non-stationary with break(s). In this regard 'spurious rejections' may occur. The minimum Lagrange Multiplier (LM) unit root test proposed by Lee and Strazicich not only endogenously determines structural breaks but also avoids the problems of bias and spurious rejections by allowing for (one or two) endogenous breaks both under the null and the alternative hypothesis. The alternative hypothesis unambiguously implies the series is trend stationary. We conducted the LM unit root test and the results support the conclusions of broken trend stationarity from the Zivot and Andrews 1-break and Lumsdaine and Papell 2-break cases. These are not reported here.

Finally, since trend-stationarity implies that there is no unit root in the detrended series we carry out further unit root tests for the detrended growth rate and the detrended investment share of GDP. Table 6.9 reports the results. The null hypothesis of unit root is rejected decisively for both detrended series at 1% significance. These results confirm our findings above that China's GDP per capita growth rate and the investment rate are indeed both characterized as segmented-trend stationary processes.

Table 6.9   Aggregate economy: unit root tests on detrended series

China (1950–2004)	Augmented Dickey-Fuller			DF-GLS	
	Test statistic	Lags	P value	Test statistic	Lags
Growth rate	−6.249***	4	0.0000	−5.847***	4
Investment/ RGDP	−3.882***	1	0.0000	−5.199***	1

Note: Min SC for lag length selection. *P* value refers to the approximate Mackinnon *P* value associated with the test statistic. (***) and (*) denote the 1% and 5% levels of significance respectively.

Correlation and Causality Tests: In this last segment on the aggregate Chinese economy, we wish to test the hypothesis that the correlation between the investment rate and the growth rate is positive, as this is what the AK model implies: a broadly defined rate of investment exerts a positive effect on the long-run rate of growth. The test we use is from D. Li (2002) and is described below. Let us consider the regression:

$$g_t = a + C(1)i_t + C'(L)\Delta i_t + \varepsilon_t \tag{6.12}$$

where a is a constant; $C(1)$ is the long-run effect of the investment rate on the growth rate; and $C'(L)$ is a polynomial of order q in the lag operator L. Using ordinary least squares (OLS) to estimate this equation will lead to bias and inconsistency in the estimators, because the independent variable i and its lagged values may be correlated with the disturbance term. There may exist cyclical fluctuations in the economy that tend to make both growth and investment rates deviate from their trend values. The bias in OLS estimators may also stem from possible reverse causality from output to investment. A procedure for dealing with this bias is adopted by D. Li and involves running the regression:

$$g_t = a + C(1)i_t + E(L)\Delta i_{t+q} + v_t \tag{6.13}$$

where $E(L)$ is a polynomial of order $(2 \times q)$ in the lag operator L. On the basis of this modified equation the error is uncorrelated with the investment rate and its leads and lags, and the test of the AK model becomes a test of the null hypothesis, $C(1) = 0$, against the alternative hypothesis, $C(1) > 0$. OLS estimates of $C(1)$ would be consistent and asymptotically efficient. We conduct this regression for 2 through 6 leads and lags of the first difference of the investment rate i. The results are in Table 6.10. The estimates of the correlation between China's investment rate and growth rate are positive and differ significantly from zero and are robust to changes in the lengths of leads and lags. We can conclude that contemporaneous investment rates are positively correlated with growth after correcting for possible endogeneity.

Next, we conduct bivariate Granger causality tests proposed by Granger (1969) and popularized by Sims (1972) in Table 6.11. These

Table 6.10 Long-run effect of the investment rate on growth rate: China (1950–2004)

Long-run effect [C (1)]	Number of leads and lags
0.659***	2
(4.01)	
0.809***	3
(4.56)	
0.883***	4
(5.41)	
0.865***	5
(4.89)	
1.05***	6
(5.01)	

Note: The long-run effect is the estimated coefficient C(1) of the investment-rate variable i in the regression:

$$g_t = a + C(1)i_t + E(L)\Delta i_{t+q} + v_t$$

where g is the growth rate and q denotes the number of leads and lags included.

t-statistics are reported in parentheses. (***) denotes the 1% level of significance.

Table 6.11   Bivariate granger causality test results: China (1950–2004)

	F (1, 51) = 6.937	chi2 (1) = 22.037
Lag Length = 1	**Prob > F = 0 .011**	**Prob > chi2 = 0.0000**
Lag Length = 2	F (2, 49) = 4.604	chi2 (2) = 15.221
	Prob > F = 0 .015	Prob > chi2 = 0.0005
Lag Length = 3	F (3, 47) = 5.267	chi2 (3) = 18.155
	Prob > F = 3.2e-03	Prob > chi2 = 0.0004
Lag Length = 4	F (4, 45) = 4.124	chi2 (4) = 14.848
	Prob > F = 6.2e-03	Prob > chi2 = 0.0050

H0: investment rates do not granger cause growth rates

F-tests are used to study whether lagged information on investment rates provide any statistically significant information about current growth rates in the presence of lagged growth rates. We interpret investment to be Granger-causing growth when a prediction of growth on the basis of its past history can be improved by further taking into account the previous period's investment.

Let the null hypothesis be 'investment-rates do not Granger-cause growth'. Assuming a particular autoregressive lag length p, we estimate the following unrestricted and restricted equations by OLS and calculate the sum of squared residuals (RSS):

$$g_t = \sum_{j=1}^{p} \alpha_j g_{t-j} + \sum_{j=1}^{p} \beta_j i_{t-j} + u_t; \ \ \text{RSS}_1 = \sum_{t=1}^{T} \hat{u}_t^2 \tag{6.14}$$

$$g_t = \sum_{j=1}^{p} \alpha_j g_{t-j} + \varepsilon_t; \ \ \text{RSS}_0 = \sum_{t=1}^{T} \hat{\varepsilon}_t^2 \tag{6.15}$$

$$H_0 = \beta_1 = \beta_2 = \beta_3 = \beta_4 = \cdots = \beta p$$

If the test statistic

$$\frac{(\text{RSS}_0 - \text{RSS}_1)/p}{(\text{RSS}_1)/(T - 2p - 1)} \sim F_{p, T-2p-1}$$

is greater than the specified critical value, then we reject the null hypothesis that investment-rates do not Granger-cause growth. An asymptotically equivalent test is given by

$$\frac{T(\text{RSS}_0 - \text{RSS}_1)}{(\text{RSS}_1)} \sim \chi^2(p)$$

T is the number of observations in the sample. Granger-causality tests are very sensitive to the choice of lag length p. In this chapter we report the results of causality tests for up to 4 lags. The null hypothesis that investment rates in the preceding period have no explanatory power with respect to growth in the current period given past history of growth is rejected decisively for 1 through 4 lags. The test of the alternate null hypothesis that 'growth rates do not granger cause investment-GDP' cannot be rejected at less than 4 lags and have not been reported. We conclude that past investment shares granger cause current growth for at least as far back as four years in China for 1950–2004. Investment shares of GDP have good predictive ability in forecasts of growth for the Chinese economy.

6.4.3. Tests and findings using sectoral Chinese data

Unit root tests with breaks are also conducted for the agricultural and non-agricultural sectors of China. The results are presented in Table 6.12. We find that the agriculture sector growth rate is difference stationary. All other series are segmented trend-stationary. Thus the growth rate and investment rate series in agriculture fail to pass the necessary criterion for the AK model and we reject the hypothesis that the data in the agriculture sector are consistent with the AK model. The similarities in the dynamic natures of growth and investment rates for the non-agriculture sector indicate consistency with the AK model. Conducting unit root tests on the detrended series (Table 6.13) we find that the non-agriculture series again rejects the unit root null. We conclude that the necessary condition for consistency with the AK model is satisfied *only in the non-agricultural sector* of the economy. We were however unable to conduct correlation and causality tests on the disaggregated series because of insufficient data points.

6.5. Conclusions

Taken as a whole, our findings appear to run contrary to the general prediction of AK-type models. Less than 8% of the countries in our sample satisfy the AK model's predictions according to our empirical criteria. Output growth is generally mean stationary whereas the

Table 6.12   Disaggregate economy

China (1978–2004)	Model	Break date(s)	$t\alpha$	Lags, k
Agriculture	C	–	–3.79	7
Growth rate	CC	1993, 2000	–19.10***	8
Non-agriculture	C	1989	–6.42***	7
Growth Rate	CC	1996, 2001	–150.98***	8
Agriculture	C	1994	–6.02***	7
Investment/RGDP	CC	1990, 2000	–58.89***	8
per worker				
Non-agriculture	C	1991	–6.27***	6
Investment/RGDP	CC	1992, 1998	–434.89***	8
per worker				

Table 6.13   Disaggregate economy: unit root tests on detrended series

China (1950–2004)	Augmented Dickey-Fuller			DF-GLS	
	Test statistic	Lags	P value	Test statistic	Lags
Agriculture Growth rate	−2.630*	1	0.0673	−2.972	1
Non-agriculture Growth rate	−4.074***	1	0.0011	−4.442***	1
Agriculture Investment/RGDP per worker	−3.231**	1	0.0183	−3.207*	1
Non-agriculture Investment/RGDP per worker	−3.866***	3	0.0023	−3.055***	3

Note: Min SC for lag length selection. P value refers to the approximate Mackinnon P value associated with the test statistic. (***) and (*) denote the 1% and 5% levels of significance respectively.

investment rates in total physical capital and producer durables are generally non-stationary.

Two questions arise regarding the select economies in Table 6.3. First, we have seen evidence that for Gabon (Figure 6.1(b)) and Ecuador (Figure 6.1(c)) the AK model holds because of significant negative trends in both the data series and in China it holds because of significant positive trends. Does this indicate that consistency with the AK model is likely to be seen in cases where there has been either a 'disaster' or a 'miracle' in terms of growth and investment? Do such strong extreme conditions favor the possibility of the AK type of endogenous growth?

Second, how strong is the evidence in favor of the AK model? The inference from the time series tests for the Slovak Republic may not be even preliminarily conclusive because the time series used are considerably short spanned. Gabon and Ecuador are both oil-exporting countries. The jointly (negatively) trending nature of the growth and investment rate series led us to conclude that these economies may have followed an AK model in section 6.3. However, closer inspection reveals that the growth rate series for both countries closely correlate to world oil prices – in fact the significant trends in the series appear only in years when oil price shocks and debt crises affected the economy adversely. Back-of-the-envelope calculations using average growth and investment rate data and depreciation rates of 5% and 10% indicate that the imputed 'A' or capital productivity (if the AK model were true) changes by a factor of at least 10 when comparing the pre-debt crisis to post-debt crisis periods. This invalidates the necessary condition in AK models where A is assumed to be constant over time. Excluding China, the remaining six cases in Table 6.3 are only 'weakly' consistent with the predictions of the AK model – for these economies, there have been no statistical trends in either growth or investment rate time series.

The results for China (Figure 6.2) in section 6.3 seem to be by far the most relevant and interesting. This finding persuaded a closer look at China's growth and investment trends over the past half-century using more sophisticated unit root tests and tests for correlation and causation between the series in section 6.4. We required the following necessary conditions for consistency with the AK model:

(a) Growth and investment rates must both be trend stationary, with the same direction of trend. If breaks exist in either series, they must occur at the same approximate time in the history of the economy and must correspond to significant or meaningful events.
(b) The multiplier of investment on growth must be positive and significant.
(c) Past levels of investment/RGDP must be linked causally to present growth rates.

With our testing strategy we show that both series (at the aggregate and industrial levels) are of the same dynamic natures – i.e., they are both segmented trend stationary with the same direction of trend and approximately the same pivotal years of structural break.[11] The segmented trend stationarity of the time series data indicate that policy initiatives and stabilization policies undertaken by the government can result in a change in trend that will last for a relatively long time until a new, large shock occurs. We also provide evidence that there is stable correlation between investment rates and growth rates and that the direction of causality runs strongly from high past investment shares of GDP to current per capita GDP growth. This is support for the investment-led growth theory discussed in numerous studies on China that pronounce China's growth to be predominantly driven by accumulation of physical capital.

Why did China turn out to be the only country that satisfied the basic necessary conditions for the investment-growth hypothesis? The unique underlying political and social circumstances that this economy faced may be the reason. The Maoist period believed that capital-intensive heavy industry would bring guaranteed prosperity. This led to fiscal policy that forced savings and supported high investment/GDP ratios at the expense of current consumption.

Studying the data, we also realize that the crucial assumptions of the AK model seem to be reasonably upheld in China. The AK model takes the output elasticity with respect to capital as one, which may be supported by China's historically high levels of unemployment. Secondly, we know that the linearity between growth and investment rates in the AK model requires a constant ratio of capital to output as described by the underlying production function. The capital–output ratio has been fairly constant and stable in China (Figure 6.4) with trends closely mimicking the trends in the non-agricultural sector. According to He, Zhang and Shek (2007) China's capital–output ratio fluctuated before 1980 but hovered around 3 thereafter (average 3.36), with some minor ups and downs around 1990. In recent years there has been no clear sign of the capital–output ratio increasing in China, and the ratio is comparable to the levels observed in Japan and Korea in the late 1980s and early 1990s. The evolution of post-1978 industrialization may be the reason behind why China's capital – output ratio performs better than other High Performing Asian Economies (Zhang 2003). The inverse of the capital–output ratio, the marginal product of capital at the aggregate level, has been relatively high and comparable to that of major industrialized economies and the East Asia region in the past two decades, and has not shown any clear signs of decline. Again, these facts are consistent with the model's assumption that marginal and average productivities of capital are constant and that technological progress is not required for growth in output. The studies on TFP growth for China indicate that the role of TFP in growth has been very low, the estimates lying between 1.4% and 3.9% (Table 6.1, He et al. 2007). He et al. (2007) also find that the correlation between the growth of investment and the marginal product of capital has been increasing, implying that the allocative efficiency of investment has improved in China.

Turning to the sectoral analysis, China's economic growth seems to historically depend more on the rapid expansion of its manufacturing sector than on agriculture.[12] Zhang (2003) stated that during its rapid development phase the value added by the industrial sector accounted for 45% of China's GDP on the average, at par with that of Korea and Singapore. Zhang also showed that since the 1980s all of the Chinese manufacturing industries experienced a rapidly growing share of investments except the textile industry and some other smaller industries. According to China's National Bureau of Statistics (NBS) the share of industry in GDP rose from 38% in 1990 to 53% in 2004. Kuijs and Wang (2005) showed that over 90% of the growth in industry in 1993–2004 was led by large-scale investment effort and increased capital–labor ratios that encouraged labor productivity growth. On the other hand, with rapid industrialization, the share of agriculture in China's GDP has been on the decline since the late 1970s and is now only roughly 10%. It is the manufacturing rather than the agriculture sector that seems to be the backbone of economic growth in China and it is where we find data consistent with an AK-type endogenous growth model.

Thus, the empirical evidence suggests that while the AK model may not provide a good description of the historical economic growth process in most of the economies considered, it cannot be rejected for the economy of China. Our results indicate that concerted physical investment activity was indeed associated with China's growth performance and that growth may have been predominantly driven by investment in heavy industry and services. The singular circumstances and political-economic realities of China seem to have been favorable for the general specifications of the AK model.

Notes

1. This framework is widely used, explicitly or implicitly, by many Government planning agencies and international funding agencies like the Asian Development Bank to study and forecast investment and aid requirements in the developing world.
2. Source: Heston, A., Summers, R. and Aten, B. (2006) Center for International Comparisons of Production, Income and Prices at the University of Pennsylvania, September.

3. Although the distribution of the ADF test statistic does not depend on the lag order asymptotically, it can be sensitive to the lag order in finite samples. Cheung and Lai (1995) use response-surface analysis to examine the roles of sample size and lag order in determining the approximate finite-sample critical values of the ADF test. Their study demonstrates that ADF critical values may be biased if their dependence on the lag order is ignored. We thus verify our preliminary ADF results by using calculated response surface critical values obtained from the equations in Cheung and Lai (1995) such that the effect of varying lag lengths on the critical values is corrected for (results not shown here). The conclusions regarding stationarity of the series were not contradicted by this exercise.

4. Note that unit root processes with trend are unrealistic. We can rule them out on a priori grounds as they imply that the change in the economic variable follows a deterministic ever-increasing ($\eta > 0$) or decreasing ($\eta < 0$) path (Nelson and Plosser 1982; Perron 1988; Holden and Perman 1994).

5. Detailed test results are available in Appendix Tables A1 and A2.

6. Available at http://guillaumevdb.net/China-Data.pdf

7. Monte Carlo studies suggest that the Phillips – Perron test generally has greater power than the ADF test (Banerjee et al. 1993). The DF-GLS test proposed by Elliot, Rothenberg, and Stock (1996) is a modified version of the Dickey-Fuller t-test and substantially improves the power of the unit root test compared to the ADF in small samples.

8. Li (2000) conducted unit root tests with two structural breaks to investigate whether annual data for China's real GDP and its sectoral components between 1952 and 1998 could be modeled more accurately as a stationary process around a breaking trend as opposed to a unit root process. His conclusion was that China's output data was indeed trend stationary rather than difference stationary.

9. For equation (6.10), DU_t is a dummy variable for a mean shift occurring at time TB, and DT is the corresponding trend shift variable, where $DU_t = 1$ if $t > $ TB and 0 otherwise; $DT_t = t$-TB if $t > $ TB and 0 otherwise. For equation (6.11), DU1t and DU2t are dummy variables for mean shifts occurring at times TB1 and TB2, respectively, where TB2 > TB1+2 and DT1t and DT2t are the corresponding trend shift variables; (DU1$_t$ = 1 if $t > $ TB1 and DU2$_t$ = 1 if $t > $ TB2 > TB1) and 0 otherwise; (DT1$_t$ = t-TB1 if $t > $ TB1 and DT2$_t$ = t-TB2 if $t > $ TB2 > TB1) and 0 otherwise. The break point TB is searched for over the range of the sample ($0.15T$, $0.85T$) where T is the sample size and is selected by choosing the value of TB for which the absolute value of the t-statistic for α is maximized.

10. The finding that the breaks for Models C and CC coincide is similar to results obtained in Lumsdaine and Papell's (1997) analysis of the Nelson and Plosser (1982) data set. For a range of macroeconomic variables in the Nelson and Plosser data set, they found that one of the breaks in the two-break case corresponded to, or was within a year or two of, Zivot and Andrews' (1992) break year in the one-break case.

11. In Table 6.7, a break in the growth rate series is reported in 1963 for the one-break case and in 1963 and 1977 when two breaks are allowed in the alternative hypothesis of the unit root test. For the investment rate series, the break occurs in 1969 for the one-break and 1963 and 1969 for the two-break test. It appears that both the growth and investment rate series suffered a break in 1963 during a period of adjustment and recovery after the devastating famine that followed the Great Leap Forward of 1958. Growth rates underwent a second break in 1977 after the death of Mao and during a shift in political regimes that heralded the introduction of market reforms in China. The second break for the investment rate series in 1969 coincides with the tumultuous events of the Cultural Revolution of China that lasted from 1966 to 1976. Turning to the disaggregated sector-wise study (1978–2004), the breaks in the data for the non-agriculture sector are in the early and late 1980s and 1990s (Table 6.11), which correspond to several prominent economic events including the Tiananmen Square protests of 1989 and the austerity reign that followed. The primary goal of these austerity measures was to reduce economic growth and included such measures as limiting joint ventures, curtailing capital investment, tightening fiscal and monetary controls, re-imposing centralized control on local construction projects and cuts in capital investment. The growth rate of GNP was planned to average 6% per annum, and government investment was to be drawn away from national construction programs toward agriculture, transportation and communications. The austerity measures led to rising unemployment, stagnation of industrial output and a breakdown of the Chinese financial system because of debt defaults. Increasing investment in capital construction programs and Township and Village Enterprises (TVEs) was the government's solution to reviving the economy in mid-1990s. This was also an era of huge investments in large-scale coalmines and power plants. These events in the 1980s and 1990s may have triggered the structural breaks in the non-agricultural data that we see in Table 6.11.
12. Except for the early 1980s when agricultural growth rates sky-rocketed in response to the household responsibility system.

Appendix

Table A1 Comparative study: PWT 5 (1950–88) [in Jones (1995)] with PWT 6.2 (1950–2004) [current study]; Time series properties of GDP per capita growth rates and Investment/RGDP

	GDP per capita growth rates				Total investment as a %RGDP			
	Time trend		ADF		Time trend		ADF	
	Jones	Current study	Jones	Current study	Jones	Current study	Jones	Current study
Australia	−0.010	0.002	0.290	−1.418	−0.083	0.026	0.559	−0.472
	(−0.15)	(−0.09)	(−6.46)***	(−8.83)***	(−1.50)	(0.89)	(−2.27)	(−3.14)
Austria	−0.110	−0.085	0.070	−0.790	0.279	0.074	0.748	−0.279
	(−2.53)**	(−3.73)***	(−8.59)***	(−4.40)***	(4.46)***	(2.49)	(−1.72)	(−2.64)
Belgium	−0.032	−0.037	0.230	−0.694	0.034	0.003	0.794	−0.216
	(−0.68)	(−2.08)**	(−7.26)***	(−3.87)***	(0.410)	(−0.15)	(−2.06)	(−2.34)
Canada	0.020	−0.003	0.370	−1.015	0.083	0.078	0.531	−0.599
	(−0.38)	(−0.14)	(−6.25)***	(−5.66)***	(1.91)*	(4.65)***	(−2.95)	(−4.00)**
Denmark	−0.029	−0.032	0.040	−0.750	−0.018	0.054	0.882	−0.177
	(−0.41)	(−1.16)	(−8.83)***	(−3.24)**	(−0.11)	(1.43)	(−1.41)	(−2.26)
Finland	−0.036	−0.059	0.230	−0.863	−0.068	−0.176	0.618	−0.201
	(−0.63)	(−1.58)	(−7.27)***	(−5.69)***	(−0.69)	(−3.54)***	(−2.57)	(−2.26)
France	−0.087	−0.062	0.240	−0.556	0.166	0.072	0.916	−0.126
	(−2.38)**	(−3.75)***	(−7.18)***	(−3.63)***	(1.68)	(2.20)**	(−1.17)	(−1.94)
Germany	−0.153	−0.042	0.020	−0.962	−0.146	−0.212	0.769	−0.364
	(−3.26)***	(−1.42)	(−9.05)***	(−4.66)***	(−2.12)**	(−5.04)***	(−2.27)	(−2.80)

Italy	−0.095	−0.100	0.270	−0.492	−0.095	−0.145	0.797	−0.229
	(−2.63)**	(−6.46)***	(−6.93)***	(−3.19)**	(−0.85)	(−3.52)***	(−2.53)	(−3.03)
Japan	−0.182	−0.177	0.120	−0.279	0.426	0.244	0.899	−0.037
	(−3.07)***	(−6.30)***	(−8.10)***	(−2.59)*	(2.84)***	(3.50)***	(−1.41)	(−0.80)
Netherlands	−0.075	−0.038	0.190	−0.988	−0.140	−0.098	0.823	−0.199
	(−1.40)	(−1.18)	(−7.57)***	(−5.97)***	(−1.36)	(−2.62)	(−2.21)	(−2.39)
Norway	0.025	−0.016	0.000	−0.773	−0.036	−0.239	0.573	−0.241
	(−0.73)	(−0.89)	(−9.20)***	(−4.70)***	(−0.64)	(−6.86)***	(−3.02)	(−2.71)
Sweden	−0.033	−0.028	0.220	−0.694	−0.033	−0.077	0.819	−0.246
	(−1.00)	(−1.42)	(−7.39)***	(−4.47)***	(−0.43)	(−2.90)***	(−1.82)	(−2.78)
UK	0.002	−0.001	0.240	−1.010	0.158	0.101	0.723	−0.203
	(−0.06)	(−0.07)	(−7.19)***	(−5.73)***	(2.71)**	(4.59)***	(−2.62)	(−2.55)
USA	0.001	0.000	0.246	−1.064	0.068	0.108	0.028	−0.443
	(−0.10)	(−0.02)	(−7.98)***	(−5.45)***	(2.18)**	(5.29)***	(−5.74)***	(−3.96)**

Continued

Table A1 Time series properties of GDP per capita growth rates and producer durables investment/RGDP Continued

	GDP per capita growth rates				Producer durables investment as %RGDP			
	Time trend		ADF		Time trend		ADF	
	Jones	Current study	Jones	Current study	Jones	Current study	Jones	Current study
Australia	−0.010	0.002	0.290	−1.418	0.030	0.113	0.8	0.007
	(−0.15)	(−0.09)	(−6.46)***	(−8.83)***	(1.60)	(5.38)***	(−1.71)	(0.07)
Austria	−0.110	−0.085	0.070	−0.790	0.071	−0.051	0.420	−0.302
	(−2.53)**	(−3.73)***	(−8.59)***	(−4.40)***	(3.82)***	(−2.48)**	(−3.59)*	(−2.93)
Belgium	−0.032	−0.037	0.230	−0.694	–	0.112	–	−0.227
	(−0.68)	(−2.08)**	(−7.26)***	(−3.87)***	–	(13.5)***	–	(−2.60)
Canada	0.020	−0.003	0.370	−1.015	0.077	0.143	0.810	−0.239
	(−0.38)	(−0.14)	(−6.25)***	(−5.66)***	(3.85)***	(8.98)***	(−1.71)	(−2.73)
Denmark	−0.029	−0.032	0.040	−0.750	0.096	0.174	0.651	−0.123
	(−0.41)	(−1.16)	(−8.83)***	(−3.24)**	(5.55)***	(12.5)***	(−2.66)	(−1.58)
Finland	−0.036	−0.059	0.230	−0.863	0.042	−0.016	0.677	−0.253
	(−0.63)	(−1.58)	(−7.27)***	(−5.69)***	(1.22)	(−0.63)	(−2.84)	(−2.64)
France	−0.087	−0.062	0.240	−0.556	0.113	0.144	0.902	−0.244
	(−2.38)**	(−3.75)***	(−7.18)***	(−3.63)***	(5.69)***	(16.1)***	(−1.28)	(−2.89)
Germany	−0.153	−0.042	0.020	−0.962	0.086	0.017	0.659	−0.520
	(−3.26)***	(−1.42)	(−9.05)***	(−4.66)***	(6.18)***	(0.95)	(−3.48)*	(−4.41)***
Italy	−0.095	−0.100	0.270	−0.492	0.037	0.072	0.374	−0.515
	(−2.63)**	(−6.46)***	(−6.93)***	(−3.19)**	(3.69)***	(8.05)***	(−4.30)**	(−4.08)**

Japan	−0.182	−0.177	0.120	−0.279	0.159	0.190	0.820	−0.339
	(−3.07)***	(−6.30)***	(8.10)***	(−2.59)*	(7.76)***	(21.8)***	(−1.56)	(−3.60)**
Netherlands	−0.075	−0.038	0.190	−0.988	0.008	0.077	0.854	−0.441
	(−1.40)	(−1.18)	(−7.57)***	(−5.97)***	(0.21)	(8.56)***	(−1.69)	(−4.15)**
Norway	0.025	−0.016	0.000	−0.773	−0.155	−0.465	0.666	−0.220
	(−0.73)	(−0.89)	(−9.20)***	(−4.70)***	(−2.62)**	(−10.7)***	(−2.73)	(−2.30)
Sweden	−0.033	−0.028	0.220	−0.694	0.052	0.122	0.443	−0.303
	(−1.00)	(−1.42)	(−7.39)***	(−4.47)***	(6.08)***	(7.59)***	(−3.61)**	(−3.61)**
UK	0.002	−0.001	0.240	−1.010	0.066	0.082	0.605	−0.445
	(−0.06)	(−0.07)	(−7.19)***	(−5.73)***	(5.48)***	(9.01)***	(−2.73)	(−3.63)**
USA	0.001	0.000	0.246	−1.064	0.080	0.147	0.712	−0.153
	(−0.10)	(−0.02)	(−7.98)***	(−5.45)***	(5.90)***	(8.07)***	(−2.43)	(−2.45)

Table A2 Time series properties of GDP per capita growth rates and Investment/RGDP per capita;
PWT 6.2 (1950–2004)

| Country | Time trend test | | ADF test | | Conclusion: consistent with AK theory? |
	Growth rate	I/RGDP	Growth rate	I/RGDP	(Yes/no)
Category: Remaining OECD economies not considered by Jones (1995)					
Czech Rep.	0.531	0.509	−1.561	−0.504	NO
	(−1.79)	(−4.87)***	(−1.61)	(−2.45)	
Greece	−0.092	−0.008	−0.363	−0.102	NO
	(−2.59)*	(−0.10)	(−2.13)	(−1.90)	
Hungary	−0.037	−0.004	−0.650	−0.178	NO
	(−0.56)	(−0.05)	(−3.06)**	(−1.99)	
Iceland	−0.039	−0.091	−0.986	−0.379	NO
	(−0.89)	(−1.96)	(−5.60)***	(−3.04)	
Ireland	0.072	0.130	−0.531	−0.185	NO
	(−2.22)*	(−3.63)***	(−3.85)***	(−2.16)	
Luxembourg	0.051	−0.149	−0.916	−0.305	NO
	(−1.64)	(−4.27)***	(−5.06)***	(−2.92)	
Mexico	−0.063	0.004	−0.874	−0.369	NO
	(−2.40)*	(−0.17)	(−4.93)***	(−3.63)**	
New Zealand	0.001	0.003	−1.137	−0.514	YES, WEAK
	(−0.03)	(−0.09)	(−6.04)***	(−3.47)*	
Poland	−0.035	−0.337	−0.338	−0.138	NO
	(−0.28)	(−2.57)*	(−2.93)*	(−2.51)	
Portugal	−0.084	0.157	−0.653	−0.398	NO, trends are opposite
	(−3.20)**	(−5.5)***	(−4.06)***	(−3.78)**	
Slovak Rep.	0.536	0.068	−0.435	−0.747	YES, STRONG
	(−1.91)	(−0.95)	(−0.45)	(−3.06)	
Spain	−0.101	0.120	−0.701	−0.148	NO
	(−3.08)**	(−3.75)***	(−4.28)***	(−2.39)	
Switzerland	−0.068	0.065	−0.842	−0.263	NO
	(−2.90)**	(−1.62)	(−5.14)***	(−2.78)	
Turkey	−0.062	0.226	−1.130	−0.459	NO
	(−1.05)	(−11.67)***	(−5.57)***	(−3.39)*	

Continued

Table A2 Continued

	Time trend test		ADF test		Conclusion: consistent with AK theory?
Country	Growth rate	I/RGDP	Growth rate	I/RGDP	(Yes/no)
Category: Africa					
Algeria	−0.026	−0.088	−1.613	−0.130	NO
	(−0.23)	(−0.95)	(−8.67)***	(−1.83)	
Benin	−0.012	−0.022	−1.105	−0.350	NO
	(−0.29)	(−1.64)	(−4.78)***	(−2.51)	
Botswana	−0.207	−0.187	−1.079	−0.654	NO
	(−2.20)*	(−1.83)	(−4.38)***	(−3.26)*	
Burkina Faso	0.096	0.144	−1.062	−0.206	NO
	(−2.09)*	(−4.03)***	(−5.56)***	(−1.76)	
Burundi	−0.082	0.084	−1.320	−0.251	NO
	(−1.02)	(−8.29)***	(−5.56)***	(−1.98)	
Cameroon	−0.003	0.008	−0.434	−0.261	NO
	(−0.05)	(−0.4)	(−2.70)*	(−2.48)	
Cape Verde	0.057	−0.019	−0.789	−0.713	YES, WEAK
	(−0.62)	(−0.32)	(−3.68)***	(−4.98)***	
Central African Rep	0.047	−0.344	−0.917	−0.269	NO
	(−0.36)	(−3.10)**	(−3.88)***	(−2.86)	
Chad	0.087	0.258	−1.114	−0.432	NO
	(−0.95)	(−2.06)*	(−4.87)***	(−1.24)	
Cote d'Ivoire	−0.137	−0.206	−1.282	−0.209	NO
	(−3.12)**	(−5.35)***	(−5.52)***	(−2.07)	
Dem Rep of Congo	−0.022	0.119	−0.945	−0.301	NO
	(−0.11)	(−1.3)	(−3.43)**	(−1.42)	
Djibouti	0.428	0.048	−1.209	0.294	NO
	(−1.39)	(−0.33)	(−3.48)**	(−1.60)	
Egypt	0.026	−0.151	−1.288	−0.218	NO
	(−0.89)	(−4.28)***	(−6.26)***	(−2.99)	
Equatorial Guinea	0.592	0.680	−0.210	0.819	NO
	(−1.57)	(−3.62)***	(−0.39)	(−0.57)	
Eritrea	−0.749	0.166	−0.670	−0.367	YES, STRONG

Continued

Table A2 Continued

	Time trend test		ADF test		Conclusion: consistent with AK theory?
Country	Growth rate	I/RGDP	Growth rate	I/RGDP	(Yes/no)
	(–1.61)	(–0.77)	(–1.23)	(–0.86)	
Ethiopia	0.005	0.044	–1.240	–0.346	NO
	(–0.1)	(–4.05)***	(–5.17)***	(–3.04)	
Gabon	–0.337	–0.244	–0.881	–0.288	YES, STRONG
	(–4.74)***	(–3.07)**	(–4.10)***	(–3.76)**	
Gambia	–0.057	0.297	–0.802	–0.309	NO
	(–0.55)	(–7.08)***	(–3.28)**	(–2.61)	
Ghana	–0.19	–0.734	–1.167	–0.475	NO
	(–1.04)	(–4.96)***	(–4.64)***	(–3.06)	
Guinea Bissau	–0.052	0.14	–3.387	–0.222	NO
	(–0.45)	(–1.17)	(–5.35)***	(–1.49)	
Kenya	–0.026	–0.115	–1.209	–0.264	NO
	(–0.74)	(–3.64)***	(–5.83)***	(–2.59)	
Lesotho	–0.002	0.610	–1.368	–0.237	NO
	(–0.03)	(–6.01)***	(–5.42)***	(–1.92)	
Liberia	0.095	–0.232	–0.530	–0.550	NO
	(–0.21)	(–3.65)***	(–2.50)	(–4.62)***	
Madagascar	–0.044	–0.013	–1.151	–0.108	NO
	(–1.34)	(–0.70)	(–4.75)***	(–0.64)	
Malawi	–0.026	–0.027	–1.111	–0.183	NO
	(–0.52)	(–0.44)	(–5.75)***	(–1.77)	
Mali	0.112	–0.039	–1.319	–0.355	YES, WEAK
	(–1.95)	(–0.99)	(–5.35)***	(–3.29)*	
Mauritania	0.023	–0.282	–0.762	–0.255	NO
	(–0.25)	(–3.08)**	(–2.77)*	(–2.31)	
Mauritius	0.138	–0.084	–0.646	–0.437	NO
	(–3.15)**	(–2.26)*	(–3.51)**	(–2.97)	
Morocco	–0.029	–0.036	–0.810	–0.274	NO
	(–0.57)	(–0.70)	(–4.02)***	(–2.85)	
Mozambique	0.056	0.094	–0.868	–0.453	NO
	(–0.73)	(–6.66)***	(–4.25)***	(–3.13)	
Namibia	0.075	–0.105	–1.901	–0.621	NO
	(–1.32)	(–2.43)*	(–5.17)***	(–2.88)	

Continued

	Time trend test		ADF test		Conclusion: consistent with AK theory?
Country	Growth rate	I/RGDP	Growth rate	I/RGDP	(Yes/no)
Niger	−0.039	0.140	−1.173	−0.200	NO
	(−0.75)	(−5.6)***	(−5.67)***	(−2.23)	
Rep of Congo	−0.202	−0.927	−0.903	−0.573	NO
	(−1.61)	(−5.92)***	(−4.24)***	(−5.23)***	
Rwanda	0.125	0.057	−1.551	−0.590	NO
	(−1.03)	(−8.06)***	(−6.29)***	(−2.72)	
Sao Tome & Principe	−0.18	−0.476	−1.007	−0.298	NO
	(−1.35)	(−4.83)***	(−3.31)**	(−2.42)	
Senegal	0.046	0.096	−1.620	−0.486	NO
	(−1.09)	(−4.93)***	(−6.57)***	(−2.17)	
Sierra Leone	−0.126	−0.015	−0.778	−1.291	NO
	(−1.12)	(−0.80)	(−3.22)**	(−0.11)	
Somalia	−0.05	0.084	−1.513	−0.741	NO
	(−0.48)	(−2.88)**	(−6.11)***	(−3.45)*	
South Africa	−0.022	−0.039	−0.803	−0.230	NO
	(−0.98)	(−2.28)*	(−4.79)***	(−2.43)	
Sudan	0.008	−0.281	−1.043	−0.239	NO
	(−0.09)	(−3.21)**	(−4.43)***	(−3.13)	
Swaziland	−0.191	−0.209	−0.771	−0.652	NO
	(−2.03)	(−7.99)***	(−3.50)**	(−3.42)*	
Tanzania	0.131	0.080	−0.882	−0.148	NO
	(−0.95)	(−2.15)*	(−3.98)***	(−1.55)	
Togo	−0.152	0.079	−0.688	−0.266	NO
	(−2.34)*	(−1.67)	(−3.51)**	(−2.80)	
Tunisia	−0.019	0.517	−1.022	−0.241	NO
	(−0.46)	(−11.09)***	(−2.36)	(−2.23)	
Uganda	0.042	0.024	−0.775	−0.222	NO
	(−0.99)	(−4.28)***	(−4.35)***	(−2.30)	
Zambia	−0.109	−1.873	−1.202	−0.186	NO
	(−1.28)	(−7.27)***	(−5.41)***	(−1.99)	
Zimbabwe	−0.13	−0.153	−0.807	−0.384	NO
	(−1.74)	(−2.61)*	(−3.93)***	(−3.37)*	

Continued

Country	Time trend test		ADF test		Conclusion: consistent with AK theory?
	Growth rate	I/RGDP	Growth rate	I/RGDP	(Yes/no)
Category: South America					
Argentina	−0.022	−0.018	−1.156	−0.251	NO
	(−0.45)	(−0.57)	(−6.17)***	(−2.70)	
Bolivia	0.026	−0.047	−0.847	−0.615	YES, WEAK
	(−0.79)	(−1.73)	(−4.56)***	(−3.92)**	
Brazil	−0.104	−0.134	−0.513	−0.189	NO
	(−4.38)***	(−5.44)***	(−3.17)**	(−2.07)	
Chile	0.055	−0.155	−0.852	−0.196	NO
	(−1.68)	(−2.33)*	(−4.43)***	(−1.93)	
Colombia	−0.019	−0.038	−0.480	−0.413	YES, WEAK
	(−0.98)	(−1.34)	(−3.17)**	(−4.06)**	
Ecuador	−0.071	−0.276	−0.537	−0.503	YES, STRONG
	(−2.72)**	(−5.81)***	(−3.33)**	(−4.21)***	
Paraguay	−0.037	0.163	−0.549	−0.099	NO
	(−1.31)	(−4.54)***	(−3.54)**	(−1.37)	
Peru	−0.082	−0.490	−0.794	−0.186	NO
	(−1.58)	(−5.51)***	(−5.27)***	(−2.37)	
Suriname	0.286	0.350	−0.849	−0.904	NO
	(−1.17)	(−2.84)**	(−2.89)*	(−3.66)**	
Uruguay	0.002	−0.075	−0.798	−0.222	NO
	(−0.04)	(−2.34)*	(−4.78)***	(−2.92)	
Venezuela	−0.092	−0.431	−1.001	−0.358	NO
	(−2.34)*	(−8.54)***	(−5.26)***	(−3.04)	
Category: Developing Southeast and South Asia					
Afghanistan	−0.34	0.088	−0.900	−0.769	NO
	(−1.16)	(−3.98)***	(−5.04)***	(−3.44)*	
Bangladesh	0.107	0.221	−1.120	−0.313	NO
	(−2.14)*	(−7.14)***	(−4.02)***	(−2.02)	
Bhutan	−0.034	0.188	−1.255	−0.651	NO
	(−0.38)	(−2.90)**	(−4.73)***	(−3.17)	

Continued

Country	Time trend test		ADF test		Conclusion: consistent with AK theory?
	Growth rate	I/RGDP	Growth rate	I/RGDP	(Yes/no)
Brunei	−0.131	0.116	−0.641	−0.276	NO
	(−1.08)	(−5.44)***	(−2.30)	(−2.03)	
Cambodia	0.478	0.083	−0.499	−0.586	NO
	(−7.22)***	(−3.94)***	(−2.37)	(−1.08)	
China	0.163	0.254	−0.725	−0.652	YES, STRONG
	(3.01)***	(5.55)***	(−4.03)***	(−5.88)***	
India	0.055	0.080	−0.888	−0.333	NO
	(2.57)**	(5.04)***	(−4.58)***	(−2.81)	
Indonesia	−0.008	0.241	−0.648	−0.056	NO
	(−0.12)	(2.74)***	(−2.99)**	(−0.84)	
Laos	0.065	0.63	−1.113	−0.113	NO
	(−0.69)	(−8.02)***	(−4.04)***	(−2.31)	
Malaysia	0.019	0.371	−0.846	−0.249	NO
	(−0.45)	(4.53)***	(−4.39)***	(−2.18)	
Maldives	−0.2	0.057	−1.123	1658.771	NO, trends are opposite
	(−4.06)***	(−2.44)*	(−4.31)***	(11.69)***	
Nepal	0.042	0.412	−1.725	−0.180	NO
	(−1.56)	(−12.71)***	(−6.79)***	(−1.53)	
Pakistan	0.016	0.05	−0.741	−0.120	NO
	(−0.56)	(−0.80)	(−3.93)***	(−2.14)	
Philippines	−0.055	0.041	−1.056	−0.291	NO
	(−1.80)*	(2.26)**	(−5.09)***	(−3.11)	
Sri Lanka	0.055	−0.105	−1.182	−0.283	NO
	(−1.59)	(−4.98)***	(−5.62)***	(−2.23)	
Thailand	0.075	0.325	−0.599	−0.155	NO
	(−1.02)	(2.58)**	(−3.76)***	(−2.10)	
Vietnam	0.011	0.911	−0.963	−1.095	NO
	(−0.1)	(−12.74)***	(−2.11)	(−1.16)	

Table A2 Continued

	Time trend test		ADF test		Conclusion: consistent with AK theory?
Country	Growth rate	I/RGDP	Growth rate	I/RGDP	(Yes/no)
Category: East Asian Tigers					
Hong Kong	−0.173	−0.091	−0.710	−0.261	NO
	(−2.90)***	(−1.31)	(−4.19)***	(−3.05)	
Singapore	−0.068	−0.354	−0.767	−0.169	NO
	(−0.97)	(−3.23)***	(−3.81)***	(−1.34)	
South Korea	0.057	0.690	−0.757	−0.183	NO
	(−1.22)	(8.61)***	(−4.07)***	(−1.81)	
Taiwan	−0.024	0.257	−0.627	−0.118	NO
	(−0.68)	(5.65)***	(−3.93)***	(−1.62)	
Category: Other developed nations					
Bermuda	−0.07	0.218	−0.991	−0.247	NO
	(−1.23)	(−5.58)***	(−3.88)***	(−1.81)	
Cyprus	−0.057	−0.452	−0.961	−0.549	NO
	(−0.35)	(−7.56)***	(−4.96)***	(−3.26)*	
Israel	−0.069	−0.200	−0.935	−0.288	NO
	(−1.46)	(−3.31)**	(−6.46)***	(−3.65)**	
Malta	−0.315	−0.162	−0.382	−0.572	NO
	(−2.92)**	(−2.09)*	(−2.15)	(−3.77)**	

Notes for Table A1 and A2:

Jones used data from 1880–1987 in his time trend analysis for the US.

The time trend test reports the coefficient of the trend variable in a regression of gdp per capita's growth rate (%) on a constant and a trend. The test statistic is the t–statistic corresponding to the Newey West corrected standard error and tests whether the above coefficient is 0. A lag length of 2 is chosen in this annual time series analysis.

The ADF test statistic is reported. The lag length is determined using the min Schwarz Information Criterion.

References

Chapter 1

Bernstein, J. and P. Mohnen (1994). International R&D spillovers between US and Japanese R&D intensive sectors. *Working Paper,* No. 4682, Cambridge, Massachusetts: NBER

D'Aveni, R.A. (1994). *Hyper Competition: Managing the Dynamics of Strategic Maneuvering.* New York: Free Press

Folster, S. and G. Trofimov (1997). Industry evolution and R&D externalities. *Journal of Economic Dynamics and Control* 21, 727–46

Hofbauer, J. and K. Sigmund (1998). *Evolutionary Games and Population Dynamics.* Cambridge: Cambridge University Press

Grossman, G.M. and E. Helpman (1991). *Innovation and Growth in its Global Economy.* Cambridge, Massachusetts: MIT Press

Jones, C.I. (1995). Time series test of endogenous growth models. *Quarterly Journal of Economics* 110, 495–525

Lucas, R.E. (1993). Making a miracle. *Econometrica* 61, 251–72

Romer, P.M. (1986). Increasing returns and long run growth. *Journal of Political Economy* 94, 1002–37

—— (1990). Endogenous technological change. *Journal of Political Economy* 98, 71–102

Nandi, I. (2009). Time Series Tests of the AK Model of Endogenous Growth, UCSB *Working Title*, in this Book. (Chapter 6).

Otto, S. and T. Day (2007). *A Biologist's Guide to Mathematical Modeling in Ecology and Evolution.* Princeton: Princeton University Press

Rebelo, S. (1991). Long run policy analysis and long run growth. *Journal of Political Economy,* 99, 500–21

Schumpeter, J. (1942). Capitalism, socialism and democracy. New York: Harper Brothers

Sengupta, J.K. (2005). India's Economic Growth. New York: Palgrave Macmillan

Sengupta, J.K. and C. Neogi (2009). *India's New Economy: Industry Efficiency and Growth.* New York: Palgrave Macmillan

Solow, R. (1957). Technical change and the aggregate production function. *Review of Economics and Statistics* 39, 312–20

Spence, M. (1984). Cost reduction, competition and industry performance. *Econometrica* 52, 101–22

Wang, J. and K. Tsai (2002). Productivity growth and R&D expenditure in Taiwan's manufacturing firms. In T. Ito and A. Rose, eds. *Growth and Productivity in East Asia.* Chicago: University of Chicago Press

Chapter 2

Arthur, W. (1994). *Increasing Returns and Path Dependence in the Economy.* Ann Arbor: University of Michigan Press

Aghion,P. and P. Howitt (1992) A model of growth through creative destruction. *Econometrica* 60,323–51

Cellini, R. and L. Lambertini (2008). Dynamic R&D with spillovers: competition and cooperation. *Journal of Economic Dynamics and Control* 32, 628–43

Cohen, W. and D. Levinthal (1989). Innovation and learning: the two facets of R&D. *Economic Journal* 99, 569–96

Corley, M., Michie, J. and Oughton, C. (2002). Technology, growth and employment. *International Review of Applied Economics* 16, 265–75

D'Aveni, R.A. (1994). *Hyper Competition: Managing the Dynamics of Strategic Maneuvering.* New York: Free Press

Dosi, G. (1984). *Technical Change and Industrial Transformation.* New York: Macmillan

Freeman, C. (1982). *The Economics of Industrial Innovation.* London: Francis Pinter

Grossman, G.M.A. and E. Helpman (1991). Quality ladders and the product cycles. *Quarterly Journal of Economics,* 106, 557–86

Gort, M. and K. Konakayama (1982). A model of diffusion in the production of an innovation. *American Economic Review,* 72, 1111–20

Grossman, G. and E. Helpman (1993). Endogenous Innovation in the Theory of Growth. *Working Paper,* No. 4527, NBER, Cambridge, Massachusetts

Jaffe, A.B. (1986). Technological opportunity and spillovers of R&D: evidence from firms, patents, profits and market value. *American Economic Review* 76, 984–1001

Jones, C.I. (2002). *Introduction to Economic Growth.* New York: W.W. Norton.

Lucas, R.E. (1993). Making a miracle. *Econometrica* 61, 251–72

Lukach, R., J. Plasmans and P.M. Kort (2005). Innovation strategies in a competitive dynamic setting. *Working Paper,* No. 1395. Center for Economic Studies, Munich Germany

Mankiw, N.G., D. Romber and D.N. Weil (1992). A contribution to the empirics of economic growth. *Quarterly Journal of Economics,* 107, 407–38

Nachum, L. (2002). International Business in a World of Increasing Returns. *Working Paper, No. 224, Center for Business Research.* University of Cambridge, UK

Palokangas, T. (2007). Employment cycles in a growth model with creative destruction. In B. Jensen and T. Palokangas, eds. *Stochastic Economic Dynamics.* Copenhagen: Copenhagen Business School Press

Porter, M. (1998). *The Competitive Advantage of Nations.* New York: Free Press

Prahalad, C.K. and G. Hamel (1994). *Competing for the Future.* Cambridge: Harvard University Press

Romer, P.M. (1990). Endogenous technological change. *Journal of Political Economy* 98, 71–102

Rosenberg, N. (1972) *Technology, Economics and History.* Cambridge, Cambridge University Press.

Schumpeter, J. (1934). *The Theory of Economic Development.* Cambridge: Harvard University Press

Sengupta, J.K. (2004). *Competition and Growth: Innovations and Selection in Industry Evolution.* New York: Palgrave Macmillan

—— (2005). *India's Economic Growth.* New York: Palgrave Macmillan

Sengupta, J.K. and B. Sahoo (2006). *Efficiency Models in Data Envelopment Analysis.* New York: Palgrave Macmillan

Sengupta, J.K. and C. Neogi (2009). *India's New Economy: Industry Efficiency and Growth.* New York. Palgrave Macmillan

Spence, M. (1984). Cost reduction competition and industry performance. *Econometrica* 52, 101–22

Teece, D. (1986). Profiting from technological innovation, collaboration, licensing and public policy. *Research Policy* 15, 285–305

Thomas, J. (2009). Innovation in India and China. In G. Parayil and A. P.D'Costa, eds. *The New Asian Innovation Dynamics.* New York: Palgrave Macmillan

Young, A. (1991). Learning by doing and the dynamic effects of international trade. *Quarterly Journal of Economics* 106, 369–406

Chapter 3

Aghion, P. and P. Howitt (1992). A model of growth through creative destruction. *Econometrica* 60, 323–51

Arrow, K.J.I. (1962). The economic implications of learning by doing. *Review of Economic Studies* 29, 155–74

Aumann, R.J. (1974). Subjectivity and correlation in randomized strategies. *Journal of Mathematical Economics* 1, 67–96

Bharucha-Reid, A.T. (1960). *Elements of the Theory of Markov Processes and Their Applications.* New York: McGraw Hill

Binder, M. and M.H. Pesaran (1996). Stochastic Growth. *Working Paper,* No. 96–18, University of Maryland, Department of Economics

Bradford, C.I. (1987). Trade and structural change: nics and next-tier nics as transitional economics. *World Development* 15, 30–45

Caballero, R.J. and R.K. Lyons (1992). In A. Cukierman, Z. Hercowitz and L. Leidermann, eds. *Political Economy: Growth and Business Cycles.* Cambridge, Massachusetts: MIT Press

Cohen, W.M. and D.A. Levinthal (1989). Innovation and learning: the two faces of R&D. *Economic Journal* 99, 569–96

Goodwin, R.M. (1990). *Chaotic Economic Dynamics.* Oxford: Clarendon Press

Gregory, A., A. Paganand and G. Smith (1993). Estimating linear quadratic models with integrated processes. In P.C.B. Phillips, ed. *Models, Methods and Applications in Econometrics* Cambridge: Blackwell Publishers

Grossman, G.M. and E. Helpman (1991). *Innovations and Growth in the Global Economy.* Cambridge. Massachusetts: MIT Press

—— (1994). Endogeneous innovation in the theory of growth. *Journal of Economic Perspectives* 8, 23–44

Helpman, E. (1997). R&D and Productivity: The International Connection. *Working Paper,* No. 165, Harvard Institute of Economic Research.

Jovanovic, B. (1997). Learning and growth. In D.M. Kreps and K.F. Wallis, eds. *Advances in Economics and Econometrics: Theory and Applications.* Cambridge: Cambridge University Press

Kellman, M. and P.C. Chow (1989). The comparative homogeneity of the East Asian NIC Exports of Similar Manufacturers. *World Development* 17, 65–74

Kennan, J. (1979). The estimation of partial adjustment models with rational expectations. *Econometrica* 47, 1441–57.

Kennedy, C. (1964). Induced bias in innovation and the theory of distribution. *Economic Journal* 74,150–62

Krugman, P. (1991). History versus expectations. *Quarterly Journal of Economics* 106, 651–67

Lorenz, E. (1963). Deterministic nonperiodic flow. *Journal of the Atmospheric Sciences* 20, 130–41

Lucas, R.E. (1993). Making a miracle. *Econometrica* 61, 251–72

May, R.M. (1973). *Stability and Complexity in Model Ecosystems.* Princeton, New Jersey: Princeton University Press

Nordhaus, W.D. (1967). The optimal rate and direction of technical change. In K. Shell, ed. *Essays on the Theory of Optimum Economic Growth.* Cambridge. Massachusetts: MIT Press

Norsworthy, J.R. and S.L. Jang (1992). *Empirical Measurement and Analysis of Productivity and Technical Change.* Amsterdam: North Holland.

Ohyama, M. and Y. Fukushima (1995). Endogeneous dualistic structure. Marshallian externalities and industrialization. In S. Chang and S. Katayama, eds. *Imperfect Competition in International Trade.* Dordrecht, Netherlands: Kluwer Academic Publishers

Romer, P.M. (1990). Endogenous technological change. *Journal of Political Economy* 98, S7I-S102.

Schumpeter, J.A. (1934). *The Theory of Economic Development.* Cambridge Massachusetts: Harvard University Press

Sengupta, J.K. (1983). Optimal control in limit pricing under uncertain entry. *International Journal of Systems Science* 14, 1–18

—— (1993). Growth in NICs in Asia: some tests of new growth theory. *Journal of Development Studies* 29, 342–57

Sengupta, J.K. and P. Fanchon (1997). *Control Theory Methods in Economics.* Dordrecht: Kluwer Academic Publishers

Sengupta, J.K. and K. Okamura (1996). Learning by doing and openness in Japanese growth. *Japan and the World Economy* 8, 43–64

Sengupta, J.K. and Y. Zheng (1995). Empirical tests of chaotic dynamics in market volatility. *Applied Financial Economics* 5, 291–300

Solow, R.M. (1994). Perspectives on growth theory. *Journal of Economic Perspectives* 8, 45–54

Tintner, G. and Sengupta, J.K. (1972). *Stochastic Economics.* New York: Academic Press

Treadway, A.B. (1974). The globally optimal flexible accelerator. *Journal of Economic Theory*1, 17–39

Young, A. (1991). Learning by doing and the dynamic effects of international trade. *Quarterly Journal of Economics* 106, 369–406

Chapter 4

Bradford, C. (1987). Trade and structural change: NICs and next-tier NICs as transitional economies. *World Development* 15, 299–316

Chow, P.C. (1987). Causality between export growth and industrial development. *Journal of Development Economics* 15, 55–63

Feder, G. (1982). On exports and economic growth. *Journal of Development Economics* 12, 59–73

Honglin, K.Z. (2004). Why does China receive so much Foreign Direct Investment (FDI)? In the Institute of World Economics and Politics: China: Going Global: London: Marshall Cavendish Academic.

Hung-gay, F., H. Yu-Sheng, P. Changhongand and S. Jingian (2004). In the Institute of World Economics and Politics: *China: Trading with the Dragon*. London Marshall Cavendish Academic

Jones, C.I. (1995). Time series test of endogenous growth models. *Quarterly Journal of Economics* 110, 495–525

Kwon, J.K. (1986). Capital utilization, economies of scale and technical change in the growth of total factor productivity. *Journal of Development Economics* 24, 75–89

Lucas, R.E. (1990). Why does net capital flow from rich to poor countries. *American Economic Review* 80, 92–6

Nandi, I. (2009). Time series tests of the AK model of endogenous growth. UCSB *Working Title*, in this Book. (Chapter 6)

Porter, M. and I. Stern (2004). A report on global competitiveness. In M. Porter, ed. *Global Competitiveness Report*. New York: World Economic Forum

Sengupta, J.K. (2000). *Dynamic and Stochastic Efficiency Analysis*. Singapore: World Scientific

—— (2005). *India's Economic Growth*. New York. Palgrave Macmillan

Solow, R. (1957). Technical change and the aggregate production function. *Review of Economics and Statistics* 39, 312–20

Spence, M. (1984). Cost reduction, competition and industry performance. *Econometrica* 52, 101–22

World Bank (1996). *The Chinese Economy*. Washington D.C. World Bank.

World Economic Forum (2004). Global Competitiveness Report. Edited by M. Porter and I. Stern, New York: World Economic Forum

Wu, Y. (2004). *China's Economic Growth: A Miracle with Chinese Characteristics*. London: Routledge Curzon

Yao, S. (2005). *Economic Growth, Income Distribution and Poverty Reduction in Contemporary China*. London: Routledge Curzon

Chapter 5

Besanko, D., D. Dranove, M. Shanely and S. Schaefer (2010). *Economics of Strategy.* New York: John Wiley

Cabral, L. and M. Riordan (1994). The learning curve, market dominance and predatory pricing. *Econometrica* 62, 1115–40

Cellini, R. and L. Lambertini (2008). Dynamic R&D with spillovers: competition and cooperation. *Journal of Economic Dynamics and Control* 32, 628–43

Corley, M., J. Michie and C. Oughton (2002). Technology, growth and employment. *International Review of Applied Economics* 16, 265–76

D'Costa, A.P. and G. Parayil (2009). China, India and the New Asian Innovation Dynamics: An Introduction. In G. Parayil and A.P. D'Costa, eds. *The New Asian Innovation Dynamics: China and India in Perspective.* New York: Palgrave Macmillan

Encaoua, D., P. Geroski and A. Jacquemim (1986). Strategic competition and the persistence of dominant firms: A survey. In J. Stigler and G. Mathewson, eds. *New Developments in the Analysis of Market Structure.* New York: Cambridge University Press

Folster, S. and G. Trofimove (1997). Industry evolution and R&D externalities. *Journal of Economic Dynamics and Control* 21, 1727–46

Griliches, Z. (1984). *R&D, Patents and Productivity.* Chicago. University of Chicago Press

Jorgenson, D.W. and K.J. Stiroh (2000). *Raising the Speed Limit: US Economic Growth in the Information Age.* In Brookings Papers on Economic Activity Washington D.C., Brookings Institution

Kessides, I.N. (1990). The persistence of the profits in US manufacturing. In D.C. Mueller, ed. *The Dynamics of Company Profits.* New York: Cambridge University Press

Lu, D. and A. Hu (2008). China's regional variations in patenting. In E. Thompson, and J. Sigurdson, eds. *China's Science and Technology Sector and the Forces of Globalization.* Singapore: World Scientific

Norsworthy, J.R. and Jang, S.L. (1992). *Empirical Measurement and Analysis of Productivity and Technological change.* Amsterdam: North Holland.

Porter, M.E. (1990). *The Competitive Advantage of Nations.* New York: Free Press

Sengupta, J.K. (2004). Dynamic efficiency with learning by doing. *International Review of Applied Economics* 18, 381–95

—— (2005). *India's Economic Growth.* New York: Palgrave Macmillan

Sengupta, J.K. and B. Sahoo (2006). *Efficiency Models in Data Envelopment Analysis.* New York: Palgrave Macmillan

Sutton, J. (1998). *Technology and Market Structure.* New York: Cambridge University Press

Wang, J. and K. Tsai (2002). Productivity, growth and R&D expenditure in Taiwan's manufacturing firms. In T. Ito, and A.K. Rose, eds. *Growth and Productivity in East Asia.* Chicago: Chicago University Press

Chapter 6

Banerjee, A., J.J. Dolado, W. Galbraith, and D.F. Hendry (1993). *Co-Integration, Error Correction and the Econometric Analysis of Non-Stationary Data*. Oxford: Oxford University Press

Ben-David, D. and D.H. Papell (1995). The great wars, the great crash, and steady state growth: some new evidence about an old stylized fact. *Journal of Monetary Economics* 36, 453–75

Bond, W., Leblebicioglu, T., and Schiantarelli, R. (2004). Capital accumulation and growth: a new look at the empirical evidence. IZA Discussion Paper, 1174.

Cheung, Y.W. and K.S. Lai (1995). Lag order and critical values of the augmented Dickey-Fuller test. *Journal of Business & Economic Statistics* 13, 277–80

Chow, G. (1993). How and why China succeeded in her economic reform. *China Economic Review* 4, 117–28

Dekle, R. and G. Vandenbroucke (2006). A quantitative analysis of China's structural transformation, usc institute for economic policy research (IEPR). Research Paper Series.

Dickey, D.A. and W.A. Fuller (1979). Distribution of the estimators for autoregressive time-series with a unit root. *Journal of the American Statistical Association* 74, 427–31

Elder, J. and P.E. Kennedy (2001). Testing for unit roots: what should students be taught? *Journal of Economic Education* 32, 137–46

Elliot, G., T. Rothenberg and J. Stock (1996). Efficient tests for an autoregressive unit root. *Econometrica* 64, 813–36

Engle, R. and C.W.J. Granger (1987). Co-integration and error correction: representation, estimation, and testing. *Econometrica* 55(2), 251–76

Granger, C.W.J. (1969). Investigating causal relations by econometric methods and cross-spectral methods. *Econometrica* 34, 424–38

Hall, D. (1994). Testing for a unit root in time series with pretest data based model selection. *Journal of Business and Economic Statistics* 12, 95–102

He, D., W. Zhang and J. Shek (2007). How efficient has been China's investment? Empirical evidence from national and provincial data. *Pacific Economic Review* 12, 597–617

Heytens, P. and H. Zebregs (2003). *How Fast Can China Grow?* Washington, D.C.: International Monetary Fund

Holden, D. and R. Perman (1994). Unit roots and co-integration for the economist. *Cointegration for the Applied Economist* 47–112

Jones, C.I. (1995). Time-series tests of endogenous growth-models. *Quarterly Journal of Economics* 110, 495–525

Krugman, P. (1994). The myth of Asia's miracle. *Foreign Affairs* 73, 62–78

Kuijs, L. and T. Wang (2005). China's pattern of growth: moving to sustainability and reducing inequality. *China and the World Economy* 13, 45–64

Kuijs, L. (2006). *How Will China's Savings-Investment Balance Evolve?* Beijing: World Bank China Office

Kwan, A., Y. Wu and J. Zhang (1999). Fixed investment and economic growth in China. *Economics of Planning* 32, 67–79

Lee, J. and M.C. Strazicich (2003). Minimum Lm unit root test with two structural breaks. *Review of Economics and Statistics* 63, 1082–9

—— (2004). *Minimum Lm Unit Root Test With One Structural Break*. Department of Economics, Appalachian State University

Li, D. (2002). Is the Ak model still alive? The long-run relation between growth and investment re-examined. *The Canadian Journal of Economics/ Revue Canadienne d'Economique* 35, 92–114

Li, X.M. (2000). The great leap forward, economic reforms and the unit root hypothesis: testing for breaking trend functions in China's GDP data. *Journal of Comparative Economics* 28, 814–27

Lumsdaine, R.L. and D.H. Papell (1997). Multiple trend breaks and the unit root hypothesis. *Review of Economics and Statistics* 79, 212–18

MacKinnon, J. (1991). Critical values for cointegration tests. *Long-Run Economic Relationships: Readings in Cointegration* 35, 267–76

McGrattan, E.R. (1998). A defense of AK growth models. *Federal Reserve Bank of Minneapolis Quarterly Review* 22, 13–27

Nelson, C. and C. Plosser (1982). Trends and random walks in macroeconomic time series: some evidence and implications. *Journal of Monetary Economics* 10, 139–62

Ng, S. and P. Perron (2001). Lag length selection and the construction of unit root tests with good size and power. *Econometrica* 69, 1519–54

Perron, P. (1988). Trends and random walks in macroeconomic time series. *Journal of Economic Dynamics and Control* 12(2), 297–332

—— (1989). The great crash, the oil price shock, and the unit root hypothesis. *Econometrica* 57, 1361–401

Perron, P. and T.J. Vogelsang (1992). Testing for a unit root in a time series with a changing mean: corrections and extensions. *Journal of Business and Economic Statistics* 10, 467–70

Romero-Avila, D. (2006). Can the AK model be rescued? New evidence from unit root tests with good size and power. *The BE Journal of Macroeconomics* 6, 3.

Sims, C. (1972). Money, income and causality. *American Economic Review* 62, 540–52

Yu, Q. (1998). Capital investment, international trade and economic growth in China: evidence in the 1980–1990s. *China Economic Review* 9, 73–84

Zhang, J. (2003). Investment, investment efficiency, and economic growth in China. *Journal of Asian Economics* 14, 713–34

Zivot, E. and D. Andrews (1992). Further evidence of the great crash, the oil-price shock and the unit-root hypothesis. *Journal of Business and Economic Statistics* 10, 251–70

Index